Islamic Mysticism

IBN AL RAWANDI

Islamic Mysticism

A Secular Perspective

Prometheus Books

59 John Glenn Drive
Amherst, New York 14228-2197

Published 2000 by Prometheus Books

Inquiries should be addressed to
Prometheus Books, 59 John Glenn Drive, Amherst, New York 14228–2197.
VOICE: 716–691–0133, ext. 207.
FAX: 716–564–2711.
WWW.PROMETHEUSBOOKS.COM

04 03 02 01 00   5 4 3 2 1

Library of Congress Cataloging-in-Publication Data

Ibn al-Rawandi.
        Islamic mysticism : a secular perspective / Ibn al-Rawandi.
            p. cm.
        Includes bibliographical references and index.
        ISBN 1–57392–767–8
        1. Sufism. 2. Islam and secularism. I. Title.

BP189 .I36 2000
297.4—dc21   99–057689
                                                                   CIP

Printed in the United States of America on acid-free paper

For my mother
(1903–)

Contents

Part I: Origins

Part II: Islam

Part III: Sufism or Islamic Mysticism

Part IV: Islam in the Modern World

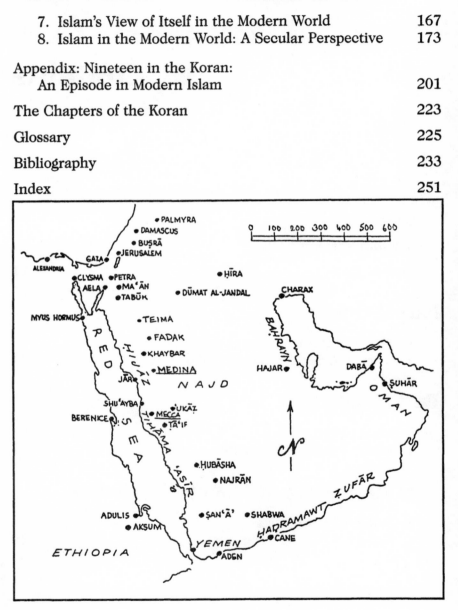

Chronology

570 Birth of Muhammad

578 Muhammad placed in the care of his uncle Abu Talib

595 Marriage of Muhammad to Khadija

610 First revelation of the Koran and vision of Gabriel

615 Emigration of Muslims to Abyssinia

619 Death of Khadija

622 Emigration (*hijrah*) of Muslims to Medina; arrival of Muhammad in Medina. Beginning of Islamic era

624 Battle of Badr

625 Battle of Uhud

627 Siege of Medina/Battle of the Trench (*al-Khandaq*)

628 Attempt at *umra* (minor pilgrimage to Mecca); pact of Hudaybiyah

629 Fulfillment of postponed *umra*; battle of Muta/raid on Syria

630 Muslim conquest and occupation of Mecca. Battle of Hunayn; expedition to Tabuk and Ayla

632 Farewell Pilgrimage (*hajj*). Death of the Prophet. Election of Abu Bakr as successor and representative (caliph)

633 Suppression of Apostasy (*ar-ridda*); conquest of Yemen

634 Death of Abu Bakr; Umar becomes caliph

9

10 CHRONOLOGY

635 Fall of Damascus
638 Surrender of Jerusalem
641 Capture of Babylon
642 Occupation of Alexandria; capture of Isfahan; capture of Rei
643 Capture of African Tripoli
644 Caliph Umar assassinated; accession of Uthman to caliphate
649 Conquest of Cyprus
650 Capture of Persepolis
656 Murder of Caliph Uthman; Ali chosen as caliph
658 Seizure of Egypt
661 Assassination of Ali

Personalities

Abd al-Muttalib, Muhammad's grandfather
Abdallah Ibn Muttalib, Muhammad's father
Amina bint Wahb, Muhammad's mother
Abu Talib, Muhammad's uncle
Ali Ibn abi Talib, Muhammad's cousin, brought up in his house. Fourth caliph
Zayd Ibn Haritha, Muhammad's adopted son, freedman of Khadija
Khadija, Muhammad's first wife
Abu Bakr, friend of Muhammad. First caliph
Aisha, daughter of Abu Bakr, wife of Muhammad
Umar Ibn al-Khattab, Muhammad's principal supporter after Abu Bakr. Second caliph
Abu Sufyan, leader of the Quraysh
Fatima, Muhammad's youngest and favorite daughter, wife of Ali
Hasan and Husain, sons of Ali and Fatima, grandsons of the Prophet, second and third Imams of Shia Islam.

The Caliphate
The Orthodox or Rightly Guided Caliphs
(Al-Khulafa ar-Rashidun)
11–40/632–61

A.H./C.E.

11/632	Abu Bakr
13/634	Umar b. al-Khattab
23/644	Uthman b. Affan
35/656	Ali b. Abi Talib
40/661	

The Umayyad Caliphs
41–132/661–749

41/661	Mu'awiya I b. Abi-Sufyan
60/680	Yazid I
64/683	Mu'awiya II
64/684	Marwan I b. al-Hakam
65/685	Abd al-Malik
86/705	al-Walid I
96/715	Sulaiman
99/717	Umar b. Abd al-Aziz
101/720	Yazid II
105/724	Hisham
125/743	al-Walid II
126/744	Yazid III
126/744	Ibrahim
127/744	Marwan II al-Himar
132/749	

The Abbasid Caliphs
In Iraq and Baghdad 132–656/749–1258

132/749	as-Saffah
136/754	al-Mansur
158/775	al-Mahdi
169/785	al-Hadi
170/786	Harun ar-Rashid
193/809	al-Amīn
198/813	al-Ma'mūn
201–3/817–19	Ibrāhīm b. al-Mahdī, in Baghdad
218/833	al-Mu'taṣim
227/842	al-Wāthiq
232/847	al-Mutawakkil
247/861	al-Muntaṣir
248/862	al-Musta'ī̄n
252/866	al-Mu'tazz
255/869	al-Muhtadī
256/870	al-Mu'tamid
279/892	al-Mu'taḍid
289/902	al-Muktafī
295/908	al-Muqtadir
320/932	al-Qāhir
322/934	ar-Rāḍī
329/940	al-Muttaqī
333/944	al-Mustakfī
334/946	al-Muṭī'
363/974	aṭ-Ṭā'i'
381/991	al-Qādir
422/1031	al-Qā'im
467/1075	al-Muqtadī
487/1094	al-Mustaẓhir
512/1118	al-Mustarshid
529/1135	ar-Rāshid
530/1136	al-Muqtafī
555/1160	al-Mustanjid

566/1170	al-Mustaḍī'
575/1180	an-Nāṣir
622/1225	aẓ-Ẓāhir
623/1226	al-Mustanṣir
640–56/1242–58	al-Mustaʿṣim
	Mongol sack of Baghdad

Acknowledgments

I would like to thank the following: Jim Herrick, editor of *New Humanist*, for first suggesting that I write a book on Islam; Ibn Warraq, whose enthusiasm ensured that this work finally reached publication; the editorial staff at Prometheus Books for coping with the original typescrpt; Mark Koslow, for supplying and allowing me a free hand with unpublished material on the Schuon cult; Robert Burns, of Goldsmiths' College, London, for invaluable guidance in religious studies and showing me the importance of both skepticism and trust; Mike Magee, for convincing me that the "unseen" can certainly be seen by some; Muhammad ar-Ramdani and Dawud Relf, for showing me the human face of Islam; and last but not least, Janet Audley Charles, for being a beautiful, unknowing, amusing muse.

Introduction

Alterius non sit, qui suus esse potest.
(Let no man who can belong to himself belong to another.)
—Paracelsus

The writing and publishing of books on Islam has become something of a growth industry in recent years. There are several reasons for this, and together they amount to the fact that Islam now impinges on the Western consciousness in ways that it never did in times past. Formerly, the average Westerner would have become aware of Islam only if he happened to travel abroad in Islamic lands. Now, however, practically everyone will have met Muslims at school, at work, socially, or as next-door neighbors. Even those who do not know Muslims personally cannot fail to be aware of their immediate presence through their often distinctive dress, shops, and places of worship.

Beyond the personal level, the Western world has been made aware of Islam and the Arab peoples in recent times through terrorism, the oil crisis, the Arab-Israeli wars, the Gulf War, and by the *fatwa* issued against author Salman Rushdie by the late Aya-

tollah Khomeini. It is this latter affair that has forced into promi-
nence the profound social and religious differences between Westerners and those born and raised in a Muslim environment. Westerners and Muslims may now live on the same street and pass
politely by each other in social discourse, but this often disguises
an immanent cultural and intellectual abyss.

The more obvious differences between Islam and Western
ways of life—the attitude toward women, feasts and fasts, punish-
ments and prayers—have been treated in numerous recent and
not-so-recent books, many of them aimed at the general reader.
The traditional story of the origin of Islam and the life of Muhammad have been told over and over as real history. Most of these
books repeat the same material in an uncritical way and serve, in
effect, as apologies for Islam. From such works the uninformed
reader would get no idea that there is any doubt at all about the
origin of Islam and the career of the Prophet, whereas the truth is
that the whole traditional picture has been undermined by recent
Western scholarship. Much of this critical material is out of reach
of most people in obscure and expensive academic books and
journals. However, recent criticisms have been aimed at a popular
readership. Andrew Rippin, himself a radical scholar in the field
of Islamic origins, gives full references in his *Muslims*,[1] and the
same material is given its due by Ibn Warraq in *Why I Am Not a
Muslim*.[2] Both books are among the few that take an unapologeti-
cally critical stance toward Islam.

As yet the insubstantiality of the traditional account of the origins of Islam has had little impact on popular views of the religion,
which would be reason enough for another book that makes the
point. However, another book is needed since Islam has many
aspects that have so far received little or no critical attention,
aspects that carry considerable weight in their appeal to both life-
long Muslims and converts.

The heading under which most of these aspects fall is Sufism,
or Islamic mysticism. Despite how it may appear to outsiders,
Islam is not wholly a religion of rigid rules and unforgiving
severity, unlikely tales and unthinking belief, but it has a heart

made of poetry and art, vision and devotion, which can be fully known only from within. It is this side that has attracted many Western intellectuals and that they often present in their writings as Islam's only or truest face. Sufism raises many of the deepest questions that can be asked about metaphysics and religious experience, questions that have received considerable attention in recent debates in the philosophy of religion.

Here, perhaps, a personal statement may be in order. Having long been drawn to the mystical aspects of Islam through the writings of traditionalist authors, I made contact in the mideighties with a group of Western converts centered around a Sufi sheikh from Cyprus. I was initiated in 1985, and for three years thereafter I led the Muslim life as far as possible in full, including fasts, prayers, and prohibitions. As time went on, however, it became plain to me that I was leading a double life. Some of my personal reservations about Islam, Sufism, and religion in general were not shared by other members of the group, liberal as they were in comparison with Muslims in general. This situation led to my gradual disillusionment, distancing, and "dropping out" of activities. About this time the Rushdie affair broke, and I was forced to decide whose side I was on. Needless to say, it was not the side of the Muslims.

Regardless of the eventual outcome, my experience of close contact with the mystical side of Islam was of incomparable worth to me in affording insights into the mentality of Muslims in general, yet it left me with feelings of nostalgia and regret, as for an innocent childhood inevitably outgrown. For these reasons, this book will not be an anti-Islamic tirade. The intention will be, as it should be in all good intellectual debate, to pay attention to the opponent's best arguments as well as his worst.

Since this book is aimed at the general reader, no prior knowledge of Islam is assumed, and the subject is introduced step by step. At each stage the Islamic tradition is first allowed to speak for itself, either from primary sources or from sympathetic contemporary interpreters, and thereafter critical and oppositional views are stated. Those readers familiar with Islam might well proceed directly to the critique offered in the second chapter of each part. The final section serves as a summary and overview, questioning the position of Islam in the modern world.

Notes

1. See A. Rippin, *Muslims: Their Religious Beliefs & Practices*, vol. 1: The Formative Period (London: Routledge, 1990), chaps. 1, 2, 3, and 4.

2. See Ibn Warraq, *Why I Am Not a Muslim* (Amherst, N.Y.: Prometheus Books, 1995), chap. 3 and passim.

Part I

Origins

Chapter 1

The Traditional Account

His nature was as the Koran.
　　　　　　　　—Aisha, wife of the Prophet

According to the traditional account, Muhammad was born at Mecca in the southern Hijaz, the southwestern part of the Arabian peninsula, on the twelfth or seventeenth of the month *Rabi al-awwal*, in year 570 C.E. He was born into the Arab tribe of the Quraysh, defined as the descendants in the male line of Fihr Ibn (son of) Malik, who lived eleven generations before Muhammad. Originally the Quraysh lived scattered among the other Arab tribes without a territorial center of their own, but five generations before Muhammad a member of the tribe called Qusayy, by means of alliances, diplomacy and war, obtained possession of the sanctuary at Mecca.

This sanctuary, known as the Kaaba, was built originally by Abraham, the patriarch of monotheism and father of both Arabs and Jews. Despite Abraham's monotheistic message, by Muhammad's time the vast majority of Arabs had fallen into a state of idolatry, constituting what came to be known later as *al-*

23

jahiliyyah, the age of ignorance. The only exceptions to this general state were a small number of Jewish and Christian monotheists, called in the Koran *hanifs* or *hunafa*. Paralleling the religious decadence, Mecca at this time was a city of great wealth and prosperity based on trade.

Muhammad was the son of Abdallah, the son of Abd al-Muttalib, the son of Hashim, the son of Abd Manaf, the son of Qusayy. Hashim, the patriarch of the family, was a prominent person in Mecca and traded as far away as Syria and Yemen. Abd al-Muttalib, Muhammad's grandfather, apportioned the water of the sacred well of Zamzam at Mecca and was the custodian of the Kaaba. Abdallah, Muhammad's father, like the rest of the family, was engaged in trade with Syria and died at Medina on his way back from a trading expedition shortly before his son was born. Amina bint (daughter of) Wahb, Muhammad's mother, was of the clan of Zuhrah of the Quraysh and was connected with several of the principal families of Mecca.

Being a posthumous child, Muhammad was put under the protection of his grandfather Abd al-Muttalib. Since it was the custom among the Meccan upper classes to give their children to wet-nurses of the nomadic tribes, this was done with Muhammad for two or more years. It is said that his wet-nurse was Halimah of the clan of Sa'd b. Bakr of the tribe of Hawazin. When Muhammad was six, his mother died, and two years later his grandfather died. He was then put under the protection of his uncle Abu Talib, with whom he made the journey to Syria. During this journey, which took place when Muhammad was about twelve years old, he met the Christian monk Buhayra, who predicted that he would be a great prophet who would illuminate the world. The war of the Fijar took place when he was between fifteen and twenty, and Muhammad played a part in the fighting at the side of his uncles.

These are the main events of Muhammad's life before his marriage. Such an illustrious life could not be without supernatural indications of its coming greatness, however. When he was four years old and in the keeping of Halimah, a significant event occurred. As Muhammad later related it:

There came unto me two men, clothed in white, with a gold basin full of snow. Then they laid hold upon me, and splitting open my breast they brought forth my heart. This likewise they split open and took from it a black clot which they cast away. Then they washed my heart and my breast with the snow.[1]

In explaining this event, he said: "Satan toucheth every son of Adam the day his mother beareth him, save only Mary and her son."[2]

Because of his outstanding moral character, sense of justice, and reputation for honesty, Muhammad was invited by Khadijah, a wealthy widow of Mecca, to take charge of her affairs, acting as her agent on a caravan journey to Syria. Khadijah was so pleased with the results that she made him an offer of marriage, which he accepted. Muhammad was at this time twenty-five and Khadijah forty. The marriage produced seven children—al-Qasim, Ruq-qayah, Zaynab, Umm Kulthum, Fatimah, Abdallah (at-Tayyib), and at-Tahir. All the boys (al-Qasim, Abdallah, and at-Tahir) died young, while all the girls lived to maturity. Muhammad's youngest daughter, Fatima, was of special importance to him and married his cousin Ali.

Following his marriage to Khadijah and prior to the first Koranic revelations, Muhammad became increasingly involved with the affairs of the Meccan community. He was held in very high regard and was invited to oversee the raising of the sacred Black Stone into the corner of the Kaaba when it was rebuilt. He ordered that the stone be placed on a piece of cloth and then asked members of all the tribes to lift together, thus avoiding disputes and feuds. Muhammad was at this time thirty-five years of age.

Not long after these events Muhammad began to experience certain powerful inward signs of his authority and mission. He spoke of visions that came to him in his sleep and were "like the breaking of the light of dawn."[3] As a result of these experiences, solitude became dear to him, and he adopted the habit of making spiritual retreats in a cave on Mount Hira on the outskirts of Mecca.

In Muhammad's fortieth year, in the holy month of Ramadan, one night alone in the cave on Mount Hira, an angel in the form of a man came to him and said: "Recite," and he replied: "I am not a reciter." Thereafter, as Muhammad later described it,

the Angel took me and whelmed me in his embrace until he had reached the limit of mine endurance. Then he released me and said: "Recite!" I said: "I am not a reciter," and again he took me and whelmed me in his embrace, and again when he had reached the limit of mine endurance, he again released me and said: "Recite!" and again I said: "I am not a reciter." Then a third time he whelmed me as before, then released me and said:

Recite in the name of thy Lord who created!
He createth man from a clot of Blood.
Recite; and thy Lord is the Most Bountiful,
He who hath taught by the pen,
taught man what he knew not. (K.96: 1–5)[4]

Muhammad recited these words after the angel, who then left him. This was the first revelation of the Holy Koran. Afterward Muhammad said: "It was as though the words were written on my heart."[5] Despite the overwhelming nature of the experience, Muhammad feared that he had become a man possessed, as a poet is possessed by a spirit (*jinn*). He fled from the cave, but on his way down the mountain he heard a voice above him saying: "O Muhammad, thou art the Messenger of God, and I am Gabriel."[6] He looked around him, and the angel filled the whole horizon.[7]

On returning to Mecca, Muhammad related these events to Khadijah, who reassured him and believed. Khadijah then took Muhammad to his cousin Waraqah, who, on hearing his story, agreed that he had received a genuine revelation.

These human reassurances were followed by a reassurance from heaven in the form of a second revelation (K.68:1–4), and, after a barren period when no revelations came, they resumed with a third (K.93), confirming his mission.[8]

After Khadijah, the first to believe in the genuineness of the revelations were Muhammad's cousin Ali, who was then only nine or ten years of age, his friend Abu Bakr, and the freedman Zayd. As yet no summons to Islam had been made in public; nevertheless, there was soon a small but growing band of believers, most of them young and many of them Muhammad's cousins, though none of his uncles were convinced. Eventually Muhammad made public pronouncements on the basis of the revelations concerning the true religion, ways of worship, and modes of conduct. The chief of these, which was the main cause of offense and opposition among the Quraysh, was the condemnation of idol worship.

Arab historian Ibn Ishaq describes the situation:

When the Quraysh saw that he [Muhammad] would not yield to them and withdrew from them and insulted their gods and that his uncle treated him kindly and stood up in his defense and would not give him up to them, some of their leading men went to Abu Talib. . . . They said, "O Abu Talib, your nephew has cursed our gods, insulted our religion, mocked our way of life and accused our forefathers of error; either you must stop him or you must let us get at him, for you yourself are in the same position as we in opposition to him and we will rid you of him." He gave them a conciliatory reply and a soft answer and they went away.

Not being able to attack Muhammad directly, the Quraysh then turned upon his followers:

The Quraysh incited people against the companions of the Apostle who had become Muslims. Every tribe fell upon the Muslims among them, beating them and seducing them from their religion. God protected his Apostle from them through his uncle, who, when he saw what the Quraysh were doing, called upon the Banu Hashim and the Banu Abd al-Muttalib to stand with him in protecting the Prophet. This they agreed to do, with the exception of Abu Lahab, the accursed enemy of God.[9]

Because of this persecution by the Quraysh, while Muhammad himself was under the protection of Abu Talib, he ordered the

Muslims to emigrate to Abyssinia. The reason for this move is described by Arab historian At-Tabari:

> In Abyssinia there was a righteous king called the Negus in whose land no one was oppressed and who was praised for his righteousness. Abyssinia was a land with which the Quraysh traded and in which found an ample living, security and a good market. When the Messenger of God commanded them to do this, the main body of them went to Abyssinia because of the coercion they were being subjected to in Mecca. His fear is that they would be seduced from their religion. He himself remained and did not leave Mecca. Several years passed in this way, during which the Quraysh pressed hard upon those of them who had become Muslims.[10]

This was the first emigration (*Hijra*) in Islam.

After some time a rumor reached the emigrants in Abyssinia that the Quraysh at Mecca had converted and become Muslims, so some decided to return. Unfortunately, although two powerful and important men among the Quraysh, Hamza Ibn Abd al-Muttalib and Umar Ibn al-Khattab, had converted, most were still opposed to the Muslims and continued the persecution. The Quraysh then decided to impose a boycott on the Banu Hashim and Banu Muttalib to the effect that "no one should marry their women nor give women for them to marry; and that no one should buy from them or sell to them."[11] Shortly after this, Muhammad's uncle and protector, Abu Talib, and his wife, Khadija, died. At this time the Prophet was fifty years old and at the lowest point of his life. After the death of Khadija, Muhammad married Sawda, the wife of one of his followers who had died in Abyssinia, and became betrothed to Aisha, the young daughter of Abu Bakr.

Because of the difficulty of his position at Mecca, Muhammad now looked for opportunities to spread Islam elsewhere. He first tried the nearby town of at-Taif but was rebuffed by its citizens. He then approached the nomadic tribes but was no better received. His words and reputation did, however, strike a responsive chord in Yathrib (Medina), a town of mixed Arab and Jewish population two hundred miles north of Mecca. The dominant group at Medina were the Banu Qayla, later known as the *Ansar* ("Helpers"). They were divided into the related stems of the Aws and the Khazraj, each of which was further divided into clans and subclans. Two other important groups in Medina were the Banu Qurayza and the Banu Nadir, together with a smaller grouping called the Banu Qaynuqa, all of whom adhered to the Jewish faith.

The Aws and the Khazraj were frequently in dispute, and during several pilgrimages to Mecca members of the factions made contact with Muhammad, and many became Muslims. Thereafter they pledged their support for Muhammad and invited him to come to Medina to settle their quarrels. As a result, the Prophet encouraged the Muslims of Mecca to remove themselves to Medina, which they did in numerous small groups, the Muslims in Medina providing the emigrants (*Muhajirun*) with lodging. Before long only Muhammad, Abu Bakr, and Ali were left in Mecca. In order to foil a plot against his life, Muhammad left Ali in his own bed one night while he and Abu Bakr slipped away to a cave on Mount Thawr to the south of Mecca. This is when the famous incident of the cave occurred. When the Quraysh came looking for Muhammad and Abu Bakr, they found the cave in which they were hiding but didn't go in because a spider had spun a web over the entrance and a rock dove had built a nest on the ledge in front of it, so they concluded that no one could possibly have entered it recently. Soon, Abu Bakr's son Abdallah arrived with camels and provisions and they set off for Medina by devious paths, arriving at Quba on the outskirts of the Meccan oasis on Monday, September 27, 622.[12] This event is known as the *Hijra* and marks the beginning of the Islamic era.

Perhaps the most important early outcome of Muhammad's residence in Medina was the drawing up of a document known as the Constitution of Medina. Ibn Ishaq introduces it:

And the Apostle of God wrote a document [*kitab*] between the Migrants [*Muhajirun*] and the Helpers [*Ansar*], and in it he made a peace [wada'a] with the Jews and a pact ['ahada] with them, and he confirmed/established them according to their religion/law ['ala dinihim] and properties and laid down obligations due to them, and imposed obligations upon them.

The document begins:

In the Name of God, the Compassionate, the Merciful. This is a document from Muhammad the Prophet [concerning the relations] between the believers and the Muslims of the Quraysh and Yathrib [Medina], and those who followed them and joined them and labored with them. They are one community [umma] to the exclusion of all men.

This is followed by forty-seven clauses, including the stipulation that "Whenever you differ about a matter, it must be referred to God and Muhammad."[13]

In the first two years of the *hijra* the Muslims in Medina engaged in many expeditions or campaigns (*maghazi*) against the caravans of the Quraysh passing between Mecca and the north. Most of these raids were on a small scale and without significant result, but in the year 624 (2 A.H.) the first great victory of Islam occurred at the battle of Badr.

News reached Muhammad that a large caravan in the charge of Abu Sufyan was passing southward from Palestine toward Mecca. In the expectation that God would give success, the Prophet exhorted the Muslims in Medina to go out and attack it. Word of his intentions reached the Quraysh, who in response assembled forces to defend the caravan. The Meccan force, led by the notorious Abu Jahl, a sworn enemy of Islam, numbered about 950 men, while the Muslims amounted to 324, consisting of 238 *Ansar* and 86 *Muhajirun*; the date of the battle was 17, 19 or 21 of Ramadan (= March 13, 15, or 17).[14] On the previous night, aware that Abu Jahl was heading for the wells at Badr, Muhammad blocked them all up but one, around which he stationed his forces. On the morning of the battle the presence of the Muslims at the wells took the Quraysh by surprise. Fights between champions and exchanges of arrows were followed by a general melee, which culminated in the Quraysh fleeing the field. Between forty-five and seventy Quraysh were killed, including Abu Jahl and several other Meccan leaders, and many others were taken prisoner, including Muhammad's uncle Abbas. The victory of such a small force over one almost three times its size convinced the Muslims that it could not have been achieved without heavenly assistance in the form of angels, as the Koran confirms (K.3:123–25).

After the battle of Badr the Banu Qaynuqa were accused of breaking the pact they had made with Muhammad, and as a consequence the Muslim forces attacked them in their stronghold at Medina and defeated them. The survivors were then driven from the town and forced to leave their property in the hands of the Muslims.

In the following year, 625 (3 A.H.), the Meccans attempted to avenge their defeat at Badr. A force of three thousand foot soldiers and two hundred cavalry were assembled under the command of Abu Sufyan and marched toward Medina. They reached the town on Thursday, March 21, and selected a site for their camp near the hill of Uhud, after which the ensuing battle was named. In order to provoke the Muslims into attacking them, the Meccans deliberately pastured their animals in nearby fields of corn. This strategy worked in that the Muslims left the safety of Medina and approached the Meccan camp. The battle took place on Saturday, March 23, and, in short, the Muslims got the worst of it. Ibn Ishaq describes the crucial events:

> The Muslims were put to flight and the enemy slew many of them. It was a day of trial and testing in which God honored several with martyrdom, until the enemy got at the Messenger who was struck with a stone so that he fell on his side and one of his teeth was smashed, his face gashed and his lip injured.[15]

Fortunately for the Muslims, after the battle the Meccans chose to return home rather than sack Medina. They could, however, comfort themselves with the revelation that "What befell you on the day when two hosts met was by the permission of God, and in order that He might know the believers and in order that He might know the hypocrites" (K.3:166). As after Badr, after Uhud Muhammad turned against the Jews of Medina. This time he expelled the Banu Nadir on the grounds of a plot against his life.

In the years 625–27, the only signficant event was an inconclusive raid on Dumat al-Jandal, the present-day oasis of al-Jawf. In 627, however, some of the Banu Nadir who had gone into exile at Khaybar took the initiative. A party of them went to Mecca and invited the Quraysh to join in an attack on Muhammad in Medina in order to finish him off, to which they readily agreed; they then went on to enlist the help of the Ghatafan of Qays Aylan with equal success. News of these plans reached Muhammad, who then ordered a ditch or trench to be dug around Medina where it was vulnerable to attack by cavalry. The Quraysh arrived at Medina on March 31 with ten thousand black mercenaries, plus their allies from the Banu Kinana, Tihana, and Ghatafan, while Muhammad could muster about three thousand.[16] The two forces faced each other for more than twenty days with little more fighting than the exchange of volleys of arrows. Six of the *Ansar* are reported to have been killed, and three Meccans. The morale of neither side was high, but that of the Meccans was worse, and eventually their alliances began to break up, and they decided to withdraw.

After the inconclusive "battle" of the trench (*al-Khandaq*) comes the notorious affair of the Banu Qurayza, the last major Jewish presence in Medina. According to Muslim tradition, the Banu Qurayza were bound by treaty not to assist the enemies of the Prophet, which is precisely what they did during the siege of Medina at the instigation of Huyay Ibn Akhtab, leader of the Banu Nadir. Whatever the political reasons for pursuing the Banu Qurayza may have been, action against them was made imperative by divine intervention. As Ibn Ishaq relates:

> According to what al-Zuhri told me, at the time of the noon prayers Gabriel came to the Messenger wearing an embroidered

turban and riding on a mule with a saddle covered with a piece of brocade. He asked the Messenger if he had abandoned fighting, and when he said he had, Gabriel said that the angels had not yet laid aside their arms and that he had just come from pursuing the enemy. "God commands you, Muhammad, go to the Banu Qurayza. I am about to go to them and shake their stronghold."[17]

The same army that had withstood the siege of Medina now proceeded to besiege the Banu Qurayza. After twenty-five nights Kalb Ibn Asad, the leader of the Banu Qurayza, offered to surrender on the same terms granted to the Banu Nadir but was told that he and his tribe must surrender unconditionally. The Aws, as former patrons of the Banu Qurayza, then begged Muhammad to show mercy. As a result, the Prophet agreed that sentence should be passed on them by a member of the Aws, and a certain Sa'd Ibn Mu'adh was chosen for the task. His verdict was that "the men should be killed, the property divided, and the women and children taken as captives."

Then the Banu Qurayza surrendered themselves and the Messenger confined them in the compound of Bint al-Harith, a woman of the Banu al-Najjar. Then the Messenger went out to the market of Medina—which is still the market today—and dug trenches in it. Then he sent for them and struck off their heads in those trenches as they were brought out to him in batches. Among them was the enemy of God Huyay ibn Akhtab and Kalb Ibn Asad their chief. There were 600 or 700 in all, though some put the figure as high as 800 or 900. As they were being taken out in batches to the Apostle, they asked Kalb what he thought would be done to them. He replied, "Will you never understand? Don't you see that the summoner never stops and those who are taken away never return? By God, it is death." This went on until the Messenger made an end to them.[18]

Harsh as this might seem, its justice was confirmed by revelation:

The worst of beasts in the sight of God are those who reject Him:
they will not believe. They are those with whom you made a
pact, then they break their compact every time and they fear not
God. So if you come up against them in war, drive off through
them and their followers, that they may remember. And if you
fear treachery from any group, dissolve it with them equally, for
God does not love the treacherous. (K.8:55–58)

Soon after dealing with the Banu Qurayza, Muhammad had a
dream that convinced him that he should perform the *umra*, or
lesser pilgrimage to Mecca. He set off with about 19,500 men and
reached al-Hudaybiyah, on the edge of the sacred territory, where
he halted. The Meccans would not allow him to enter the city
since they suspected his intentions, so he sent Uthman, the future
third caliph of Islam, to negotiate on his behalf. The eventual
result was a truce known as the Pact of Hudaybiyah (March 628),
in which the Quraysh agreed to refrain from war for ten years and
to allow the *umra* in the following year. This gave Muhammad a
free hand against the settlements north of Medina, particularly the
Jewish settlement of Khaybar, which fell into his hands, together
with Fadak, during a seven-week campaign. In February of the following year (629=7A.H.), the delayed *umra* was fulfilled, after
which Muhammad returned to Medina for the next five or six
months. In September he made a daring raid deep into Byzantine
territory in Syria, with disastrous results at the hands of the Greek
and Arab forces of Heraclius. This incident is mentioned by the
Byzantine historian Theophanes (d. 818) and is the first event in
the history of Muhammad and his community to be reported in a
source outside Muslim tradition.[19]
    The cause of the breach of the truce of Hudaybiyah was not
any event directly involving the main parties, that is, the Meccans
and the Muslims, but a quarrel between two of their bedouin
allies. Although negotiation was possible, Muhammad felt that the
tide of events was in his favor, and he decided to move against the
Meccans. On the first day of January 630 he set out with an army
of about ten thousand men, made up of contingents from

numerous tribes he had won to his cause. They encamped at Marr az-Zahran, about two short stages from Mecca, and lit ten thousand fires to give the impression of an overwhelming force. At this point the event that was the key to their imminent triumph occurred: The important Meccan leader Abu Sufyan came out from the town and made submission. The following night they camped nearer to Mecca, and in the morning, with forces divided into four columns, they advanced into the town from four directions. Only one column met any resistance, and this was soon overcome. Twenty-four Quraysh and four Hudhayl were killed, as were two Muslims. This event became known as the *Fat'h*, or the conquest. The date was about January 11, 630 (20/9/8 A.H.).[20]

After the majority of Meccans had accepted Islam and the idols of the Kaaba and the shrines around Mecca had been destroyed, less than a month after the conquest, Muhammad faced another test in an alliance against him by the bedouin tribes of the Hawazin and Thaqif. They collected an army of twenty thousand, twice the size of Muhammad's, only two or three days' march away, and although the Prophet was able to add only two thousand men to his force, he judged himself strong enough to give battle. Leaving Mecca on January 27, 630 (6/10/8 A.H.), on the evening of the thirtieth, the Muslim army camped near the valley of the Hunayn, close to the enemy. Next morning the Muslims moved down the valley into the midst of their foes. At first things went badly, but without warning the tide of the battle turned in their favor, and the enemy was overwhelmed. The reason for this sudden change of fortune was subsequently made apparent by revelation:

> God has given you victory on many fields, and on the day of Hunayn, when you exulted in your numbers, though they availed you nothing, and the earth, vast as it was, was straitened for you. Then you turned back in flight. Then God sent down His peace of reassurance on His Messenger and upon the believers, and sent down hosts you could not see, and punished those who did not believe. Such is the reward of disbelievers. (K.9:25–26)

After the battle of Hunayn, remnants of the Banu Thaqif fled back to the protection of their fortified city of al-Ta'if. Though Muhammad laid siege, the taking of a walled city was beyond his powers, so he retired to al-Ji'ranah, close to Mecca, to divide the spoils of his victory. He remained there until until March 9, 630, when he left for Mecca to make the *umra*, after which he returned to Medina. Muhammad now turned his attention once again to the north and made an expedition to Tabuk and Ayla, then later Aqaba, where he made a treaty with the governor. The Hijri year, which began in April 630 (9 A.H.) is known as the year of deputations, since each tribe sent its *wafd*, or deputation, to Muhammad to profess Islam and to become members of the *umma*, the community of the Prophet.

Although Muhammad completed the *umra*, or lesser pilgrimage, in March 630, he did not perform the *hajj*, or greater pilgrimage. In 631 the *Hajj* was led by Abu Bakr, and it was not until *Dhu al-Hijja* (March) 632, the year of his death, that Muhammad went on his one and only *hajj*, known as the Pilgrimage of Farewell. The *hajj* was an ancient pre-Islamic custom, and the Prophet turned it, by means of his own example, into a properly Muslim rite. As Ibn Ishaq says:

> The Apostle completed the *Hajj* and showed men the rites and taught them what God had prescribed as to their *Hajj*, the "standing," the throwing of stones, the circumambulation of the temple and what He had permitted and forbidden. It was the pilgrimage of completion and the pilgrimage of farewell because the Apostle did not go on pilgrimage after that.[21]

This was in fact a restoration of the original form of the *hajj* initiated by Adam and Abraham, and thereafter all pagans and non-Muslims were excluded.

It was while at Mecca on the *hajj* that Muhammad preached what came to be known as the Farewell Sermon, which concluded: "I have left amongst you that which, if ye hold fast to it, shall preserve you from all error, a clear indication, the Book of

God and the word of His Prophet. O people, hear my words and understand."²² He then spoke the final revelation, twenty-three years after the first:

> This day the disbelievers despair of prevailing against your religion, so fear them not, but fear Me! This day have I perfected for you your religion and fulfilled My favor unto you, and it hath been My good pleasure to choose Islam for you as your religion. (K.5:3)

On returning to Medina and not long after ordering the preparation of a raid on Syria, the Prophet showed sudden signs of illness. As Ibn Ishaq describes:

> The Prophet began to suffer from the illness by which God took him to what honor and compassion He intended for him shortly before the end of [the month of] Saffar or the beginning of First Rabi'a. It began, so I have been told, when he went to the Gharqad cemetery in the middle of the night and prayed for the dead. Then he returned to his family and in the morning his sufferings began. . . . Aisha [the Prophet's young wife] said: The Messenger came back to me from the mosque that day and lay on my lap. A man of Abu Bakr's family came in to me with a toothpick in his hand. The Messenger looked at it in such a way that I knew he wanted it, and when I asked him if he wanted me to give it to him, he said yes. So I took it and chewed it to soften it for him and gave it to him. He rubbed his teeth with it more energetically than I had ever seen him rub them before. Then he laid it down. I found him heavy on my breast, and as I looked into his face, lo his eyes were fixed and he was saying, "No, the most Exalted Companion is of Paradise." I said, "You were given the choice and you have chosen, by Him who sent you with the truth!" And so the Messenger was taken. . . . When the preparations for his burial had been completed on the Tuesday, he was laid upon his bed in his house. Some were in favor of burying him in his mosque, while others wanted to bury him with his (already fallen) companions. Abu Bakr said, "I heard the Apostle

say, 'No prophet dies but he is buried where he died.' " So the bed on which he had died [in Aisha's house] was taken up and they made a grave beneath it. Then the people came to visit the Prophet, praying over him by companies: first came the men, then the women, then the children. No man acted as prayer-leader in the prayers of the Apostle. The Apostle was buried in the middle of the night of the Wednesday.[23]

After the death of the Prophet, Abu Bakr was elected caliph (*khalifa*, representative). He was forced to take immediate action in face of a rebellion, known as the apostasy (*ar-ridda*), when the tribes who had pledged allegiance to Muhammad refused to pay the alms tax (*zakat*) or abide by the treaties to which they were parties. Also at this time, in various parts of Arabia, other claimants to prophetic status had arisen and gained followers among the tribes. Abu Bakr had the advantage of an army raised to attack the Roman Empire and a general of genius, Khalid Ibn al-Walid, the "Sword of God," who, with a succession of victories, subdued the *ridda* and began the conquest of the settled lands in the north, east, and west.

Abu Bakr died in 634 and was succeeded by Umar (634–644), Uthman (644–656), and Ali (656–661). These four leaders of the Islamic community, all of whom were intimate companions of the Prophet, are known as the rightly guided caliphs (*al-khulafa ar-rashidun*). During this period and for long thereafter the extent of Islamic territory (*dar al-Islam*) increased in a spectacular and providential fashion.

Notes

1. Ibn Sa'd, *Kitab at-Tabaqat al-Kabir* (The Great Book of Classes), 1/1, p. 96, quoted by M. Lings, *Muhammad: His Life Based on the Earliest Sources* (London: George, Allen & Unwin, 1983), p. 26.

2. al-Bukhari, *Al-Jami as-Sahih* (The Sound Comprehensive Work), 50/54, quoted by Lings in ibid.

3. Bukhari, *Al-Jami*, 1/3; Lings, *Muhammad*, p. 43.

4. Bukhari, *Al-Jami*, 1/3; Lings, *Muhammad*, p. 44.

5. Ibn lshaq, *Sirat Rasul Allah* (Life of the Messenger of God), p. 153, quoted in Lings, *Muhammad*, p. 44.

6. Bukhari, *Al-Jami*, 1/3; Lings, *Muhammad*, p. 44.

7. This crucial event will be discussed in part II.

8. Lings, *Muhammad*, p. 45; cf. W. M. Watt, *Muhammad at Mecca* (Oxford: Oxford University Press, 1953), p. 41; and F. E. Peters, *Muhammad and the Origins of Islam* (New York: SUNY Press, 1994), pp. 147–52.

9. A. Guillaume, *The Life of Muhammad*, translation of Ibn Ishaq's *Sirat* (Oxford: Oxford University Press, 1955), pp. 118–20.

10. At-Tabari, *Annals*, ed. and trans. W. M. Watt and M. V. McDonald (New York: SUNY Press), vol. 6, pp. 98–99.

11. Ibn Ishaq in Guillaume, *Life of Muhammad*, p. 159.

12. Lings, *Muhammad*, p. 123; cf. Watt, *Muhammad at Mecca*, p. 151, and Peters, *Muhammad and the Origins*, pp. 188–89.

13. Ibn Ishaq in Guillaume, *Muhammad*, pp. 231–32.

14. Ibn Sa'd, *Tabaqat*, quoted in W. M. Watt, *Muhammad at Medina* (Oxford: Oxford University Press, 1956), p. 10.

15. Ibn Ishaq in Guillaume, *Life of Muhammad*, p. 380.

16. Watt, *Muhammad at Medina*, p. 36.

17. Ibn Ishaq in Guillaume, *Life of Muhammad*, p. 461.

18. Ibid., p. 464; cf. Lings, *Muhammad*, ch. 61, esp. p. 232.

19. See Peters, *Muhammad and the Origins*, pp. 231–33.

20. Ibn Hisham, *Kitab Sirat Rusul Allah*, and al-Waqidi, *Kitab al-Maghazi*, summarized by Watt, *Muhammad at Medina*, p. 66.

21. Ibn Ishaq in Guillaume, *Life of Muhammad*, p. 652.

22. Lings, *Muhammad*, p. 334.

23. Ibn Ishaq in Guillaume, *Life of Muhammad*, pp. 678–88.

Chapter 2

Origins:
A Secular Perspective

Variant versions (of stories) do not always survive, and even when they do, the Islamic tradition is so huge that one has not always read or recognized them: most of what passes for factual information about the rise of Islam is derived from stories read in isolation from their counterparts. The Islamic tradition on the rise of Islam in fact consists of nothing *but* stories, and the massive information that can be derived from these stories never represents straightforward fact.

—Patricia Crone

Chapter 1 gave the account of the life of Muhammad that Muslims have told themselves for over twelve hundred years. It is the story that is presented to any potential convert and offered generally as reliable information on the origin of Islam. As presented here, the emphasis has been put on mundane events — battles, treaties, dates—the kind of thing looked for by historians seeking to know what actually happened. The transcendent aspects of the story, such as Muhammad's ascent to heaven (*miraj*) and the circumstances surrounding the Koranic revelations (*asbab an nusul*), will be dealt with in parts II and III.

41

It is important to realize that the story as told above is but the barest bones of what is supposed to be known to have happened. Many events and characters have not been mentioned at all, and even those referred to have been described with minimal detail. The material on these matters to be found in the works of the Arab historians is of formidable proportions and incredible detail: everything from the names and lineages of the most minor characters to the inner thoughts and motivations of the major protagonists, everything, in short, that anyone who enjoys a good story might want to know. Some idea of the detail available can be gathered from Martin Lings's book *Muhammad: His Life Based on the Earliest Sources*. Lings, a pious Muslim, presents it all without the least hint of doubt or reservation, but a life of Muhammad "based on the earliest sources" is precisely the problem for the secular historian since the sources are not really early at all but late and tendentious.

The way that Muslims like to imagine the situation with regard to our knowledge of the life of Muhammad is well illustrated by a passage from a contemporary introduction to Islam aimed at young Muslims:

> The life of Muhammad is known as the *Sira* and was lived in the full light of history. Everything he did and said was recorded. Because he could not read and write himself, he was constantly served by a group of 45 scribes who wrote down his sayings, instructions and his activities. Muhammad himself insisted on documenting his important decisions. Nearly three hundred of his documents have come down to us, including political treaties, military enlistments, assignments of officials and state correspondence written on tanned leather. We thus know his life to the minutest details: how he spoke, sat, sleeped [sic], dressed, walked; his behaviour as a husband, father, nephew; his attitudes toward women, children, animals; his business transactions and stance toward the poor and the oppressed; his engagement in camps and cantonments, his behaviour in battle; his exercise of political authority and stand on power; his personal

habits, likes and dislikes—even his private dealings with his wives. Within a few decades of his death, accounts of the life of Muhammad were available to the Muslim community in written form. One of the earliest and the most famous biographies of Muhammad, written less than [a] hundred years after his death, is *Sirat Rasul Allah* by Ibn Ishaq.[1]

In contrast, the following is the verdict of John Burton, professor emeritus of Islamic studies at the University of St. Andrews, on the translation of a volume of at-Tabari's *History* dealing with the early life of Muhammad:

In this series of translations of the History of at-Tabari, four volumes on the life of Muhammad are projected, of which this, the first, covers the part from birth to early fifties. None will fail to be struck by the slimness of a volume purporting to cover more than half a century in the life of one of History's giants. Ignoring the pages tracing his lineage all the way back to Adam and disregarding the merely fabulous with which the author has padded out his book, is to realize how very meagre is the hard information available to the Muslims for the life of the man whose activities profoundly affected their own as well as the lives of countless millions. Of the childhood, the education of the boy and the influences on the youth, all of which set the pattern of the development of the man, we know virtually nothing. We simply have to adjust to the uncomfortable admission that, in the absence of contemporary documents, we just do not and never shall know what we most desire to learn. To admit that we do not know as much as we thought we did is the sign of maturity, and have we not been told that of that whereof we cannot speak, we must perforce be silent? Otherwise we speculate. There is nothing wrong with speculation, as long as it is not called History.[2]

The gulf between the attitudes represented by these two quotations forms the theme for the rest of this book.

The claim that Ibn Ishaq's life of Muhammad was "written less than a hundred years after his death" is disingenuous, not to say deliberately misleading. When this kind of statement is found in books written by Muslims, it is hard to know whether they are the result of ignorance, wishful thinking, or a conscious desire to deceive. It is indeed true that the earliest biography of Muhammad is the *Sirat Rasul Allah* by Ibn Ishaq. It is also true that he was born about 717 and died in 767. Ibn Ishaq was the oldest of the sources for the life of Muhammad relied upon by at-Tabari (d. 992) and, as Burton says, "was himself a man who died as much as a century and a half after the time of the Prophet. Born some eighty-five years after Muhammad's arrival at Medina, Muhammad b. Ishaq would have reached his teens only as much as one hundred years after the events he affects to portray."[3]

The only way to ameliorate the effect of Ibn Ishaq's debilitating remoteness from the time of the purported events of Muhammad's life is to claim he had access to reliable sources who were themselves eyewitnesses or hearers of eyewitnesses. This amounts to a claim for the reliability of the chain of transmission (*isnad*) of the traditions of the Prophet (*hadith*), a claim without foundation, as we shall see in part II. In any case, as Burton goes on to say:

> To demonstrate the feasibility of the *isnad* is to say nothing about the authenticity of the matter being transmitted. . . . In judging the content, the only resort of the scholar is to the yard-stick of probability, and on this basis, it must be repeated, virtually nothing of use to the historian emerges from the sparse record of the early life of the founder of the latest of the great world religions. . . . So, however far back in the Muslim tradition one now attempts to reach, one simply cannot recover a scrap of information of real use in constructing the human history of Muhammad, beyond the bare fact that he once existed— although even that has now been questioned.[4]

So much for the life "lived in the full light of history." In addition to these devastating caveats, we do not possess Ibn Ishaq's *Sira* in its original form but in the redaction of Ibn Hisham

(d. 833), who edited it so as to omit "things which it is disgraceful to discuss; matters which would distress certain people; and such reports as al-Bakka'i told me he could not accept as trustworthy."[5]

The Muslims' delusion that they have eyewitness reports for every aspect of Muhammad's life is similar to the delusion of fundamentalist and evangelical Christians that in the Gospels they have eyewitness reports of every moment of the life of Jesus. Likewise, Orthodox Jews are convinced they have a record of all that is worth knowing about the life of Moses in the Pentateuch and the Talmud. The motivation for all these fantasies is the same. Believers, of necessity, need something to believe, and if the information is not at hand, there are always those ready to supply it, not always or necessarily in a spirit of deliberate falsification and conscious deceit, but as a natural product of the hothouse that is the pious imagination given their view of God, man, history, and the scraps of information about the past that they happened to have. What we have in such documents as the Pentateuch, the New Testament, and the *Sira* is not history as understood by modern secular historians but something that is best called salvation, or sacred history, the history of God's plan for humankind; that is, not history at all in the sense of a record of real events in the ordinary world, but an imaginative literary genre.

This view of the Muslim sources for the life of Muhammad and the origins of Islam has been advocated by John Wansbrough of the London School of Oriental and African Studies in his two books: *Quranic Studies* (1977) and *The Sectarian Milieu* (1978). Wansbrough's achievement was to bring to the Koran and to Islam the same healthy skepticism developed in modern biblical and historical studies. This was needed in order to counteract a certain overeagerness to attain positive results that had become predominant in Islamic studies, an overeagerness that tended to ignore or dismiss the achievements of an older generation of scholars who had shown how untrustworthy the Muslim sources are.

The first chapter of *The Sectarian Milieu* is devoted to a study of Muslim historiography, particularly the *Sira* of Ibn Ishaq and the *Maghazi* of Waqidi (d. 822). Wansbrough concludes that the primary components of salvation history to be found in these works were "largely derived from the discourse of interconfessional polemie,"[6] the sectarian milieu of the title. By means of narrative techniques that Wansbrough calls "historicization" and "exemplification," these components or topics (*topoi*) were introduced into the *Sira* as incidents in the life of the Arabian Prophet, thus giving them an apparently authentic life situation (*Sitz im Leben*). Most of these standard topics, twenty-three in all, appear in one passage of the *Sira* (i 544–72) summarizing Muhammad's purported encounter with the Jews in Medina.

The six most basic themes are adduced as anecdotes in the following forms: (1) prognosis of Muhammad in Jewish scripture, (2) Jewish rejection of that prognosis, (3) Jewish insistence upon miracles for prophets, (4) Jewish rejection of Muhammad's revelation, (5) Muslim charge of scriptural falsification, and (6) Muslim claim to supersede earlier dispensations.

The most important of these themes, which became a habitual and hackneyed topic in Muslim polemics against their Jewish and Christian opponents, was that of scriptural falsification. It was hardly original. The same thing had been alleged between Jews and Samaritans, Jews and Christians, Pharisees and Saducees, Karaites and Rabbinites, and the accusation that fabricated passages were introduced into scripture by satanic intervention, as in the notorious "satanic verses," was an Ebionite accusation against the Pentateuch. In the Muslim case the last is to do with the doctrine of divine annulment of "false" revelation, that is to say, the necessity of superseding or abrogating previous prescriptions. As Wansbrough says: "It is not unlikely that what became the doctrine of abrogation (*naskh*) was originally a polemical topos employed to justify a new dispensation, and hence readily transferable within the sectarian milieu."[7]

After dozens of pages of this kind of analysis, nothing is left of the *Sira-Maghazi* literature as evidence for what actually happened in early Islam. Radical as this conclusion is, even more devastating for the traditional picture of Islamic origins is Wansbrough's view of what the underlying motive was for the production of all this polemical literature. It is mentioned in passing in *Quranic Studies* and might easily be overlooked. It is that "Tafsir [Koranic exegesis] traditions, like traditions in every other field, reflect a single impulse: to demonstrate the Hijazi origins of Islam."[8]

Why would the Hijazi origin of Islam need to be demonstrated if the traditional view of the origin of Islam is correct? The obvious answer is that it was a matter for dispute in the sectarian milieu of the eighth and ninth centuries. It was not generally known or believed at that time that Islam had originated in the Hijaz, because it was not yet entirely clear, either to Muslims or to non-Muslims, exactly what Islam was. It was still in the process of definition, and that definition took the form of an extended and simultaneous literary exercise in the fields of history (*Sira, tarikh*), law (*sharia, fiqh*), and religion (*Koran, hadith*). This alters the whole traditional picture of the origin of Islam and the purported life of its Prophet.

Wansbrough's views on the historical value of the Muslim sources and the likely geographical location for the self-definition of Islam had a profound effect on two scholars who have produced the most radical version of Islamic origins. Patricia Crone and Michael Cook first presented their views at a colloquium on the first century of Islamic society held at Oxford in 1975, which were later published as *Hagarism: The Making of the Islamic World* (1977). In the preface to this work the authors admit that without exposure to "the sceptical approach of Dr. John Wansbrough to the historicity of the Islamic tradition . . . the theory of Islamic origins set out in this book would never have occurred to us."[9] Recognition of this approach led to a theory that is "not one which any believing Muslim can accept: not because it in any way belittles the historical role of Muhammad, but because it presents him in a role quite different from that which he has taken on in the Islamic tradition. This is a book written by infidels for infidels, and it is based on what from any Muslim perspective must appear an inordinate regard for the testimony of infidel sources."[10]

The "infidel sources" are the non-Muslim historians of the period of the Islamic conquests. The reasons for resorting to them are set out in the opening paragraph, which well summarizes the situation in Islamic studies that called for the book to be written:

> Virtually all accounts of the early development of Islam take it as axiomatic that it is possible to elicit at least the outlines of the process from the Islamic sources. It is however well-known that these sources are not demonstrably early. There is no hard evidence for the existence of the Koran in any form before the last decade of the seventh century, and the tradition which places this rather opaque revelation in its historical context is not attested before the middle of the eighth. The historicity of the Islamic tradition is thus to some degree problematic: while there are no cogent internal grounds for rejecting it, there are equally no cogent external grounds for accepting it. In the circumstances it is not unreasonable to proceed in the usual fashion by presenting a sensibly edited version of the tradition as historical fact. But equally, it makes some sense to regard the tradition as without determinate historical content, and to insist that what purport to be accounts of religious events in the seventh century are utilizable only for the study of religious ideas in the eighth. The Islamic sources provide plenty of scope for the implementation of these different approaches, but offer little that can be used in any decisive way to arbitrate between them. The only way out of the dilemma is thus to step outside the Islamic tradition altogether and start again.[11]

In other words, the book represents a leap of unfaith, both in the Muslim sources and in the scholarly establishment in Islamic studies.

The reconstruction that resulted from this alternative approach has Muhammad alive during the conquest of Palestine and acting as the herald of a coming Jewish messiah, Umar al-Faruq. This Muhammad was the leader of a movement to retake Jerusalem and the Holy Land, the participants in which were known as *Magaritai* (Greek), *Mahgraye* (Syriac), or *muhajirun* (Arabic), indicating that they were associated with Hagar and that the original *hijra* was to Jerusalem. With the Arabs' increasing success, the need for a break with the Jews became pressing, and this was occasioned by a quarrel over building on the temple site at Jerusalem. After a flirtation with Christianity that precipitated a respect for Jesus as prophet and messiah and Mary as virgin, Islamic identity finally asserted itself in identification with an Abrahamic monotheism independent of and ancestral to both Judaism and Christianity. This notion was filled out by borrowing from Samaritanism the idea of a scripture limited to the Pentateuch, a prophet like Moses, a holy book revealed like the Torah, a sacred city with nearby mountain and shrine of an appropriate patriarch, plus a caliphate modeled on an Aaronid priesthood. In short, up until about the time of the caliph Abd al-Malik (685–705), Hagarism was a Jewish messianic movement intent on reestablishing Judaism in the Promised Land, with little Arabic about it apart from the language.

As was surely anticipated, these ideas stirred up a hornets' nest, not so much among affronted Muslims as among the old school of established authorities in the field, who had, for the most part, been content to go along with the traditional account. This is not to say that many, even among the skeptics, were convinced by Crone and Cook's reconstruction. Wansbrough, for one, could see no more reason to believe the Jewish and Christian version of events than the Muslim, since they were just as much a part of the sectarian milieu and involved in the production of polemical literature.[12] The great achievement of the book was to explode the academic consensus and demolish deference to the Muslim view of things, thus making it possible to propose radical alternative hypotheses for the origins of Islam.

Patricia Crone went on to write several more books challenging accepted views on early Islam. *Slaves on Horses* (1980) asked why it was that ninth-century Muslim rulers in the Middle East chose to place military and political power in the hands of imported slaves. The conceptual framework was still that of *Hagarism*, and the book was regarded by its author as an overextended footnote to that work, even though it was based firmly on the Muslim sources.

The historiographical introduction contains many astute observations on Islamic origins and the state of Islamic studies.

Of Ibn Ishaq's *Sira,* Crone says:

> The work is late: written not by a grandchild, but a great grandchild of the Prophet's generation, it gives us the view for which classical Islam had settled. And written by a member of the *ulama,* the scholars who had by then emerged as the classical bearers of the Islamic tradition, the picture which it offers is also one sided: how the Umayyad caliphs remembered their Prophet we shall never know. That it is unhistorical is only what one would expect, but it has an extraordinary capacity to resist internal criticism . . . characteristic of the entire Islamic tradition, and most pronounced in the Koran: one can take the picture presented or one can leave it, but one cannot *work* with it.[13]

As for the reputed fabulous memories of the bedouin: "the immediate disciples of a man whose biography was for some two hundred years studied under the title of *ilm al-maghazi,* the Prophet's campaigns, are unlikely to have devoted their lives to the memorization of *hadith*![14]

The constitution of Medina preserved in the *Sira* "sticks out like a piece of solid rock in an accumulation of rubble."[15] The document itself "depicts a society of Muhajirun, Arab tribes and Jewish allies preparing for war in the name of a creed to which there is only the most cursory reference. The *Sira* nonetheless has Muhammad arrive as a peacemaker in Medina, where he spends a substantial part of his time expounding Islam to the Arab tribes and disputing with Jewish rabbis."[16]

The religious tradition of Islam is in fact "a monument to the destruction rather than the preservation of the past," and it is "in the *Sira* of the Prophet that this destruction is most thorough, but it affects the entire account of the religious evolution of Islam until the second half of the Umayyad period."[17] Furthermore, it is a tradition full of "contradictions, confusions, inconsistencies and anomalies." For example:

There is nothing, within the Islamic tradition, that one can do with Baladhuri's statement that the *qibla* [direction of prayer] in the first Kufan mosque was to the west [opposite direction to Mecca]: either it is false or else it is odd, but why it should be there and what it means God only knows. It is similarly odd that Umar [second caliph] is known as the Faruq [Redeemer], that there are so many Fatimas, that Ali [Muhammad's cousin] is sometimes Muhammad's brother, and that there is so much pointless information. . . . It is a tradition in which information means nothing and leads nowhere; it just happens to be there and lends itself to little but arrangement by majority and minority opinion.[18]

This is evidenced by the work of modern historians with this material:

reinterpretations in which the order derives less from the sources than from our own ideas of what life ought to be about —modern preoccupations graced with Muslim facts and foot- notes. . . . [M]aybe Muhammad was a Fabian socialist, or maybe he merely wanted sons; maybe the Umayyad feuds were tribal or maybe that was how Umayyad politicians chose to argue. What difference does it make? We know as little as and understand no more than before.[19]

In the end, just about the only positive conclusion to be drawn is that

There is of course no doubt that Muhammad lived in the 620s and 630s, that he fought in wars, and that he had followers some of whose names are likely to have been preserved. But the pre- cise when, what and who, on which our interpretations stand and fall, bear all the marks of having been through the mill of rabbinic arguments and subsequently tidied up.[20]

In *God's Caliph* (1986), written with Martin Hinds, Crone examines the nature of religious authority in early Islam. The con- ventional view is that under Abu Bakr, Umar, and Uthman, all of whom were companions of the Prophet, religious and political powers were united, but that under Ali this situation changed so that the caliph became a political figure only, and the transmission of Muhammad's religious and legal legacy was left in the hands of his remaining companions and their successors. Crone and Hinds argue that this picture of early Islamic history was invented by the *ulama* (scholarly elite) two or three centuries later to support their own position and power by claiming that things had always been that way.

The authors find the demonstration of this theory in the substitution of the title *khalifat rasul Allah*, deputy of the Prophet of God, for the title *khalifat Allah*, deputy of God. Whereas the latter implies the inheritance of power directly from God, the former implies that it comes via the Prophet, or the Prophet's latter-day representatives, the *ulama*. If this is correct, it would mean that the original conception of the caliphate was of political and religious authority concentrated in the single person of the caliph, not divided between secular and religious authorities. This in turn would mean that it is the Sunni, not the Shia, version of the caliphate that is the deviation from the original conception.

Once again, the book is full of evidence and argument that undermines the traditional picture of early Islam and the role of Muhammad in its formation. For instance: "It is a striking fact that such documentary evidence as survives from the Sufyanid period (661–684) makes no mention of the messenger of God at all. The papyri do not refer to him. The Arabic inscriptions of the Arab-Sasanian coins only invoke Allah, not his *rasul*."[21]

It also appears that early *hadith* reflect a stage at which God's law was indeed formulated by God's caliph:

> . . . [I]t is clear that the caliphs were free to make and unmake *sunna* as they wished. 'We do not know of anyone who adjudicated on the basis of this rule before Abd al-Malik,' a transmitter remarks without in any way wishing to depreciate the validity of the rule in question; in other words, it was valid because a caliph had made it, not because it went back to the Prophet or a companion.[22]

The earliest form of *sunna* was thus not the *sunna* of the Prophet, let alone something documented in *hadith*: "As for *sunna*, it was good practice in general and that of prophets and caliphs in particular. Among the prophets David and Solomon have pride of place. . . ."[23] In short, *sunna* was originally simply ancestral custom or the established way of doing things, but with the advent of the *ulama* it became Muhammad's way of doing things, and against that there was no appeal, even by the caliphs.

This view of the development of Islamic law is confirmed in *Roman, Provincial and Islamic Law* (1987). Here Crone examines the cultural origins of the *Sharia* by comparing Sunni, Shia, and Ibadi law to Roman law and provincial law in Byzantine Syria and Egypt. She concludes that the Islamic institution of the *Sharia* is the result of a long process of adjustments by the *ulama*, who inherited its substance from the Umayyad caliphate in general and Muawiya in particular. What the Arab invaders reshaped into the *Sharia* was essentially provincial law as they found it: "substantially it was of ancient Near Eastern and Greek origin, or in other words it was the indigenous law of the Near East as it had developed after Alexander. The Muslims sifted and systematized this law in the name of God, imprinting it with their own image in the process."[24]

Uncongenial as the conclusions of these four books may be to the way that Muslims like to imagine their past and the origin of their religion, they are incidental compared with the implications of Crone's innocuously titled *Meccan Trade and the Rise of Islam* (1987). We have already noted how John Wansbrough concluded that the underlying purpose of all Muslim traditions, whether historical, legal, or religious, was "to demonstrate the Hijazi origins of Islam." The implication of such a propaganda exercise is that in reality Islam did *not* originate in the Hijaz, and more specifically, did *not* originate at Mecca.

There has long been an undercurrent of unease among Western students of Islam about the part played by Mecca in the Muslim account of Islamic origins. As we have seen, Mecca is portrayed in the Muslim sources as a wealthy trading center, full of merchants exchanging goods by caravan with Yemen in the south and Syria and the Roman Empire in the north. Yet there is no mention anywhere in the non-Muslim sources of a Mecca placed where the Mecca we know today is placed, that is to say, in the southern Hijaz. Before the First World War, D. S. Margoliouth noted that "[T]he classical geographers, who devote considerable attention to Arabia, are apparently not acquainted with this settlement; for the Makoraba of Ptolemy (VI. vii. 32) is derived from a different root."[25] Yet such is the weight of the traditional Muslim account among Islamicists, and such the general inertia in Islamic studies, that we still find the following in a book published in 1988: "Mecca is known to the ancient geographers as Macoraba."[26] The identification of Macoraba with Mecca is demolished by Crone in *Meccan Trade*. After examining the various theories, she says: "The plain truth is that the name of Macoraba has nothing to do with that of Mecca, and that the location indicated by Ptolemy for Macoraba in no way dictates identification of the two. . . . [I]f Ptolemy mentions Mecca at all, he calls it Moka, a town in Arabia Petraea,"[27] that is to say, a town in the northern part of Arabia in the area of the city of Petra in present-day Jordan.

Crone well describes the odd silence of the non-Muslim sources on Meccan trade:

> . . . it is obvious that if the Meccans had been middlemen in a long-distance trade of the kind described in the secondary literature, there ought to have been some mention of them in the writings of their customers. Greek and Latin authors had, after all, written extensively about the south Arabians who supplied them with aromatics in the past, offering information about their cities, tribes, political organization, and caravan trade; and in the sixth century they similarly wrote about Ethiopia and Adulis. The political and ecclesiastical importance of Arabia in the sixth century was such that considerable attention was paid to Arabian affairs, too; but of Quraysh and their trading center there is no mention at all, be it in the Greek, Latin, Syriac, Aramaic, Coptic, or other literature composed

outside Arabia before the conquests. This silence is striking and significant.[28]

Furthermore:

... this silence cannot be attributed to the fact that sources have been lost, though some clearly have. The fact is that the sources written after the conquests display not the faintest sign of recognition in their accounts of the new rulers of the Middle East or the city from which they came. Nowhere is it stated that Quraysh, or the "Arab kings," were the people who used to supply such-and-such regions with such-and-such goods: it was only Muhammad himself who was known to have been a trader. And as for the city, it was long assumed to have been Yathrib. Of Mecca there is no mention for a long time; and the first sources to mention the sanctuary fail to give a name for it, whereas the first source to name it fails to locate it in Arabia (The *Continuatio Arabica* gives Mecca an Abrahamic location between Ur and Harran, nt. 21). Jacob of Edessa knew of the Ka'ba toward which the Muslims prayed, locating it in a place considerably closer to Ptolemy's Moka than to modern Mecca or, in other words, too far north for orthodox accounts of the rise of Islam; but of the commercial significance of this place he would appear to have been completely ignorant. Whatever the implications of this evidence for the history of the Muslim sanctuary, it is plain that the Qurashi trading center was not a place with which the subjects of the Muslims were familiar.[29]

Crone concludes that if Qurashi trade existed at all, the silence of the classical sources must be due to its totally insignificant nature.

It was assumed by practically all Islamicists before Crone that Mecca must have been involved in the spice trade, presumably because spices are indelibly linked in the Western mind with the romance of Araby. By careful examination of the documentary evidence on the classical spice trade, Crone shows that Mecca, even if it existed as a trading center, could not have been involved at all.

To begin with, it is simply not true that Mecca, that is, Mecca in the location that we know today, was situated at the crossroads of major Arabian trade routes. Neither was it a natural stopping-place on the so-called incense route from south Arabia to Syria. "[A]s Bulliet points out (Camel & Wheel, p. 105), these claims are quite wrong. Mecca is tucked away at the edge of the peninsula: 'only by the most tortured map reading can it be described as a natural crossroads between a north-south route and an eastwest one.' And the fact that it is more or less equidistant from south Arabia and Syria does not suffice to make it a natural halt on the incense route."[30] What is more, "Why should caravans have made a steep descent to the barren valley of Mecca when they could have stopped at Ta'if? Mecca did, of course, have both a well and a sanctuary, but so did Ta'if, which had food supplies, too."[31] In fact, it would appear that Mecca was not on the incense route at all, since going from south Arabia to Syria via Mecca would have involved a substantial detour from the natural route. Indeed, "the incense route must have bypassed Mecca by some one-hundred miles. Mecca, in other words, was not just distant and barren; it was off the beaten track, as well.[32]

If Mecca does not make sense as a trading center for spices, incense, or any other conceivable commodity, what of its purported role as a sanctuary and place of pilgrimage? On examination of the sources, Crone confirms the conclusion of Wellhausen, reached as long ago as 1887, that "[t]he pre-Islamic Arabs did trade during the pilgrimage. But they did not go to Mecca during the pilgrimage, because the pilgrimage did not go to Mecca before the rise of Islam."[33] Moreover, the Hubal-Allah sanctuary at Mecca, of which the Quraysh are supposed to have been the guardians, does not make any sense either. In fact, "There would seem to be at least two sanctuaries behind the one depicted in the tradition, and Quraysh do not come across as guardians of either."[34]

Taking all these factors into account, Crone summarizes the problems surrounding Mecca and the rise of Islam:

We seem to have all the ingredients for Muhammad's career in northwest Arabia. Qurashi trade sounds perfectly viable, indeed more intelligible, without its south Arabian and Ethiopian extensions, and there is a case for a Qurashi trading center, or at least diaspora, in the north. One might locate it in Ptolemy's Moka. Somewhere in the north, too, there was a desert sanctuary of pan-Arabian importance, according to Nonnosus. . . . Jewish communities are well attested for northwest Arabia. Even Abrahamic monotheism is documented there, and the prophet who was to make a new religion of this belief was himself a trader in northwest Arabia. Yet everything is supposed to have happened much further south, in a place described as a sanctuary town inhabited since time immemorial, located, according to some, in an unusually fertile environment, associated with southern tribes such as Jurhum and Khuza'a, linked with Ethiopia and the Yemen, and endowed with a building accommodating Hubal and his priests. Why? What is the historical relationship between these places?[35]

Nobody knows. All we do know is "the sources on the rise of Islam are wrong in one or more fundamental respects."[36]

In the process of examining these sources, Crone has already had occasion to remark that "[t]he tradition asserts both A and not A, and it does so with such regularity that one could, were one so inclined, rewrite most of Montgomery Watt's biography of Muhammad in reverse."[37] In her penultimate chapter she subjects that tradition to a further withering analysis. Examining the contradictory traditional exegesis of the chapter of the Koran called "Quraysh," she concludes that the Islamic commentators had no more idea of what it means than we do today.[38] The numerous purported historical events that are supposed to have occasioned a revelation (Badr, Uhud, Hudaybiya, Hunayn, and so on) owe many of their features, and often their very existence, to the Koran itself; that is to say, wherever the Koran mentions a name or an event, stories were invented to give the impression that somehow, somewhere, someone knew what they were about. This means that "much of the classical Muslim understanding of the Koran rests on the work of popular storytellers, such storytellers being the first to propose particular historical contexts for particular verses."[39] In short: "What the tradition offers is a mass of detailed information, none of which represents straightforward facts."[40]

This manufacture of detail is well illustrated by the steady growth of apparent information.

> It is obvious that if one storyteller should happen to mention a raid, the next storyteller would know the date of this raid, while the third would know everything that an audience might wish to hear about it. This process is graphically illustrated in the sheer contrast of size between the works of Ibn Ishaq (d. 767) and Waqidi (d. 823), that of Waqidi being much larger for all that it covers only Muhammad's period in Medina.

This fact naturally leads to the thought that "if spurious information accumulated at this rate in the two generations between Ibn Ishaq and Waqidi . . . even more must have accumulated in the three generations between the Prophet and Ibn Ishaq."[41]

Now it might be suggested in mitigation of these negative conclusions that although the storytellers may have embroidered their stories somewhat, underneath it all there is a core of true memory of real events, a sound tradition. Crone totally rejects this idea: "[I]t was the storytellers who created the tradition: the sound historical tradition to which they are supposed to have added their fables simply did not exist." Nobody remembered any of these events, "but nobody remembered anything to the contrary either,"[42] so there was nobody to deny them. The only reason the sources agreed on the historicity of certain characters and events is because there were well-known stories about them, not because there was an unbroken transmission of a sound historical tradition. "There was no continuous transmission. Ibn Ishaq, Waqidi, and others were cut off from the past: like the modern scholar, they could not get *behind* their sources."[43]

Finally, the tradition as a whole, not just parts of it, as some have thought, is tendentious, and that tendentiousness arises from allegiance to Islam itself: "its aim being the elaboration of an Arabian *Heilsgeschichte* [salvation/sacred history]."[44] It is this that has shaped the facts as we have them.

It should not be supposed from our dependence upon Patricia Crone's analysis that she is alone in her views on the historical value of the Muslim sources and the factitious nature of Mecca in the southern *Hijaz* as the location for the origin of Islam; Crone's analysis is simply the most thorough, comprehensible, and courageous. At the same colloquium at Oxford in 1975 where Crone and Cook first presented the views published later in *Hagarism*, S. P. Brock delivered a lecture on "Syriac Views of Early Islam." In this lecture he noted that "[f]or Muhammad the title 'prophet' is not very common, 'apostle' even less so. Normally he is simply described as the first of the Arab kings, and it would be generally true to say that the Syriac sources of this period see the conquests primarily as Arab, and not Muslim."[45] Also, in another lecture on "The Origins of the Muslim Sanctuary at Mecca," the historian G. R. Hawting expressed the view that "[i]t appears that certain Muslim sanctuary ideas and certain names which Islam applies to its sanctuary at Mecca originated in a Jewish milieu, in the context of Jewish sanctuary ideas, and that they were then taken up by Islam and applied to the Meccan sanctuary."[46]

The complete unreliability of the Muslim tradition as far as dates are concerned has been demonstrated by Lawrence Conrad. After a close examination of the sources in an effort to find the most likely birth date for Muhammad, traditionally *'Am al-fil*, the Year of the Elephant, 570 C.E., he remarks that

> well into the second century A.H. scholarly opinion on the birth date of the Prophet displayed a range of variance of 85 years. On the assumption that chronology is crucial to the stabilization of any tradition of historical narrative, whether transmitted orally or in writing, one can see in this state of affairs a clear indication that *sira* studies in the second century were still in a state of flux.[47]

That is to put it politely and to say the least. If Muslim historians in the second century of the *hijra* could be that vague about Muhammad's birth date, what could they possibly have known about the date of his death or any other event in his life? Indeed, it appears that the only secure date anywhere in the whole saga of the origins of Islam is 622 C.E., which has been confirmed from dated coinage as marking the beginning of a new era. But there is no seventh-century source that identifies it as that of the *hijra*, and the only clue to its nature comes from two Nestorian Christian documents of 676 and 680 that call it the year of "the rule of the Arabs."[48]

The uncertainty of the Muslim historians about Muhammad's dates is just one indication that it was some time before Muslims were interested in him at all. As we have seen, the important Islamic concept of *sunna*, the right or established way of doing things, began as a generalized idea. There was the *sunna* of a region, the *sunna* of a group of persons, or the *sunna* of some particular distinguished person, such as David or Solomon or the caliph, even the *sunna* of Allah. It was not until the manufacture of *hadiths* (prophetic traditions) got under way in the second Islamic century that all these vague notions were absorbed and particularized in the detailed *sunnat an-nabi* (*sunna* of the Prophet). Likewise, it was only with the gradual emergence of the legend of Muhammad that places that had for well nigh two centuries gone unmarked and unregarded became places of reverence and honor. As Goldziher long ago pointed out:

> The fact that the Prophet's birthplace [at Mecca] was used as an ordinary dwelling house during Umayyad time and was made a house of prayer only by al-Khayzuran (d. 173), the mother of Harun al-Rashid, would suggest that the consecration of places associated with the legend of the Prophet did not date from the earliest period of Islam.[49]

It is likely that Muhammad, insofar as he was remembered at all, was remembered chiefly as a political and military leader who brought the Arab tribes together and urged them to conquer in the name of their ancestral deity. That is all that is needed to explain the Arab conquests and the so-called rise of Islam. In reality there was no Islam as we know it for another two or three hundred years; there was simply the barbarian conquest of civilized lands. Muhammad, as Prophet and mouthpiece for the universal deity Allah, is an invention of the *ulama* of the second and third centuries A.H. As Patricia Crone says, "In short, Muhammad had to conquer, his followers liked to conquer, and his deity told him to conquer: do we need any more?"[50]

It is important to realize that for one to two hundred years the Arab conquerors were a minority ruling a majority, and that majority was not Muslim. It has been estimated that by the middle of the eighth century only about 8 percent of the subject populations had become Muslim, whatever being Muslim involved at that time.[51] Christians, Jews, and Zoroastrians, in all their varieties, vastly outnumbered Muslims, and it was in that sectarian milieu diagnosed by Wansbrough that the forms of Islam, such as the source of its authority, the life of its Prophet, and the Koranic canon, were gradually worked out. As Gordon Newby says, confirming the analysis of this chapter, "The myth of an original orthodoxy from which later challengers fall away as heretics is most always the retrospective assertion of a politically dominant group whose aim is to establish their supremacy by appeal to divine sanction."[52]

Taking Crone and Cook's messianic Hagarism as the first stage of what later became Islam, the following scenario becomes plausible. Once the Arabs had acquired an empire, a coherent religion was required in order to hold that empire together and legitimize their rule. In a process that involved a massive backreading of history, and in conformity to the available Jewish and Christian models, this meant they needed a revelation and a revealer (prophet) whose life could serve at once as a model for moral conduct and as a framework for the appearance of the revelation; hence the Koran, the hadith, and the *sira* were contrived and conjoined over a period of a couple of centuries. After a century or so of Judeo-Muslim monotheism centered on Jerusalem, in order to make Islam distinctively Arab, the need for an exclusively *hijazi* origin became pressing. It is at this point that Islam as we recognize it today—with an inner Arabian biography of the Prophet, Mecca, Quraysh, *hijra*, Medina, Badr, and so forth—was really born *as a purely literary artifact*, an artifact, moreover, based not on faithful memories of real events but on the fertile imaginations of Arab storytellers elaborating from allusive references in Koranic texts, the canonical text of the Koran not being fixed for a hundred years or more. This scenario makes at least as much sense of the sources as the traditional account and eliminates many anomalies.

Looking back from the vantage point of the analysis carried out in this chapter, the narrative related in chapter 1 that purports to be the life of the Prophet of Islam appears as a baseless fiction. The first fifty-two years of that life, including the account of the first revelations of the Koran and all that is consequent upon that, are pictured as unfolding in a place that simply could not have existed in the way it is described in the Muslim sources. Mecca was *not* a wealthy trading center at the crossroads of hijazi trade routes, the Quraysh were *not* wealthy merchants running caravans up and down the Arabian peninsula from Syria to the Yemen, and Muhammad, insofar as he was anything more than an Arab warlord of monotheist persuasion, did his trading far north of the hijaz; furthermore, Mecca, as a sanctuary, if it was a sanctuary, was of no more importance than numerous others and was *not* a place of pilgrimage.

If we cannot believe the life of Muhammad at Mecca, we can no more believe his life at Medina either. That, too, is just as likely to be a fiction concocted for propaganda purposes, and perhaps, after all, that is just as well, since, as Margoliouth long ago observed of the *sira*: "The character which the narrator ascribes to his prophet is, on the whole, exceedingly repulsive."[53]

Notes

1. Z. Sardar and Z. A. Malik, *Muhammad for Beginners* (London: Writers & Readers, 1994), p. 30.

2. J. Burton, "Review of Watt and McDonald, *The History of at-Tabari*, vol. 1: Muhammad at Mecca," *Bulletin of the Society of Oriental & African Studies* 53 (1990): 328.

3. Ibid.

4. Ibid.

5. A. Guillaume, *The Life of Muhammad*, translation of Ibn Ishaq's *Sira* (Oxford: Oxford University Press, 1955), p. 691.

6. J. Wansbrough, *The Sectarian Milieu* (Oxford: Oxford University Press, 1978), p. 40.

7. Ibid., p. 41.

8. Ibid., p. 179.

9. P. Crone and M. Cook, *Hagarism* (Cambridge: Cambridge University Press, 1977), p. viii.

10. Ibid., pp. vi–viii.

11. Ibid., p. 3.

12. See Wansbrough, *The Sectarian Milieu*, pp. 116–17, and his review of *Hagarism in Bulletin of the School of Oriental & African Studies* 41 (1978): 155–56.

13. P. Crone, *Slaves on Horses* (Cambridge: Cambridge University Press, 1980), p. 4.

14. Ibid., p. 5.

15. Ibid., p. 7.

16. Ibid., p. 202, nt. 15.

17. Ibid., p. 7.

18. Ibid., p. 12.

19. Ibid., p. 13.

20. Ibid., p. 20.

21. P. Crone, *God's Caliph* (Cambridge: Cambridge University Press, 1986), p. 24.

22. Ibid., p. 52.

23. Ibid., p. 54.

24. P. Crone, *Roman, Provincial and Islamic Law* (Cambridge: Cambridge University Press, 1987), p. 99.

25. See the article "Mecca," in J. Hastings, ed., *Encyclopaedia of Religion & Ethics*, vol. 8, p. 511.

26. See G. Newby, *A History of the Jews of Arabia*, p. 13.

27. P. Crone, *Meccan Trade* (Oxford: Blackwell, 1987), p. 136.

28. Ibid., p. 134.

29. Ibid., p. 137.

30. Ibid., p. 6.

31. Ibid., p. 6–7.

32. Ibid., p. 7.

33. Ibid., p. 173.

34. Ibid., p. 195.

35. Ibid., pp. 196–99.

36. Ibid., p. 196.

37. Ibid., p. 111.

38. Ibid., pp. 204–14.

39. Ibid., p. 216.

40. Ibid., p. 222.

41. Ibid., pp. 223–24.

42. Ibid., p. 225.

43. Ibid., pp. 225–26.

44. Ibid., p. 230.

45. See G. H. A. Juynboll, ed., *Studies in the First Century of Islamic Society* (Carbondale: Southern Illinois University Press, 1982), p. 14.

46. Ibid., p. 25. The implications of these remarks will be explored in ch. 4.

47. See the article by L. Conrad, "Abraha and Muhammad: Some Observations Apropos of Chronology and Literary topoi in the Early Arabic Historical Tradition." *Bulletin of the Society of Oriental and African Studies* 50 (1987): 239.

48. See Crone and Cook, *Hagarism*, n. 56, p. 160.

49. See Goldziher, *Muslim Studies*, II, p. 279.

50. See Crone, *Meccan Trade*, p. 244.

51. See G. D. Newby, *The Making of the Last Prophet* (Columbia: University of South Carolina Press, 1989) p. 1.

52. Ibid., pp. 1–2.

53. See the article "Muhammad" in *Encyclopaedia of Religion and Ethics*, vol. 8, pp. 873, 877–78.

Part II
Islam

Chapter 3

Islam's View of Itself

Islam is the meeting between God as such and man as such.

—Frithjof Schuon

The Arabic word *Islam* means submission to God's will. More specifically, it designates the final religion for mankind, revealed by God (Allah) through the angel Gabriel to the Prophet Muhammad in the form of the Koran. A Muslim is someone who submits to God's will, or who follows the religion of Islam.

The universal implications of these definitions are explained by Abdel Hameed Mahmud:

> . . . [W]hether we regard the word "Islam" from its lexical or religious aspect, we find that it does not refer to a specific person, in the way Buddhism refers to the Buddha or the Zoroastrian faith to Zoroaster; it does not refer, either, to a specific people in the way Judaism refers to a specific people; nor does it denote a certain region or country, as do yet other religions. A religion which is related, or refers to a certain person, or people, or region, is necessarily limited in time by the survival of that person or people, and limited in space by their geographical

67

location. In contrast to this the word "Islam" knows no such limiting time or space, person or people. So divorced is the word from any specific location that in considering it we are taken directly to an unlimited sphere which extends beyond the bounds of the globe. Nor is it limited in history by the era of the Muhammadan mission.[1]

As the Koran says, "Abraham was neither Jew nor Christian, but he was a man of pure faith, muslimun [submitting to God]: certainly he was no idolator" (K.3:67).

In the particular historical context of its revelation, Islam is the restoration of the primordial religion (ad-din al-halif) of Abraham and beyond history of Adam in paradise, so that Adam-Abraham-Muhammad form a cyclical chain of monotheist (muwahhid) prophets transmitting God's will to mankind; Islam is thus both the first and the last religion (din).

Islam, as the form of religion brought by the Prophet Muhammad, consists of five pillars (arkan): the confession of faith (shahada); prayer (salat); almsgiving (zakat); fasting (sawm); and pilgrimage (hajj).

The first pillar, the confession of faith, or shahada, the utterance of which before witnesses is the formal public means of becoming a Muslim, consists of two formulae: La ilaha illa Llah, there is no god but God; and Muhammadun rasulu Llah, Muhammad is the messenger of God. The first formula refers to the nature of God and is known as the sentence of unity or oneness (kalimat at-tawhid), the word tawhid, meaning unity, being derived from the word wahid, meaning one. In this statement, definitive of the essence of Islam, ilah (god) is opposed to Allah (God), the former meaning anything that is worshipped and the latter meaning that which is alone worthy of worship. The formula is thus the antidote to the sin of shirk, the association of anything other than God with God. As the Koran says, "Worship God, and do not associate any others with him" (K.4:36). Whereas the first formula concerns Islam in the universal sense of submission to God, the second concerns Islam in the particular sense of the religion brought by the Prophet Muhammad. The role of

Muhammad and the other prophets will be discussed when we come to the six articles of faith.

The second pillar, prayer, or *salat*, refers to the five daily, canonical prayers, called by Muhammad the centerpole of the religion. These prayers are incumbent upon all Muslims and are performed at the following times: the evening prayer (*Maghrib*), after sunset and before the disappearance of the last light from the horizon, considered the beginning of the day in Islam and Judaism; the night prayer (*Isha*), any time from the end of the evening prayer until the dawn prayer, preferably before sleep; the dawn prayer (*Fajr*), between first light and sunrise; the noon or midday prayer (*Zuhr*), between noon and midafternoon; and the midafternoon prayer (*Asr*), from midafternoon until sunset. The validity of the prayers depends upon certain initial conditions, such as ritual purity (*tahara*), correct direction (*qibla*), correct time, and correct intention (*niyya*). All the prayers are performed in a prescribed order of standing (*qiyam*), bowing (*ruku*), and prostrating (*sajda*), combined with the recitation of verses from the Koran and other formulae. In addition, there are supererogatory prayers of the same form as the canonical prayers and personal prayers (*dua*) in which God is addressed in the worshiper's own words. The form of the canonical prayers was taught by Muhammad from divine instruction.

The third pillar, almsgiving or *zakat*, consists of a certain percentage of one's property, or profit for the year, given to the needy. In accordance with Koran 9:60, there are eight categories of people to whom the *zakat* should be given: the needy, the poor, the collectors of *zakat*, those whose hearts are inclined to Islam, captives, debtors, those fighting for Islam, and travelers.

The fourth pillar, fasting, or *sawm*, consists chiefly of the annual fast in the month of Ramadan, during which eating, drinking, smoking, and sexual activity are forbidden between sunrise and sunset. The fast is obligatory for all Muslims who have reached puberty, although certain categories, such as travelers, the sick, and pregnant or menstruating women, are temporarily exempt, the missed days having to be made up later.

The fifth and final pillar, pilgrimage, or *hajj*, consists of the journey to Mecca carried out in the last lunar month, *dhu'l hijja*. The *hajj* proper consists of a complex set of rituals performed at and around Mecca between the eighth and thirteenth of the month. All Muslims are required to make the *hajj* once in their lives, but only if they have the means.

The five pillars are primarily concerned with actions, those things that a Muslim is required to do. In addition, there are six articles of faith (*iman*), six things a Muslim is required to believe. They are mentioned in one of the most famous prophetic traditions, known as the *hadith* of Gabriel, where Muhammad says: "Faith means that you have faith in God, His angels, His books, His messengers, and the Last Day, and that you have faith in the measuring out, both its good and its evil."

The God of Islam is strictly monotheistic and unitarian. God alone has absolute being and is totally independent and self-sufficient. He alone creates the universe and maintains it in existence at every moment; he is not only the first cause but the only cause. All that is and happens, is and happens according to God's will. The concept of God in Islam has been summarized as follows by a distinguished Western convert:

> ... the God of Islam is transcendent, the all-powerful and all-knowing Creator and Lawgiver, though at the same time infinitely merciful, generous and forgiving. Man, His creature and His servant into whom He has breathed something of His spirit, stands before Him without intermediary or intercessor, meeting Him through prayer during this brief life on earth and meeting Him face-to-face when life is over. In Islam, God does not embody himself in any human being or make Himself accessible through idols and images. He is what He is, absolute and eternal, and it is as such that the Muslim worships Him.[2]

It is also the view of Islam that it is impossible for the unaided human mind to achieve an adequate conception of God as he is in his eternal and absolute being. All that mankind can know of God is what he chooses to unveil by means of revelation. In other words, all that can be known of God is what he says of himself through the prophets and the scriptures; for a Muslim, to know God is to know the Koran. The letters, words, verses, and chapters of the Koran are all God's speech and God's signs (*ayat*), containing meanings without end. Likewise, the cosmos itself is God's speech and an endless forest of signs. For the normal human being, untainted by pride and forgetfulness, the existence and reality of God is apparent and manifest by means of these signs, and no further argument is necessary. As God says in the Koran: "We have sent down upon thee signs, clear indications, and none denies their truth save the transgressors" (K.2:99).

The Arabic word for angel is *malak*, similar in form to the Hebrew *mal'ak* and in meaning to the Greek *angelos*, messenger; Islam thus inherits all the attributes of this term in Hellenism, Judaism, and Christianity. Angels are mentioned over eighty times in the Koran and innumerable times in the hadith; from these sources the cosmographer al-Qazwani (d. 682/1283) drew up a list of fourteen different angels and types of angel.[3] The key to the concept consists in recognizing that angels are inhabitants of the unseen world (*alam al-ghayb*), the intermediate reality or isthmus (*barzakh*), also known as the imaginal world or world of images and similitudes (*alam al-mithal*), between corporeal matter and the realm of pure spirit, earth and heaven, access to which in this life is a matter of piety and spiritual discipline.

By "His Books" is meant the scriptures revealed to the prophets in the Abrahamic tradition, that is to say the Torah (*Taurat*), revealed to Moses (*Musa*); the Psalms (*Zabur*), revealed to David (*Dawud*); the Gospel (*injil*), revealed to Jesus (*Isa*); and the Holy Koran, revealed to Muhammad. The Torah, the Psalms, and the Gospel no longer exist in their original forms, since they have been distorted by the interpretations of the Jews and Christians; the original texts contained the teachings found in the Koran and references to the coming of Muhammad. For these reasons the Koran now takes precedence over all former scriptures, being the undistorted final word of God to mankind.

A prophet (*nabi*) is someone chosen by God to inform and warn mankind about God. According to the traditions of the Prophet, from Adam to Muhammad, God sent 124,000 or 224,000 prophets, so that no people has been left without knowledge of God. Three hundred thirteen or 315 of these prophets were also messengers (*rasul*), founders of religions whose teachings were preserved as written or oral scriptures; all messengers are prophets, but not all prophets are messengers. The Koran mentions numerous figures from the Bible considered to be prophets by Islam including: Adam, Seth, Noah, Enoch, Abraham, Isaac, Jacob, Ishmael, Joseph, Moses, David, Solomon, Jonah, Lot, Job, Ezra, Elias, Aaron, Zakariah, John and Jesus; plus several otherwise unknown prophets, such as Hud, Salih, and Shu'aib. Adam, Noah, Abraham, Moses, Jesus, and Muhammad are all regarded as prophets and messengers who brought new dispensations and new law. The dispensation of Muhammad supersedes all previous dispensations since he holds the highest rank of all prophets and messengers.

The last day involves all the teachings of Islam that come under the heading of eschatology as it concerns both the individual and the universe as a whole. The Koran and the Hadith discuss these matters at greater length than any other scriptures, and these have been swelled further by the commentaries of the philosophers, theologians, and mystics.[4] In summary, for the individual (microcosm), death comes by the intervention of Izra'il, the angel of death. After death the dead person is aware of his body and observes the burial; this is the lesser resurrection. He is then confined to the grave, where on the first night he is questioned by the angels Munkar and Nakir concerning his faith. If satisfactory answers are given, the grave is made pleasant until the last day. If not, it is filled with whatever is dreaded most. The period between death and the last day is known as the *barzakh*, with all that that implies as described above. The last day itself, or day of the greater resurrection, the standing up (*qiyama*), corresponds to the end of the world (macrocosm), when the last judgment takes place and all returns to the original unity (*tawhid*).

The term "measuring out" (*qadar*) is usually translated as "predestination," the "fate" of the popular Western view of Islam. This translation is not incorrect and conveys the Koranic theme that God controls all things and events, regardless of how human beings might view them. The hadith of Gabriel says of the *qadar*: "the good and the evil of it," and Muslims know from the Koran that "[i]t may happen you will hate a thing which is good for you, and it may happen that you will love a thing which is evil for you, God knows and you know not" (K.2:216). In other words, it is not for mankind to decide what is good and evil apart from God's decrees. The Muslim also knows that what might appear a gratuitous evil from the human point of view is in reality a trial (*bala*) and a testing (*fitna*) of faith: "We try you with evil and good as a testing, and then unto us you shall be returned" (K.21:55). This testing is not of course for the benefit of God, who knows all things, but for those who are tested. On the return they will have no excuse or objection to the judgment meted out, since the quality of their faith has been revealed to them.

The six articles of faith were classified by theologians and philosophers under the headings of unity (*tawhid*), prophecy (*nubuwwa*), and eschatology, or return (*ma'ad*), as the three principles, or roots (*asl*), of the religion. This broad categorization is supplemented by a further classification in depth, referring to the three dimensions of *Islam*, *Iman*, and *Ihsan*.

If *Islam* comprises those acts and beliefs described under the headings of the five pillars and the six articles of belief, *Iman* is the faith with which the Muslim submits to those acts and beliefs. For the Muslim this faith is not in face of the possibility that what is done and believed might not be true, as it would be for a lukewarm Western Christian, but in the absolute certitude that it *is* true. The acts and beliefs of *Islam* are *recognized* as true because they are knowledge of the heart (*qalb*). The Prophet said that *Iman* is "a knowledge in the heart, a voicing with the tongue, and an activity with the limbs." In *Islam* the heart is not simply a metaphor for deeply felt feelings but a cognitive organ that gives access to spiritual realities; it is the heart in this sense that distinguishes the human being from the rest of creation. *Iman*, as knowledge of the heart, is the knowing as absolutely and indubitably true the primary defining feature of *Islam*—that there is one God (Allah), who is the creator and sustainer of all things. This faith or belief, amounting to apodictic certainty, is the positive pole of a number of polarities that define *Islam* vis-à-vis all that is not Islam. All these polarities are variations on the foundational polarity of *Iman-kufr*.[5]

Kufr is unbelief, and in Islam unbelief is the greatest of all sins. The meaning of the root KFR is that of covering up or denying, in the sense of knowingly and deliberately ignoring benefits that have been bestowed, and thence of being unthankful. The *kafir*, the unbeliever, is one who having received God's benefits shows no sign of gratitude, either in his words or in his deeds, and even acts rebelliously against the very idea. *Kufr* is the exact antonym of *Iman*, and in the Koran the *kafir*, the unbeliever, is the opposite of the *mu'min*, the believer or Muslim, the one who has surrendered or submitted to the reality of God. *Kufr*, as the denial of the creator, manifests itself in various acts of insolence and presumptuousness, such as *istakbana*, "to be big with pride," and *istaghna*, "to consider oneself absolutely free and independent." These traits are the opposites of humbleness (*tadarru*) and fear (*taqwa*), that the Muslim regards as the essence of religion (*din*).

The unbelievers are especially culpable not only because of their denial of God's signs (*ayat*), sent down in the Koran and in the world around them, but also because of their perverse denial of their own nature. It is revealed in the Koran that mankind has accepted a trust (*amana*) from God, the trust of vicegerency:

> When your Lord took their offspring from the loins of the children of Adam and made them bear witness concerning themselves— "Am I not your Lord?"—they said, "Yes, we bear witness!" Lest you say on the Day of Resurrection, "As for us, we were heedless of this," or lest you say, "Our fathers associated others with God before us, and we were their offspring after them. What, wilt Thou destroy us for what the vain-doers did?" (K. 7:172–73)

The Arabic word for "we bear witness" is the verb from which the word *shahada* is derived, and the event is called the covenant of alast, *alast* being the Arabic for "Am I not?" The idea that all human beings innately recognize *tawhid* is known as the *fitra*, meaning "primordial nature," or "innate disposition." The word *fitra* is used in a famous hadith in which the Prophet says: "Every child is born according to *fitra*. Then its parents make it into a Christian, a Jew, or a Zoroastrian." This means in effect that the human race is God's deputy or representative (*khalifa*) on earth, but the unbelievers pretend to be ignorant of this fact and attribute their position and abilities to themselves, not gifts bestowed by God. *Kufr* is thus the opposite not only of *Iman*, but also of *shukr*, gratitude.

If *Islam* refers to activity, and *Iman* refers to understanding, *Ihsan* refers to intentionality. In the hadith of Gabriel, Muhammad says that *Ihsan* is "to worship God as if you see him, for if you do not see Him, He sees you." *Ihsan* derives from the word *husn*, meaning good and beautiful, and in the Koran the adjective *husna*, meaning "most beautiful," is applied to God's names; the Koran also uses the word as a noun meaning "the best," referring to the reward of those who have faith. *Husna* thus refers to both the qualities and attributes of God expressed by his names and the end or recompense of those who live up to the *fitra*, implying that the faithful can come to participate in the divine qualities. The word *Ihsan* is a verb which means to do or establish the good and the beautiful, and what is most good and beautiful in *Islam* is worship (*ibada*): "I created the *jinn* and mankind only to worship Me" (K.51:56), and it is by worship that humankind assumes the divine qualities. Worshiping God "as if you see him," and not for outward show or reward, is the essence of sincerity (*ikhlas*) and the opposite of hypocrisy (*nifaq*). *Ihsan* is the special concern of Sufism, or Islamic mysticism, and the Sufi Ibn Arabi said that Sufism is to assume God's character as one's own (*al takhalluq bi akhlaq allah*). In short, *Ihsan* is the perfection of *Islam* and *Iman*.[6]

These features of Islam derive from the Koran and the Hadith. The Koran is the verbatim word of God, revealed in Arabic via the angel Gabriel to the Prophet Muhammad over a period of twenty-three years. This is known from the Koran itself, the Hadith, and the *sira*.

The Koran tells us that there are three forms of revelation: "It is not for any man that God should speak to him except by inspiration [*wahy*], or from behind a veil [*min wara 'i hijabin*], or by God's sending a messenger to communicate [*yuhiya*] by His leave what He wills" (K.42:51).[7] The third form of revelation clearly refers to Muhammad, and some idea of what it involved can be gathered from the *hadiths* on how revelation came to the Prophet.

After the first revelation[8] the circumstances of the second are recounted as follows:

> Jabir said, speaking of the temporary break in the revelation, [The Holy Prophet] said in his narrative: "Whilst I was walking along, I heard a voice from heaven and I raised up my eyes, and lo! the Angel that had appeared to me in Hira was sitting on a throne between heaven and earth and I was struck with awe on account of him and returned [home] and said, Wrap me up, wrap me up. Then Allah revealed: 'O thou who art clothed! Arise and warn, And thy Lord do magnify, And thy garments do purify, And uncleanness do shun.'"[9] Then revelation became brisk and came in succession. (Bukhari, I,1)[10]

We know that the angel was Gabriel, since God tells us in the Koran: "Say: Whosoever is an enemy to Gabriel—for he it is who has brought it down to your heart by Allah's command, confirming that which was before it and a guidance and a happy news to the believers" (K.2:97). And this is confirmed by Ibn Abbas, who tells us:

> The Messenger of Allah, used to exert himself hard in receiving Divine revelation and would on this account move his lips . . . so Allah revealed: "Move not thy tongue with it to make haste with it. Surely on Us devolves the collecting of it and the reciting of it" [K.75:16-17]. . . . So after this when Gabriel came to him the Messenger of Allah would listen attentively, and when Gabriel departed, the Prophet recited as he [Gabriel] recited it. (B.I,1)[11]

We also know the effect the revelations had on the Prophet from Aisha, who reported that

> Harith ibn Hisham asked the Messenger of Allah, O Messenger of Allah! How does revelation come to thee? The Messenger of Allah said: "Sometimes it comes to me like the ringing of a bell and that is the hardest on me, then he departs from me and I retain in memory from him what he says; and sometimes the Angel comes to me in the likeness of a man and speaks to me and I retain in memory what he says." Aishah said, And I saw him when revelation came down upon him on a severely cold day, then it departed from him and his forehead dripped with sweat. (B.I,1)[12]

And Zaid ibn Thabit said: "Allah sent down revelation on His Messenger, and his thigh was upon my thigh and it began to make its weight felt to me so much so that I feared that my thigh might be crushed" (B.8,12),[13] which precisely confirms what God says in the Koran: "Verily, We are going to cast upon thee a weighty [thaqil] word" (K.73:5).

The circumstances of the initial revelations are known to Muslim tradition, as well as the revelations for the whole period of twenty-three years. The study of these circumstances, known as the occasions of revelation (asbab an-nuzul), forms one of the Islamic sciences. The most famous work in this field is the Book of the Occasions of Revelation of the Qur'an (Kitab asbab nuzul al-Qur'an), by Abu 'l Hasan Ali ibn Ahmad al Wahidi al Nisaburi (d. 468/1075). It is also known to tradition how the Koran was collected and assembled in its canonical form. According to the Setting in Perfect Order of the Quranic Sciences (Al Itqan fi Ulum al Qur'an) of as-Suyuti (d. 911/1505), the Prophet arranged to have the revelations written down immediately after they were revealed and used to collate the material with the angel Gabriel every year; in the final year of the Prophet's life the material was collated twice. When the Prophet died the text of the Koran was already fixed, although it had not yet been written out in the form of a book. The first official recension occurred during the caliphate of Abu Bakr, and during the caliphate of Uthman a standard codex was written in the pure dialect of the Quraysh. Copies of this text were then sent to the chief centers of the Muslim empire, and all earlier versions were destroyed. It is from this second recension that all modern editions of the Koran are produced in the Muslim world.[14]

The Koran is about the same length as the New Testament. It consists of 114 chapters, or *suras*, a word meaning "a fence, enclosure, or part of a structure." The first *sura, al Fatihah*, the opening, is a short prayer used frequently by Muslims in their daily lives. The second *sura, al Baqara*, the cow, is the longest and is followed by the remaining chapters in order of roughly decreasing length. The contents of the Koran contain a doctrine of God and other spiritual beings, prophets and other religions, the last judgment and rules for the righteous life of a religious community. Much of the material is reminiscent of the Old and New Testaments in that it mentions personalities and recounts narratives from those books but described and retold from a different perspective. Many passages are allusive, referring to persons or events without further explanation, while others have a poetic quality that invites mystical interpretations. Many Muslims know the text by heart and will testify to its consoling and transformative qualities. The Koran as a book is regarded by Muslims as the inlibration of a divine archetype known as the mother of the book (*umm al kitab*, K.3:7) or the well-guarded tablet (*al lawh al mahfuz*, K.85:22).

The word "Koran" is an intensive form of the verbal root *qara'a*, meaning "to read or recite," and may be used to designate the entire book (*kitab*), or a single verse (*aya*) or passage (*juz'*). The Koran is also known as *al dhikr*, the remembrance (K.15:9; 3:58), and *al furqan*, the criterion that distinguishes falsehood from error (K.3:3). The text has two facets or dimensions, an outer or exoteric dimension (*zahir*) and an inner or esoteric dimension (*batin*); it also has verses that are unambiguous (*muhkam*) and others that are ambiguous (*mutashabih*). It is the problematic nature of much of the Koranic text that has given rise to a vast literature of exegesis (*tafsir/ta'wil*).

Tafsir means uncovering or unveiling, and it is the purpose of the *tafsir* literature to uncover or illuminate the obscurities of the Koran. For any particular verse or passage it includes the elucidation of the occasion of revelation, its place in the chapter in which it is found, its story or historical reference, whether it is ambiguous or unambiguous, whether it is abrogated (*naskh*) by another text or itself abrogating, and whether it is of Meccan or Medinan provenance. *Ta'wil* means the final end (*'aqibah*) of a matter (K.7:53; 10:39) in the sense of its purpose and ultimate significance. *Tafsir* is thus concerned primarily with the transmission (*riwayah*) of tradition and refers to the exoteric or outer (*zahir*) meaning of the text, whereas *Ta'wil* is concerned with insight into hidden meanings and refers to its esoteric or inner (*batin*) dimension. *Ta'wil*, however, is not supposed to do violence to the literal sense of the text or to undermine the prophetic tradition (*sunnah*) of Koran interpretation. Certain Shiite and Sufi exegesis is therefore disapproved by the more orthodox Sunni scholars and interpreters. In order to forestall the tendency to extravagant exegesis, it has been said by some commentators that there are only two legitimate sources for Koran interpretation— the Koran itself and the *sunna* of the Prophet transmitted through the Hadith (*tafsir bi al ma'thur*).[15]

One of the earliest and most important Koran commentaries, consisting of thirty printed volumes, is the *Jami al bayan an Ta'wil al Qur'an*, of the historian Muhammad ibn Jarir at Tabari (d. 923). Tabari adds his own interpretations to the statements of Ibn Abbas and other early authorities, complete with the chain of transmitters through whom the information has come down to him. There are sometimes more than a dozen authorities to be consulted for any single passage, and as their views often differ, Tabari expounds them all and then describes his own view and the reasons for it. Tabari's work is typical of all earlier and later Koran commentaries in that it rests on the Hadith.

Hadith is the vast body of literature on the traditions of the

Prophet of Islam, the individual elements or narratives of which are called *hadith*, "saying" (pl. *ahadith*). Virtually synonymous with Hadith is *sunna*, meaning way, path, or custom (pl. *sunan*). Whereas *hadith* refers to a written source, *sunna* refers to the words or actions recounted in that source. The provenance and validity of each *hadith* is guaranteed by its list of narrators, from the most recent back to the earliest. This chain of transmission is known as the support (*isnad*) of the *hadith*, while its content is its back or body (*matn*). The Hadith is second only to the Koran as a source for Islam.

Those close to the Prophet were known as the companions (*sahaba*), and it was they who reported his doings and sayings to the next generation of their students and associates, known as the followers (*tabi'un*). It has been estimated that all those who ever saw or heard Muhammad must have amounted to over 100,000, but in the largest collection of *hadiths*, the *Musnad* of Abu Abd al Rahman, traditions are related from only 1,300 companions. Ibn al Jawzi gave a list, amounting to 1,060 names, of all the companions who related traditions, together with the number transmitted by each. From this information it is apparent that the great mass of traditions were transmitted by less than three hundred companions; these fifty-five related one hundred or more traditions, and of these eleven were responsible for more than five hundred traditions each. Seven of these reported more than one thousand traditions each and are known as the *mukathirun*. The seven are Abu Hurayra (5,374), Abd Allah b. Umar al Khattab (2,630), Anas b. Malik (2,286), Aisha, wife of Muhammad (2,210), Abd Allah b. Abbas (1,660), Jabir b. Abd Allah (1,540), and Abu Said al Khudri (1,170).[16]

Because in the early days of Islam, the advocacy of any particular belief, attitude, or action required an authoritative source to make it effective, false *hadiths* were fabricated on a large scale by divergent parties in order to further their various causes. To counter this situation, methods were devised to sift authentic from inauthentic *hadiths*, chief among which was the institution of the *isnad*. Eventually a body of what were agreed to be authentic *hadiths* emerged in the form of the six canonical collections of sound *hadiths* (*sunan*). The most important of these are the sound collections (*sahihan*) of Muhammad al Bukhari (d. 256/870) and Muslim b. al Hajjaj (d. 261/875). Soon after Bukhari and Muslim four other collections achieved almost as much respect, namely, those of Abu Dawud al Sijistani (d. 275/889), al Tirmidhi (d. 279/892), al Nasali (d. 303/915), and Ibn Maja al Qazwani (d. 273/887). In addition to the *hadith nabawi*, wherein the Prophet speaks on his own authority, there are also *hadith qudsi*, or holy *hadiths*, wherein God is said to speak through the Prophet. These number only a few hundred and refer mainly to the mystical side of Islam expressed in the Sufi tradition.[17]

The Hadith literature serves as a basis not only for Koran commentary, but also for Islamic law (*sharia*) and jurisprudence (*fiqh*). The legal matter in the Koran consists mainly of general propositions indicating the ethical basis for a Muslim society. These range from the kind of propositions to be found in any code of law concerning basic justice and fair treatment for the weaker members of society to more specifically Islamic prohibitions such as those on alcohol and usury. In all, the legal matter in the Koran amounts to no more than six hundred verses, and the majority of these concern the religious duties of prayer, fasting, and pilgrimage; no more than eighty verses concern legal topics in the strict sense of the term, and the majority of these are to do with family law, marriage, and the status of women. The Koran establishes the principle that God is the only lawgiver, but on many legal topics it remains silent, and what it does say is often far from specific. These legal lacunae were filled by the *sunna* of the Prophet recorded in the Hadith.

The master architect of Islamic law is Muhammad ibn Idris Ash Shafi'i (d. 204/820), and it was Shafi'i who insisted in his *Risala* that the Prophet's legal rulings in the Hadith were divinely inspired, drawing this conclusion from the repeated injunction in the Koran to obey God and his Prophet, the Book and the Wisdom (*hikma*). This meant in effect that the *sunna* of the Prophet (*sunnat an nabi*) provided an explanatory commentary on the Koran with superseding authority. Shafi'i also insisted that there are four sources or roots (*usul*) of the law. Beside the Koran and the *sunna* there are also consensus (*ijmā*) and reasoning by analogy (*qiyas*). By consensus Shafi'i meant the consensus not merely of the scholars of a particular locality, but of the whole Muslim community, both lawyers and lay members alike. By analogical reasoning he meant deduction beginning with a principle set out in the Koran, *sunna*, or consensus, and therefore not reaching any conclusion that contradicted those sources. The use of reason in the widest sense in the elaboration of law was known as *ijtihad*, so *qiyas* was the special use of *ijtihad* in showing how the principles set out in the Koran, *sunna*, and consensus applied to cases not previously ruled upon.

Shafi'i's legal theory established a compromise between the divine will and human reason in the formation of the *shariah* and served as the origin for the Shafi'i school of law (*madhhab*), which represented a middle position between those who were less and those who were more enthusiastic about the role of the *sunna*. The latter group gave rise to two further schools of law that rejected the use of reason entirely. Ahmad ibn Hanbal (d. 855), founder of the Hanbalite *madhhab*, is alleged never to have eaten a watermelon because he could not find a prophetic ruling on the matter. Dawud ibn Khalaf (d. 883) declared that the sole basis for the law should be the literal (*zahir*) meaning of the Koran and the *sunna*; his school thus became known as the Zahiri, and because of its impracticable rigidity it died out in the Middle Ages. These schools were in addition to the already existing *madhhabs* of the Malikis in Medina and the Hanafis in Kufa, both of which were established on the basis of their local traditions.[18]

Islam might be described as a theocracy in the sense that all its aspects derive from and lead back to God on the principle of *tawhid*, but in practical terms it might be better described as a "divine universal nomocracy,"[19] in that the *sharia* comprehends, through the Koran and the *sunna*, God's will for the way of life of all mankind. The rulership of Islamic society derives from and rules by the *sharia* in its sense of a fence around a meadow; all within the fence is permitted (*halal*), all beyond the fence forbidden (*haram*), for the ruler and the ruled.

The question of who rules in Islam is the source of the distinction between Sunnis and Shias. After the death of the Prophet, the friends and followers of Ali were convinced that political and religious authority had passed to him. This belief was based on Ali's position in the Prophet's household as cousin, foster brother, and son-in-law and the esteem in which he was held by the companions and Muslims in general. However, another group, which was later to form the majority in Islam, ignored the claims of Ali and elected Abu Bakr as successor (*Khalifah*); those followers of Ali who protested against this decision became known as the partisans (*Shi'ah*) of Ali. The supporters of Abu Bakr regarded the caliphate as a matter of consensus, thus gaining the name of "The People of Tradition and Consensus of Opinion" (*ahl al sunnah wa 'l jama'ah*), hence Sunnis, while the followers of Ali were branded as dissidents and refusers of allegiance. Eventually, after twenty-five years, Ali became caliph for about four years and nine months, after which the caliphate passed to his son Hasan, who was soon forced to hand it over to Muawiyah, the first of the Umayyad caliphs. Ali's second son, Husain, was Imam for ten years during Muawiyah's caliphate, but when he rebelled under Caliph Yazid he was killed at Kerbala with almost all his family and aides. The anniversary of the martyrdom of Husain on the tenth of Muharram 61/680 is the high point of the Shi'ite religious calendar.

The largest group of Shias, and the second largest denomination of Muslims after the Sunnis, are the *ithna ashariyya*, the followers of Twelve-Imam Shi'ism. According to the Twelvers, after the death of Husain, the imamate remained in his descendants until the twelfth imam, Muhammad al Mahdi, who disappeared at the age of four in the year 260/873 upon the death of his father, the eleventh imam, Hasan al Askari. The disappearance of the twelfth imam, after which his will was communicated by means of four representatives, or *wakils*, is known as the lesser occultation (*al ghaybat al sughra*). This lasted until the year 399/940, when the last *wakil* failed to name a successor, after which begins the greater occultation (*al ghaybat al kubra*), which lasts to the present day. To Shi'ites the hidden imam is the pillar of the world (*axis mundi*) and lord of the age (*Sahib az Zaman*), as well as the awaited mahdi (*al Mahdi al Muntazar*) who will reappear at the end time to initiate an era of order and justice.[20]

The idea of the mahdi, the rightly guided one, also forms part of Sunni belief, although they deny that he has anything to do with any Shi'ite imam. The mahdi is mentioned in the traditions of thirty-three companions and companions of companions. All these traditions are judged by the highest authorities on Hadith to be *mutawatir*, that is to say, having sufficient independent *isnads* to guarantee authenticity.[21] The return of the mahdi is also associated with the return of Jesus and the presence of the antichrist. The Prophet is reported as saying:

> A body of my people will not cease to fight for the truth until the coming forth of the Antichrist. . . . When they are pressing on to fight, even while they straighten their lines for the prayer when it is called, Jesus the son of Mary will descend and will lead them in prayer. And the enemy of God, when he seeth Jesus, will melt even as salt melteth in water. If he were let be, he would melt into perishing: but God will slay him at the hand of Jesus, who will show them his blood upon his lance.[22]

The imminence of the end time, when these events are due to occur, is a prominent feature in contemporary Islamic mysticism, or Sufism.

Notes

1. See A. H. Mahmud, *The Creed of Islam* (London: World of Islam, 1978), pp. 14–15.

2. See Hasan abdu'l Hakim [Gai Eaton], *The Concept of God in Islam* (London: The Islamic Cultural Center, n.d.), p. 7.

3. See the essay *The Angels*, by Sachiko Murata, in S. H. Nasr, ed., *Islamic Spirituality*, vol. 1 (London: SPCK, 1989–91), pp. 324–44.

4. See the essay "Eschatology," by W. C. Chittick, in ibid., pp.

378–409; also Chittick and Murata, *The Vision of Islam* (New York: SUNY Press, 1994), pp. 193–235.

5. See T. Izutsu, *The Structure of the Ethical Terms in the Koran*, chaps. 9 and 10 (Tokyo: Keio University, 1959).

6. See T. Izutsu, *The Concept of Belief in Islamic Theology: A Semantic Analysis of Iman and Islam* (Tokyo: Yurindo Publishing, 1965) pp. 58–60.

7. See T. Izutsu, *God and Man in the Koran* (Tokyo: The Keio Institute, 1964), chap. 8, esp. pp. 176f.

8. See chap. 1, pp. 25–26.

9. K.74:1.

10. See M. M. Ali, *A Manual of Hadith* (London: Curzon, 1978), pp. 9–10.

11. Ibid., pp. 10–11.

12. Ibid., pp. 12–13.

13. Ibid., p. 15.

14. See A. Jeffrey, *Materials for the History of the Text of the Qur'an* (Leiden: Brill, 1937), p. 45; also W. M. Watt, *Bell's Introduction to the Qur'an* (Edinburgh: Edinburgh University Press, 1977), ch. 3.

15. See the introduction to N. Ayoub, *The Qur'an and Its Interpreters* (New York: SUNY Press, 1984), vol. 1, p. 140.

16. See M. Z. Siddiqi, *Hadith Literature: Its Origin, Development, Special Features and Criticism* (Calcutta: Calcutta University Press, 1961), pp. 22–37.

17. See W. A. Graham, *Divine Word and Prophetic Word in Early Islam* (The Hague: Mouton, 1977).

18. See N. J. Coulson, *A History of Islamic Law* (Edinburgh: Edinburgh University Press, 1964), part 1.

19. See D. G. Rosser-Owen, *Social Change in Islam—The Progressive Dimension* (London: The Open Press, 1975), pp. 16, 25.

20. See Nasr, trans. "Tabatabati," *Shi'ite Islam*; also Nasr, *Ideals and Realities of Islam* (London: George, Allen and Unwin, 1966), chap. 6.

21. See Siddiq, A., trans. Darwish, *Al Mahdi, Jesus and the Antichrist* (London: As-Siddiquayah, 1985).

22. Quoted in M. Lings, *The Eleventh Hour* (Cambridge: Quinta Essertia, 1987), p. 98.

Chapter 4

Islam: A Secular Perspective

What would have to occur or to have occurred to constitute
for you a disproof of the love of, or the existence of, God?
—Antony Flew

There is a sense in which Islam is like one of those endlessly repeating patterns typical of its art or like a fractal that remains the same whatever the scale of magnification. Whether it be a pillar of the religion such as the *salat* or a seemingly inconsequential element of *sunna* such as the correct foot with which to cross the threshold of a mosque, the same atmosphere prevails and the same metaphysical principles can be perceived. Once the mind has succumbed to what Paul Kurtz has called "the transcendental temptation"[1] within the ambience of Islam, all its circular assertions become plausible, and unbelief appears an incomprehensible perversion. Indeed, Islam becomes the veritable living proof that "With God all things are possible" (Matt. 19:26).

In one of his early works the traditionalist writer Frithjof Schuon gives an acute description of this Muslim mental world:

> The intellectual—and thereby the rational—foundation of Islam
> results in the average Muslim having a curious tendency to
> believe that non-Muslims either know that Islam is the truth and
> reject it out of pure obstinacy, or else are simply ignorant of it
> and can be converted by elementary explanations; that anyone
> should be able to oppose Islam with a good conscience quite
> exceeds the Muslim's imagination, precisely because Islam coin-
> cides in his mind with the irresistible logic of things.[2]

No explanations are necessary for the Muslim who quite literally
has had the Koran whispered in his ear and pounded into his
brain from birth. In a society in which the themes and phrases
of God's book are all pervading and where, until recently, a
Muslim could live his whole life without meeting an alternative
view, it is hardly surprising that Islam appears "the irresistible
logic of things."

Not only is Islam for Muslims the obvious explanation of life
and the world, it is also family and cultural heritage from which
they can sever themselves only with the utmost anguish and
danger. For such a person in such a world, rejecting Islam is not
like failing to turn up in church on Sunday. It is like a traitorous
act in time of war, a deliberate going over to an enemy for whom
no good word can be said, an act for which the only appropriate
penalty is death. That Muslims born in a Muslim culture think in
these terms is understandable; that educated Westerners voluntarily adopt it and actively promote it is a phenomenon in need of
explanation.

There has long been a kind of love affair between certain Westerners and the Arabs in which a romantic view of "the East," of
the desert and the bedouin, combines with an intellectual pursuit
of Arabic language, literature, art, and architecture. This fascina-
tion with the Arabs and Islam does not always result in conversion, but when it does it usually combines vague aspirations
toward "the spiritual," with the expression or adoption of thought
processes and attitudes that could not be respectably maintained
in any other contemporary context. Islam is in fact the last refuge

for those conservative Western intellectuals who wish it were true that the Renaissance, the Enlightenment, the Industrial Revolution, the French Revolution, in short, "the modern world," had never come about. Islam is, indeed, the only remaining mental space in which these events have not yet happened.

As we have seen, Islam is a world view in which the existence of God and the revelation of his word and will in an inerrant and infallible text are absolutely unquestionable. To raise questions about these primary items is, in effect, to put oneself outside it, and if one is Muslim-born or a convert, to become guilty of the ultimate crime of apostasy (*irtidad*), and deserving of death. In view of these facts, it might seem that the conversion of any intelligent and educated Westerners is unaccountable, but curiously enough it is precisely the uncompromising severity of Islam that is its most attractive feature for those with a psychological need for certainty in an uncertain world. In addition, there is a seductive side to Islam that consists of its mysticism and its art, and it is these features that seem to have figured largely in the conversion of many intellectuals.

There are in fact two broadly opposed ways in which Westerners approach Islam. The first, which might be described as rational-analytic, retains an overtly Western point of view, be it religious—Jewish/Christian—or secular—rational/humanist/skeptical/atheist. The second, which might be described as mystical-romantic and often leads to conversion, adopts an anti-Western posture and styles itself traditionalist, a kind of universalist religiosity that regards Islam as the final and most complete of a host of divine revelations. Despite the pretensions of the traditionalists, both approaches are indelibly Western in that neither could have arisen within the Muslim world, which is subjectively self-enclosed and seamlessly self-confirming, affording no foothold for any kind of objective assessment. These two approaches have produced two separate literatures on Islam that barely acknowledge each other's existence.

Prominent representatives of the rational-analytic approach are Ignaz Goldziher, Joseph Schacht, William Montgomery Watt,

Kenneth Cragg, Patricia Crone, Michael Cook, John Wansbrough, John Burton, Andrew Rippin, Julian Baldick, and Gerald Hawting. Prominent representatives of the mystical-romantic approach are René Guénon, Frithjof Schuon, Titus Burckhardt, Martin Lings, Toshihiko Izutsu, Michel Chodkiewicz, Annemarie Schimmel, William Chittick, Sachiko Murata, and Seyyed Hossein Nasr. Nasr is unique among this latter group in that he is an Iranian academic who has adopted as his mentors a group of Western writers who purport to know better than Muslims themselves what is the real meaning of Islam. Nasr is now the senior proponent of traditionalism in the West.

The rational-analytic group studies Islam from the outside and seeks to know how it came to be the way it is. They look critically at the evidence, or lack of evidence, for the traditional account of Islamic origins and as a result see Islam as a series of problems in need of solutions. The solutions tend to be favorable or unfavorable to Islam in direct proportion to the sympathy for religion as such; Christians, such as Watt and Cragg, are most notably sympathetic, though this is little appreciated by Muslims. The mystical-romantic group studies Islam from the inside and accepts it at its own estimation; they refuse to consider anything that might undermine faith and treat the traditional explanations as divinely guided. Because of their universalist mysticism, these too are looked at askance by many Muslims. These contrasting approaches to Islam emerge most starkly in their respective attitudes to the Koran and the Hadith.

The mystical-romantic attitude to the Koran is well described by Nasr:

> As viewed by Muslims, what is called higher criticism in the West does not at all apply to the text of the Qur'an. Elaborate sciences concerning conditions in which the verses were revealed [sha'n al-nuzul], how the Qur'an was compiled, how the verses were enumerated, as well as the science and art of the recitation of the Qur'an, have been developed by Muslim scholars over the centuries. . . . [T]hese traditional sciences provide all the

answers to questions posed by modern Western orientalists about the structure and text of the Qur'an, except, of course, those questions that issue from the rejection of the Divine Origin of the Qur'an and its reduction to a work by the Prophet. Once the revealed nature of the Qur'an is rejected, then problems arise. But these are problems of orientalists that arise not from scholarship but from a certain theological and philosophical position that is usually hidden under the guise of rationality and objective scholarship. For Muslims, there has never been the need to address these "problems" because Muslims accept the revealed nature of the Qur'an, in the light of which these problems simply cease to exist.[3]

In other words, problems cease to be problems as long as you can delude yourself that they are not there. Unfortunately, like a toothache that refuses to go away no matter how hard you try to ignore it, the problems surrounding the Koran are not so easily dismissed. If the Western scholar is prejudiced in refusing to accept that the Koran is divine revelation, and that is by no means true of them all, the Muslim scholar is even more prejudiced in accepting that it is without ever considering any alternative. But as we have seen in chapter 3, in Islam, belief (*Iman*) is the greatest virtue that overwhelms all fault, and unbelief (*kufr*) is the greatest fault that can never be forgiven.

Another advocate of the mystical-romantic view of Islam tells us that

[h]istory as such has never held much interest for most Muslims. What is important about historical events is simply that God works through them. The significant events of the past are those that have a direct impact on people's present situation and their situation in the next world. From this point of view, the one event of overwhelming significance is God's revelation of the Koran. The actual historical and social circumstances in which it was revealed relate to an extremely specialized field of learning that few scholars ever bothered with. The fact that

> Western historians have devoted a great deal of attention to this
> issue says something about modern perceptions of what is real
> and important, but it tells us nothing about Muslim perceptions
> of the Koran's significance.[4]

This is surely an oblique reference to the work done by scholars
of the rational-analytic school, such as Wansbrough, Crone, Cook,
and Hawting, on the historical origins of Islam. It is also a pre-
emptive hedging of bets. If it turns out that the work of these
scholars becomes undeniable and the traditional picture of the
origin of Islam is gone forever, it can then be claimed that that
does not really matter. All that matters is "Muslim perceptions of
the Koran's significance," rather like the liberal Christian
acknowledgment that the Gospel picture of Jesus may not be historically accurate but "the Christian message" is still God's work
and somehow wonderfully valuable and important.

Further, it is simply not true to say that the historical and
social circumstances in which the Koran was revealed "relate to
an extremely specialized field of learning that few scholars ever
bothered with." The Muslim literature on the so-called occasions
of revelation (*asbab an nuzul*) is substantial, precisely because
Muslims liked to think they knew everything that could possibly
be known about Muhammad and the circumstances surrounding
the revelation of the Koran.[5] The fact that it is all fictitious and
historically worthless tells us, in turn, something about Islamic
"perceptions of what is real and important"; namely, that believing a fantasy is better than knowing the truth or admitting
ignorance.

Andrew Rippin says of the *asbab* reports that they are cited

> . . . out of a general desire to historicize the text of the Qur'an in
> order to be able to prove constantly that God really did reveal
> his book to humanity on earth; the material thereby acts as a
> witness to God's concern for His creation. . . . The *sabab* is the
> constant reminder of God and is the "rope"—that being one of
> the understood meanings of *sabab* in the Qur'an—by which

human contemplation of the Qur'an may ascend to the highest levels even while dealing with mundane aspects of the text.

The major literary exegetical role that the *asbab* plays, however, is what could be called a "haggadically exegetical" function; regardless of the genre of exegesis in which the *sabab* is found, its function is to provide a narrative account in which the basic exegesis of the verse may be embodied.[6]

The term "haggadically exegetical" derives from Wansbrough's *Quranic Studies*. *Haggadah* is a Hebrew word meaning "the telling," and in Judaism is a book containing passages dealing with the theme of the exodus read at the Passover Seder. Generally speaking, *haggadah* refers to material of a homiletic or allegorical character, as opposed to *halakah*, another Hebrew term that refers to legal matter. The haggadic character of the *asbab* reports is most crucially apparent in the *hadiths* purporting to relate the circumstances surrounding the initial Koranic revelations. The historical insubstantiality of these reports is fully confirmed by the rational-analytic study of the *sira-maghazi* literature.

We have seen in chapters 1 and 2 the gulf that looms between the traditional and the critical accounts of the origins of Islam. The implications of this gulf are quite literally shattering. The *sira* of the Prophet Muhammad contains, perhaps as its primary raison d'être, an account of where, when, and how the Koran came to be revealed. This event is depicted as taking place at or near a town called Mecca in the southern Hijaz. As explained in chapter 2 there are very good reasons for thinking that this Mecca is a late and tendentious literary fabrication. The event could not have occurred as related in the Muslim sources because the place in which it is depicted as happening simply did not exist, at least not in the way it is described in those sources.

Furthermore, Muslims like to think they know the exact circumstances of the revelation of the Koran, because they have an account of the event from the Prophet himself as recorded in the Hadith. This, too, is a sad delusion. Despite the fact that the *hadiths* reporting the circumstances of the initial Koranic revelations are contained in the supposedly sound collections of Bukhari and others, it is quite obvious that these accounts are not independent reports originating from the Prophet or the companions, but fictions based on the Koranic text.

The *hadith* quoted in chapter 1 describing the first revelation[7] arises from the fact that the command "Recite" at the beginning of *Sura* 96 seems appropriate as an opening for a first revelation, so the story was duly invented to satisfy the curious. Likewise, the *hadith* quoted in chapter 3 describing the second revelation[8] clearly arises from the odd words "O thou enwrapped in thy robes" or "O thou shrouded in thy mantle" (*muddathir/muz amil*) that occur at the beginning of *Suras* 73 and 74 respectively. Any of these texts could plausibly be construed as first revelations, and *hadiths* were accordingly invented to that effect, which then led to the invention of further *hadiths* in order to reconcile the differences.[9] The truth is that nobody knew anything about the circumstances of the first revelations, or any of the other revelations, and the same goes for the physical effects they are supposed to have had on the Prophet. The description of Muhammad moving his lips during revelation obviously derives from the text of K.75:16–17, just as the report put into the mouth of Zaid ibn Thabit is concocted from K.73:5.[10] These *hadiths* do not explain the Koranic text; they are simply generated by it.

If the place where the first revelations are supposed to have occurred did not exist, and the precise circumstances surrounding them are fabrications based on Koranic texts, the Koran itself becomes detached from any fixed place in space and time. Its only remaining anchor is that it is somehow attached to the name Muhammad, "the richly praised one," a sobriquet that itself floats free and remains unattached to any plausible human biography. Like the early Muslim scholars who invented the historical circumstances of the birth of Islam, all we have to go on is the text of the Koran.

At this point a crucial distinction has to be made between the Koran as source (*asl*) and the Koran as document (*mushaf*). This distinction was first made by John Burton in his study of the

Muslim theories of abrogation (*naskh*).[11] In studying the sources on this topic, it becomes clear that reference to the Koran is not necessarily reference to the canonical text, since mention is made of verses and rulings that that text does not now contain. On the other hand, the liturgical function of scripture convinced Burton that it must have had an early fixed form in addition to being an authoritative source. Since on close examination the Muslim accounts of how the Koran was collected appear to be fictive and designed to exclude the Prophet from the process, Burton, somewhat perversely, concludes that "[w]hat we have in our hands today is the mushaf of Muhammad."[12] This is at odds with both Muslim tradition, which regards the text as having been fixed in the time of Caliph Uthman, and the rest of Western scholarship. John Wansbrough, in his review of the book in which this conclusion is reached, concedes the antiquity of much of the Koran's "paraenetic phraseology" but sees no reason why that should "include, or require the entire canon," and especially not those verses that seem to be "exegetical in character, namely, of *fiqh* and *sunna* at a time when scriptural 'props' for community authority were being sought (i.e., by opponents of Shafi'i's prophetical Sunna)."[13]

In his own study of the same materials, Wansbrough concludes that

> [n]o element in either the style or the structure of *halakhic* [legal] exegesis points unmistakably to the necessity, or even to the existence, of the canon as ultimately preserved and transmitted. . . . The dichotomy of "Qur'an as document" and "Qur'an as source" proposed by Burton, while not without a certain methodological utility, is misleading if meant to postulate the historical existence of the canonical text before it became a source of law.
>
> Logically, it seems to me quite impossible that canonization should have preceded, not succeeded, recognition of the authority of scripture within the Muslim community. Chronologically, the data of Arabic literature cannot be said to attest to

the existence of the canon before the beginning of the third/
ninth century.[14] . . .

It was only after the articulation of law as divinely decreed
that a scriptural canon was established, the result primarily of
polemical pressure. Once stabilized, the document of revelation
was no longer exclusively the "word of God" but also, and
equally important, a monument of the national literature. In that
capacity its service to the community, and to the cause of
polemic, was unlimited.[15]

In short, the Koran as we have it is not the work of Muhammad or
the Uthmanic redactors, much less the immaculate word of God,
but a precipitate of the social and cultural pressures of the first
two Islamic centuries.

As a piece of literature assembled over a couple of centuries by
persons unknown, the Koran exhibits "a variety of recognizable literary forms in no recognizable order."[16] From his extended analysis
of the text, Wansbrough concludes that the structure of Muslim
scripture lends little support to the theory of a deliberate edition,
not only in the examples of salvation history characterized by
variant traditions, that is, the repeated telling of the same story in
different words, but also in passages of exclusively paraenetic or
eschatological content. "[E]llipsis and repetition are such as to
suggest not the carefully executed product of one or many men,
but rather the product of an organic development from originally
independent traditions during a long period of transmission."[17]

These independent traditions appear in the canonical text as
the juxtaposition of independent pericopes unified by rhetorical
phrases, which accounts for the homogeneity of the text. The content of the pericopes consists of what Wansbrough calls "prophetical *logia*," in a number of recognizable literary forms, concerning
the means of salvation. In the text of the Koran these sayings are
expressed as the utterances of God, but outside the text they
appear as reports about such utterances. The quality of reference,
repetitious employment of rhetorical devices, and polemical tone
of these pericopes of prophetical logia all suggest "a strongly sec-

tarian atmosphere, in which a corpus of familiar scripture was being pressed into the service of as yet unfamiliar doctrine."[18] A case in point here is the Islamizing of the figure of Abraham by associating him with an Arab sanctuary at Mecca.

The Arabs were Ishmaelites, according to Jewish scripture (Gen. 17:20), and the belief that Abraham had bequeathed a monotheist religion to them, including descent from Ishmael and Hagar and prohibition of pork and other Jewish practices, is attested for northwest Arabia in a Greek source, *The Ecclesiastical History* of Sozomen, as early as the fifth century. Sozomen was a native of Gaza, and his mother tongue was Arabic, so we have testimony from a reliable source that by the fifth century, Arabs, at least in that area, were familiar with the idea that they were Abrahamic monotheists (*hanifs*) by origin; whether this was true of Arabs throughout the peninsula is impossible to say and somewhat hard to believe.[19]

In the Koran Abraham is mentioned in 245 verses in twenty-five *Suras*, outnumbered only by Moses, who appears in 502 verses in thirty-six *Suras*.[20] The Koran categorizes Abraham as a prophet (K.19:42, cf. Gen. 20:7), equips him with an autonomous religion (*din Ibrahim*) (K.16:124, 22:77) and scripture (*suhuf Ibrahim*) (K.53:35, 87:18f), and credits him, in conjunction with Ishmael, with the foundation of what Muslim tradition identified as the sanctuary at Mecca. This association of Abraham with an exclusively Arab sanctuary in the southern Hijaz is the means, at once geographical and sacerdotal, of distancing Islam from its Jewish roots in the north.

The unmistakable Jewish foundations of Islam[21] are usually explained in two ways. Either Muhammad "borrowed" these Jewish elements from his contacts with Judaism, or they are the result of the common ancestry of Jews and Arabs and their joint inheritance of a hypothetical original "Semitic religion." The Jewish elements in the Muslim sanctuary traditions, however, do not admit of either of these solutions.

In his studies of these traditions, Gerald Hawting recognized that "[t]here are certain names and terms which, with reference to the Muslim sanctuary at Mecca, have fixed and precise meanings but which sometimes occur in the traditions, in the Koran and in the poetry in a way which conflicts with their usual meanings, or at least suggests that they are being used with a different sense."[22] He concludes from this that these terms date from a time before the Muslim sanctuary was established in its classical form as we know it today, a time when Islam was much more closely conjoined with Judaism than previously supposed:

> It seems that the Muslim sanctuary at Mecca is the result of a sort of compromise between a pre-existing pagan sanctuary and sanctuary ideas which had developed first in a Jewish milieu. I envisage that Muslim sanctuary ideas originated first in a Jewish matrix, as did Islam itself. At a certain stage in the development of the new religion the need arose to assert its independence, and one of the most obvious ways in which this could be done was by establishing a specifically Muslim sanctuary. The choice of sanctuary would have been governed by already existing sanctuary ideas and when a suitable sanctuary was fixed upon these sanctuary ideas would themselves have been modified to take account of the facts of the sanctuary which had been chosen. It seems likely that the Meccan sanctuary was chosen only after the elimination of other possibilities—that in the early Islamic period a number of possible sanctuary sites gained adherents until finally Mecca became established as the Muslim sanctuary. And it also seems likely that one reason for the adoption of the Meccan sanctuary was that it did approximate to the sanctuary ideas which had already been formed—although they had to be reformulated, the physical facts of the Meccan sanctuary did not mean that already existing notions and terminology had to be abandoned.[23]

Hawting's analysis of sanctuary terms and names is too technical to detail here but confirms the conclusions of Crone, Cook, and Wansbrough that the Hijazi origin of Islam is a late literary fiction. Further confirmation of this conclusion can be found in the work of Reuven Firestone and Norman Calder on the evolution of the Abraham-Ishmael legends in Islamic exegesis.

The notoriously allusive nature of the Koran—its reference to characters and stories without providing the relevant narrative in the text is manifest in the tale of Abraham and Ishmael. In K.2:125–29, these characters are described as building what Muslim tradition interpreted as the Kaaba at Mecca, without any word as to how they arrived there from Syria, where the biblical version of the Abraham legend is set. This lack of information was more than amply offset in the exegetical literature (*tafsir*). Firestone traces at least three different legends of the transfer of Abraham and Ishmael to Mecca from Syria, attributed to three different traditionists: Ibn Abbas, Ali, and Mujahid.[24] Clearly, none of these tales is a record of real events any more than the original biblical stories that gave rise to them or their Islamized versions in the Koran.

What emerges from a close examination of the Muslim sources is that in the early days of Islam, Koran, Hadith, *tafsir*, and *sira* were fluid and interacting literary categories, not distinct entities. It is not the case that from early times there was the canonical text of the Koran and that Hadith, *tafsir*, and *sira* supplemented that bedrock as commentary and exemplification; the Koran is *tafsir* on itself and on *sunna*, the *sira* is *tafsir* of Koran and *sunna* as well as a collection of *hadiths*, and the Hadith is an alternative Koran. All these genres continually interacted, each molding the others as generation followed generation, until Islam finally defined itself in its classical form as reaction to its previous forms and its non-Muslim environment. Far from its being true, as Muhammad is made to say in his so-called farewell sermon, that "This day have I perfected for you your religion" (K.5:3), it was two or three centuries before Islam knew precisely what it was, beyond being not Judaism and not Christianity.

The fluid nature of Koran and *tafsir* appears in Norman Calder's study of the sacrifice of Abraham in early Islamic tradition. He describes the situation that produced the interaction of these two genres:

> In the course of the 7th century when Arabic speaking peoples found themselves ruling the ancient polyglot culture of the Near

East, and came thereby to constitute a new market and a new demand for story, old cycles were new-translated, amongst them the tales of the patriarchs and prophets of the Old Testament. Something of that process of Arabisation may be illustrated, for the Biblical tales, by reference to the extensive antiquarian activity of Muslim scholars in the 9th century, scholars who collected in the form of Traditions [ahadith] snippets and fragments of what the community recalled or ascribed or invented or preserved and deemed relevant to their understanding of religion. Many versions may be found of the story of Abraham's sacrifice in collections whose purpose was avowedly scriptural [Koranic] exegesis, and whose context was therefore academic.[25]

In studying the various versions of the Abrahamic sacrifice to be found in such encyclopaedists as Tabari and Suyuti, Calder found that

> [t]he actual wording of the call to Abraham, where it occurs, is always quranic but invariably introduced by the non-Quranic formula nudiya [There was a call]. The assumption must be that a standard narrative formula indicating the irruption of the supernatural has been edited and reformulated as nadayna-hu [We called him] for inclusion in a work ascribed to God. The Quranic version, if my argument is correct, is secondary to and dependent on the narratives. The stories, it may be remarked, freely refer to God as subject of action. Had they been dependent on a pre-existing Quranic text there would have been no reason to avoid mentioning the there explicitly identified caller.[26]

This confirms Wansbrough's conclusion that the Koran achieved its canonical form only in the eighth or early ninth century:

> I find the burden of his [Wansbrough's] argumentation perfectly satisfactory, and indeed consistent with what scholars working on the forms of prayer or scripture have come to expect. Such materials do not spring fully fledged into existence in their final form: they achieve a canonical form gradually over a period of

time. Clearly the sacrifice narratives, if they do not actually require a late date for the canonical text of the Qur'an, are at least consistent with such a date, c. 800.[27]

Finally, in confirmation of Hawting and Firestone, Calder concludes, "All early Arabic versions of the sacrifice narrative may, then, be analysed as built primarily out of narrative materials derived ultimately from Rabbinic sources; and as exhibiting, secondarily, interference from Arabian [Meccan sanctuary] traditions.[28]

Beside the Koran, the other source for classical Islam as we know it today is that vast body of literature known as the Hadith, and the Hadith has been subjected to an even more thorough critique by Western scholarship than the Koran. The devastating nature of that critique has been fully recognized by the mystical-romantic school of Islam. Nasr has remarked that the criticisms that European orientalists have made of the Hadith is "one of the most diabolical attacks made against the whole structure of Islam."[29]

As Nasr sees it, the danger inherent in this criticism is that it leads Muslims who accept it to the fatally dangerous conclusion that the body of Hadith is not the sayings of the Prophet and therefore does not carry his authority: "In this way one of the foundations of Divine Law and a vital source of guidance for the spiritual life is destroyed. It is as if the whole foundation were pulled from underneath the structure of Islam."[30] This assessment is, of course, perfectly correct, and Nasr expresses the hope that Muslim scholars will come to the defense of the traditional view of the Hadith. This is vital because the Western critical attitude, with which some Western educated Muslims have become imbued, "hides an a priori presumption no Muslim can accept, namely the negation of the heavenly origin of the Koranic revelation and the actual prophetic power and function of the Prophet,"[31] the same argument quoted above against Western scholarship and the Koran.

Nasr's plea for a defense of the Hadith from the traditional Muslim point of view was originally made over thirty years ago and in all that time has produced no response worthy of note. His own efforts in this direction are hardly inspiring and consist mostly of hysterical outbursts and circular assertions. The primary reply to criticism is, as always, that belief (*Iman*) cures all problems: "Were the critics of Hadith simply to admit that the Prophet was a prophet, there would be no scientifically valid argument whatsoever against the main body of Hadith." The "main body of Hadith" is a necessary caveat since even Nasr has to admit that "[t]here is of course no doubt that there are many Hadiths which are spurious," but that is all taken care of within acceptable parameters by means of the Islamic sciences of Hadith authentication (*ilm al jarh/ilm al dirayah*).[32]

However, since those ancient methods would not satisfy modern Western critics, Nasr makes an effort of his own, which perfectly exemplifies the circular nature of Muslim reasoning:

> The *Sunnah* of the Prophet and his sayings had left such a profound imprint upon the first generation and those that came immediately afterwards that a forging of new sayings, and therefore also new ways of action and procedure in religious questions that already possessed precedence, would have been immediately opposed by the community. It would have meant a break in the continuity of the whole religious life and pattern of Islam which, in fact, is not discernible. Moreover, the Imams, whose sayings are included in the Hadith corpus in Shi'ism and who themselves are the most reliable chain of transmission of prophetic sayings, survived after the third Islamic century, that is, after the very period of the collection of the well-known books of Hadith, so that they bridge the period to which the modern critics point as the "forgery" of Hadith.[33]

How does Nasr think he knows what the Prophetic *sunna* was and what the first generation of Muslims was like? His only possible way of knowing these things is by means of the Hadith! The *sunna* cannot validate the Hadith any more than the Hadith can validate the *sunna*. The *sunna* is unknown apart from the Hadith and was invented along with the first generation of Muslims who are supposed to have witnessed and reported it. As we have seen, other literary genres such as Koran, *tafsir*, and *sira* are not sources of evidence independent of Hadith, which might give us a different perspective. They are all of the same fluid and insubstantial nature, primarily concerned with differentiating Islam from Judaism and giving it an origin in the Hijaz. The Shi'ite Imams are irrelevant since the Shias were just as cut off from authentic information about the origins of Islam as were the Sunnis and had just as much of a vested interest in an idealized, fictional picture.

The credit for uncovering the spurious nature of the Hadith must go to the Hungarian scholar Ignaz Goldziher (1850–1921) in the second volume of his *Muslim Studies*, first published in German in 1889–1890. This work has never been translated into Arabic and is ignored in the Muslim world apart from a handful of scholars, such as Nasr, who happen to have had a Western education. In its basic argument the book is unanswerable and does, indeed, remove the foundations from under Islam.

We have noted Patricia Crone's remark that the Muslim sources assert A and not A with such regularity that in the end it becomes impossible to believe anything. This is also the verdict of Goldziher on the Hadith. The undisguised disagreement of the Hadith on every conceivable matter, together with the vast increase in their number with every succeeding generation, led him to conclude that

[i]n the absence of authentic evidence it would indeed be rash to attempt the most tentative opinion as to which parts of the hadith are the oldest original material, or even as to which of them date back to the generations immediately following the Prophet's death. Closer acquaintance with the vast stock of hadiths induces sceptical caution rather than optimistic trust regarding the material brought together in the carefully compiled collections. We are unlikely to have even as much confidence as Dozy regarding a large part of the hadith, but will probably consider by far the greater part of it as the result of the religious, historical and social development of Islam during the first two centuries.

The hadith will not serve as a document for the history of the infancy of Islam, but rather as a reflection of the tendencies which appeared in the community during the maturer stages of its development. It contains invaluable evidence for the evolution of Islam during the years when it was forming itself into an organized whole from powerful mutually opposed forces.[34]

These forces were political: Umayyad, Shia, Khawarij; legal, with regional groups of scholars vying for predominance; and religious, with quarrels over such issues as freewill and predestination.

Particularly devastating is Goldziher's critique of the institution of the *isnad*, the chain of authorities that supposedly takes a *hadith* back to its origin with a follower, companion, or the Prophet. The *isnad* is the only method available to Muslims for authenticating the Hadith and is wholly inadequate:

> Traditions are only investigated in respect of their outward form, and judgement of the value of the contents depends on the judgement of the correctness of the *isnad*. If the *isnad* to which an impossible sentence full of inner and outer contradictions is appended withstands the scrutiny of this formal criticism, if the continuity of the entirely trustworthy authors cited in them is complete and if the possibility of their personal communication is established, the tradition is accepted as worthy of credit. . . . Muslim critics have no feeling for even the crudest anachronisms provided that the *isnad* is correct. Muhammad's prophetic gift is used as a factor to smooth over such difficulties.[35]

This is the method used by Nasr, quoted above—all problems are solved if only it is admitted that Muhammad was a Prophet.

It turns out that not only are the *isnads* false, but they are a late innovation, which explains why they are false. In his study of Hadith, G. H. A. Juynboll says:

> In my view, before the institution of the *isnad* came into existence roughly three quarters of a century after the prophet's

death, the *ahadith* and the *Qisas* [mostly legendary stories] were transmitted in a haphazard fashion if at all, and mostly anonymously. Since the *isnad* came into being, names of older authorities were supplied where the new *isnad* precepts required such. Often the names of well-known historical personalities were chosen but more often the names of fictitious persons were offered to fill the gaps in *isnads* which were as yet far from perfect.[36] . . .

I contend that the beginning of standardization of *hadith* took place not earlier than towards the end of the first/seventh-century.[37] . . .

The overall majority of allegedly the most ancient traditions is likely to have originated at the earliest in the course of the last few decades of the first century [700s–720s], when for the first time the need for traditions became generally felt. The *isnad* as institution had just come into being and slowly but gradually the concept of *sunnat an-nabi* began to eclipse the *sunna* of a region or of a [group of] person[s].[38] . . .

On the period of the introduction of *isnads* Wansbrough is even more skeptical than Juynboll: "The supplying of *isnads*, whether traced to the prophet, to his companions, or to the successors, may be understood as an exclusively formal innovation and cannot be dated much before 200/815."[39] In any case, it must be true, as Kenneth Cragg has remarked of the collection of Hadith in general:

This science became so meticulous that it is fair (even if somewhat paradoxical) to suspect that the more complete and formally satisfactory the attestation claimed to be, the more likely it was that the tradition was of late and deliberate origin. The developed requirements of acceptability that the tradition boasted simply did not exist in the early, more haphazard and spontaneous days.[40]

Juynboll's mention of the fact that the *sunna* of the Prophet (*sunnat an nabi*) slowly came to replace the *sunna* of a region, person, or group of persons is an insight due to the other great pioneer of Hadith study after Goldziher, Joseph Schacht (1902–1969). Building on Goldziher's works but concentrating on legal *hadiths*, Schacht recognized the significance of Shafi'i's insistence on the *sunna* of the Prophet:

> Shafi'i insists time after time that nothing can override the authority of the Prophet, even if it be attested only by an isolated tradition, and that every well-authenticated tradition going back to the Prophet has precedence over the opinions of his Companions, their Successors, and later authorities. This is a truism for the classical theory of Muhammadan law, but Shafili's continual insistence on this point shows that it could not yet have been so in his time.[41]

Before Shafi'i (d. 204/820), "Islamic" law was not only not necessarily connected with the Prophet, it was not even necessarily connected with the companions and their successors.

It was also Schacht's achievement to show how *isnads* grow not only vertically, that is to say, backward in time to the earliest possible attestation, but also horizontally, that is to say, spread geographically from region to region. This last point is important in that it answers the objection of Muslims who hold that the bulk of the Hadith must be authentic because the same *hadith* is often attested with the same *isnad*, in the same generation, in regions remote from each other.[42] Finally, Schacht showed that the study of *hadiths* takes us back only to about the year 100/719, which forms a horizon, or *hadith* barrier, beyond which what went on must be surmised from material outside the Hadith.

Now, a point often made by Muslims that appears to be ceded by Burton goes as follows: "If hypocrisy lies precisely in the adoption of the external demeanour of the pious and the counterfeit testifies to the existence of the genuine coin, pseudo-*hadith* imitates real *hadith,* otherwise the exercise is pointless."[43] But this is not really so. All that is needed for the invention of false *hadiths* is knowledge that *hadiths* are the current means of gaining power and influencing people; *none of them need be true*. Because at some point coin appears that seems to be made of gold, to bear the king's head, and to come from the royal mint, it does not necessarily follow that any of that is really so, especially when there is no means of assaying the metal, no one has seen the king, and the location of the royal mint is unknown. The coin is accepted because it is a convenient means of exchange and for no other reason, so the forgers can proceed from there.

The final nail in the coffin of the Hadith comes from considering the sheer number of traditions:

> Bukhari is said to have examined a total of 600,000 traditions attributed to the Prophet; he preserved some 7,000 (including repetitions), or in other words dismissed some 593,000 as inauthentic. If Ibn Hanbal examined a similar number of traditions, he must have rejected about 570,000, his collection containing some 30,000 (again including repetitions). Of Ibn Hanbal's traditions 1,710 (including repetitions) are transmitted by the Companion Ibn Abbas. Yet less than fifty years earlier one scholar had estimated that Ibn Abbas had only heard nine traditions from the Prophet, while another thought that the correct figure might be ten. If Ibn Abbas had heard ten traditions from the Prophet in the years around 800, but over a thousand by about 850, how many had he heard in 700 or 632? Even if we accept that ten of Ibn Abbas' traditions are authentic, how do we identify them in the pool of 1,710? We do not even know whether they are to be found in this pool, as opposed to that of the 530,000 traditions dismissed on the ground that their chains of authorities were faulty. Under such circumstances it is scarcely justified to presume Hadith to be authentic until the contrary has been proved.[44]

In conclusion, if the *sharia* is based on the Hadith, it does not have even a semblance of divine sanction, and if it depends on the Koran, its case is no better, since the Koran's claim to divine origin rests on the Hadith.

Faced with the argument and evidence assembled in the present chapter and in chapter 2, believing Muslims have two options. They can avert their eyes, denounce it all as the work of *shaitan* and the enemies of Islam and go on believing the traditional account as literally true (fundamentalism), or they can adopt the posture of the mystical-romantic school. These, too, will regard the critics as the agents of *shaitan* but will go on to say that even if the criticisms are correct, which of course they are not, this cannot affect the claims of Islam, since those claims do not depend on historical origins but on an inner knowledge of God, the accompaniment and reward of piety. What makes Islam true is the spiritual life of Muslims; not religious history, but religious experience. This is the realm of Sufism, or Islamic mysticism.

Notes

1. See P. Kurtz, *The Transcendental Temptation: A Critique of Religion and the Paranormal* (Amherst, N.Y.: Prometheus Books, 1986).

2. F. Schuon, *Stations of Wisdom* (London: John Murray, 1961), p. 64, n. 1.

3. S. H. Nasr, ed., *Islamic Spirituality* (London: SPCK, 1989-91), vol. 1, p. 9, n. 1.

4. W. C. Chittick and S. Murata, *The Vision of Islam* (New York: Paragon House, 1994), pp. xiv–xv.

5. See A. Rippin, "The Exegetical Genre *Asbab Al Nuzul*: A Bibliographical and Terminological Survey," *Bulletin of the Society of Oriental and African Studies* 48 (1985): 1–15.

6. Rippin, "The Function of *Asbab Al Nuzul* in Quranic Exegesis," *Bulletin of the Society of Oriental and African Studies* 51 (1988): 2–3.

7. See p. 26.

8. See p. 76.

9. See J. Burton, *An Introduction to the Hadith* (Edinburgh: Edinburgh University Press, 1994), pp. 50–52.

10. See p. 77.

11. J. Burton, "Those are the High-Flying Cranes," *Journal of Semitic Studies* 15 (1970): 251–52, 259.

12. J. Burton, *The Collection of the Qur'an* (Cambridge: Cambridge University Press, 1977), pp.239–40.

13. J. Wansbrough, "Review of Burton's *The Collection of the Qur'an,*" *Bulletin of the Society of Oriental and African Studies* 41 (1978), p. 370.

14. J. Wansbrough, *Quranic Studies* (Oxford: Oxford University Press, 1977), pp. 201–2.

15. Ibid., p. 27.

16. Ibid., p.14.

17. Ibid., p. 47.

18. Ibid., p.20.

19. P. Crone, *Meccan Trade and the Rise of Islam* (Oxford: Blackwell, 1987), pp. 190–91.

20. Wansbrough, *Quranic Studies*, p. 49.

21. See A. Katsh, *Judaism in Islam* (New York: New York University Press, 1954), and C. Torrey, *The Jewish Foundation of Islam* (New York: Ktav, 1967).

22. G. R. Hawting, "The Origins of the Muslim Sanctuary at Mecca," in Juynboll, ed., *Studies in the First Century of Islamic Society* (Carbondale: Southern Illinois University Press, 1982), p. 24.

23. Ibid., pp. 27–28.

24. R. Firestone, *Journeys into Holy Lands* (New York: SUNY Press, 1990), chap. 8.

25. N. Calder, "From Midrash to Scripture: The Sacrifice of Abraham in Early Islamic Tradition," *Le Muséon* 101 (1988): 376.

26. Ibid., pp. 388–89.

27. Ibid., p. 389.

28. Ibid., p. 395.

29. S. H. Nasr, trans., Tabatabai, *Shi'ite Islam* (Houston: Free Islamic Literatures, n.d.), p. 119, n. 24.

30. S. H. Nasr, *Ideals and Realities of Islam* (London: George, Allen, and Unwin, 1966), p.82.

31. Ibid., p. 82.

32. Ibid., p. 80.

33. Ibid., p. 81.

34. I. Goldziher, *Muslim Studies* (London: George, Allen and Unwin, 1966–71), II, pp. 18–19.

35. Ibid., pp. 140–41.

36. G. H. A. Juynboll, *Muslim Tradition* (Cambridge: Cambridge University Press, 1983), p. 5.

37. Ibid., p. 10.

38. Ibid., pp. 72–73.

39. Wansbrough, *Quranic Studies*, p. 179.

40. K. Cragg, "Hadith, Traditions of the Prophet," in *Encyclopaedia Britannica*, vol. 22, 1974, p. 11.

41. J. Schacht, *The Origins of Muhammadan Jurisprudence*, (Oxford: Oxford University Press, 1979), p. 11.

42. See M. Azami, Studies in *Early Hadith Literature* (Indianapolis: American Trust Publications, 1987), pp. 230f, and the reply of Michael Cook, *Early Muslim Dogma* (Cambridge: Cambridge University Press, 1981), chap. 11, esp. pp. 115f.

43. Burton, *An Introduction to the Hadith*, p. xii.

44. P. Crone, *Roman, Provincial and Islamic Law* (Cambridge: Cambridge University Press, 1987), p. 33.

Part III

Sufism or Islamic Mysticism

Chapter 5

Sufism's View of Itself

*I dreamt one night that I had copulated with all the stars of
the heavens, and there was not a single star left with which
I had not copulated with supreme spiritual pleasure, and
when I had finished copulating with the stars I was given
the letters and I copulated with them.*

—Ibn Arabi

In the opening chapter of his *Book of Knowledge of the Doctrine of the Sufis* (*Kitab at ta'arruf li madhab ahl at tasawwuf*), Abu Bakr Kalabadhi (d. 385/ 995) discusses at length various possible derivations of the word "Sufi" and concludes that if it comes from the habit of wearing wool (*suf*),

> the word is correct and the expression sound from the grammatical point of view, while at the same time it has all the [necessary] meanings, such as withdrawal from the world, inclining the soul away from it, leaving all settled abodes, keeping constantly to travel, denying the carnal soul its pleasures, purifying the conduct, cleansing the conscience, dilation of the breast, and the quality of leadership.[1]

113

This conclusion has been accepted by the majority of Eastern and Western scholars.

From *suf* is derived the term *tasawwuf*, usually translated as Sufism or Islamic mysticism. *Tasawwuf* means literally "putting on a woolen garment," and figuratively it means "adhering to Sufism." The connection with wool may be derived from the fact that many Jewish and Christian ascetics covered themselves with sheepskins in imitation of John the Baptist, and this custom could have been adopted by early Muslim ascetics. It may also be significant that *tasawwuf* is numerically equivalent to the phrase *al hikmat al ilahiyyah*, divine wisdom, and there could also be a symbolic assonance with the Greek word *sophia*, meaning wisdom.[2]

The famous Baghdad Sufi Abd al Qadir al Gilani (d. 561/1160) defined the Sufi as *al mutahi*, "the one reaching the end," and strictly speaking the term should be applied only to someone reaching the end of the mystical path (*tariqa*). Anyone on the path who has not reached the end is either a beginner (*mustaswif*) or one making progress (*mutasawwif*), and all are *fuqara* (pl. of *faqir*), literally "poor men" and technically initiates. In the Muslim world there are many thousands of *fuqara*, or *fakirs*, but very few who have reached the end of the path and could rightly be called Sufis.[3]

Contrary to how things might appear to Western scholars, it is obvious to Muslims that what is now called Sufism must have existed from the beginning and have its roots in the Koran and *sunna* of the Prophet. Since Islam is by definition an integral revelation, it must from the outset have contained both outer (*zahir*) and inner (*batin*) aspects, aspects that were later named *sharia* and *tariqa*, the broad and narrow paths to salvation. All the great Sufi orders or brotherhoods (*tariqas*) that emerged from the twelfth century onward traced their chain of authorities (*silsila*) back from the present-day master, or sheikh, through the companions to the Prophet himself. Indeed, the *silsila* generally follows the sequence Allah—Gabriel—Muhammad—down to the present day, showing the descent of *tasawwuf* parallel to that of Islam itself.

In the early days of Islam, after the companions and the followers, the title of the elect (*al khawass*) fell upon certain ascetics (*zuhhad*) and devotees (*ubbad*), and it is surely among such enthusiasts that the origins of Sufism can be discerned. However, it is the distinguishing claim of Sufism that it is not concerned merely with a world-denying asceticism (*zuhd*), but in possession of an esoteric doctrine, or gnosis (*ma 'arifa/ilm*), combined with a method for realizing that doctrine in experience. Although this is true, it does not follow that this in any way exempts Sufis from the prescriptions and restraints of Islam embodied in the *sharia*. It is rather that of the three dimensions—*Islam, Iman, Ihsan*—Sufism is the practical implementation of *Ihsan* and thus the deepest possible fulfilment of all the requirements of *Islam* and *Iman*.[4]

The balance between the inner and outer religious life was not fully understood in early Islam and gave rise to the misunderstanding of Sufi esoterism by the doctors of the law (*ulama*), who considered themselves the custodians of orthodoxy. In 309/922 the Sufi al Hallaj, notorious for his ecstatic declaration "I am Truth" (*ana 'l haqq*), was executed for heresy, and the same fate befell Suhrawardi al maqtul (Suhrawardi the killed) in 587/1191. This situation prompted the composition of apologias for Sufism intended to show that Sufi doctrine was in accordance with mainstream Islam. One such was Kalabadhi's *Doctrine of the Sufis*, in which he illustrates his most important chapter on the divine unity (*tawhid*) with a long quotation from al Hallaj, not mentioned by name but called "one of the greatest Sufis."[5] Other notable efforts toward the same end are the *Nourishment of Hearts* (*Qut al Qulub*) of Abu Talib al Makki (d. 386/996) and the monumental *Revival of the Religious Sciences* (*Ihya ulum ad din*) and other works by Muhammad al Ghazali (d. 505/1111).[6]

By the twelfth century all the major strands of Islam—Koran, Hadith, *tafsir, sira, fiqh, sharia*, theology (*kalam*), philosophy (*falsafa*)—had crystallized into their classical forms. *Tasawwuf*, too, by this time had several centuries of tradition and numerous highly respected saintly and intellectual figures to its name. The stage was thus set for the appearance of the greatest figure not only in Sufism but arguably in the whole history of Islam since the days of the Prophet.

Ibn al Arabi, "The Revivifier of Religion" (*Muhyi ad din*) and "The Greatest Master" (*Sheikh al Akbar*), was born at Murcia in Spain in 560/1165 and died at Damascus in 638/1240. Tradition attributes to him some 850 different works, and modern scholarship reckons that seven hundred of these are authentic and over four hundred are still extant. Although some of these are only a few pages long, others are of immense length and contain more words than most people could write in a lifetime. Despite this staggering literary output, it was Ibn Arabi's claim that he never set out to write a single book: "On the contrary, influxes from God have entered upon me and nearly burned me alive. In order to find relief . . . I have composed works, without any intention on my part. Many other books I have composed because of a divine command given during a dream or unveiling" (*Fihrist al mu'allafat*).[7]

Ibn Arabi was born of a rich and noble family. His father, Ali, was employed by Sa'id ibn Mardanish, ruler of Murcia, and when that town was conquered by the Almohad dynasty, Ali took his family to Seville, where he was again employed in government service. In the world from which Ibn Arabi came, that did not necessarily imply ambition or worldliness but was quite compatible with piety, and there are indications from what Ibn Arabi relates of his father's death that he was one of the saints (*awliya*); at least three of his uncles were also renowned for their ascetic lives and spiritual qualities.[8] The young Ibn Arabi was promised a post as scribe to the governor of Seville and seemed destined to follow in his father's footsteps, but he also felt drawn to the spiritual life with which he was well acquainted.

According to one of his biographers, Qari al Baghdadi in his *Maraqib ibn Arabi*, the turning point came when he was attending a banquet given by a prince who was one of his father's friends. "When the goblets of wine were being passed round Ibn Arabi was about to drink when he heard a voice saying: 'Muhammad, it was not for this that you were created.' " He threw down the goblet and rushed out. As a result of this experience he went into retreat (*khalwa*) in a tomb in a cemetery on the outskirts of Seville, spending his days in invocation (*dhikr*) and coming out only to pray at the times for prayer. According to Baghdadi, ibn Arabi said of this event: "I stayed four days in that cemetery. I then came out with all this knowledge [which I now possess]." According to another, more plausible, account told to Ismail b. Sawdakin al Nuri, one of his closest disciples, he said:

> I went into retreat before dawn [*al fajr*] and I received the illu-
> mination [*fath*] before the sun rose [*qabla tulu ash shams*]. I
> remained in this place for fourteen months, and so it was that I
> obtained the secrets which I wrote about afterwards. My fath at
> that time was a state of being snatched out of myself in ecstasy
> [*wa kana fathi jadhbatu fi tilka l lahzu*].[9]

The experience of being drawn out of himself in ecstasy (*jadhba*) and illumination or opening (*fath*) is characteristic of Ibn Arabi. Such experiences are independent of the will of the experient, and in order for the result to be a balanced spiritual life, they need to be complemented by repentance and conversion (*tawba*), a conscious, voluntary act of returning to God and leaving distraction. Ibn Arabi claimed that this side of his spiritual life was overseen by the figure of Jesus, the prophet *Isa*. In the *Revelations of Mecca* (*Futuhat al Makkiya*), he says: "It was at his hands that I was converted; he prayed for me that I should persist in religion [*din*] in this low world and in the other, and he called me his beloved. He ordered me to practise renunciation [*zuhd*] and self-denial [*tajrid*]." Elsewhere he says of Jesus: "He was my first teacher, the master through whom I returned to God; he is immensely kind towards me and does not neglect me even for an instant." In further visions he saw himself as under the protection of not only Jesus, but of Moses and Muhammad as well. While Jesus urged him to more asceticism, Moses told him he would obtain the knowledge called "Ladunni," which the Koran attributes to the mysterious figure of Khidr (K.18:65), and Muhammad

told him: "Hold fast to me and you will be safe" (*istamsak bi taslam*).[10]

This phenomenon of being instructed by past prophets and masters of the Sufi path continued throughout his life. Sadruddin Qunyawi, a disciple from Qonya, said of this ability:

> Our sheikh Ibn Arabi had the Power to Meet the spirit of any Prophet or Saint departed from this world, either by making him descend to the level of this world and contemplating him in an apparitional body [*surat mithaliya*] similar to the sensible form of his person, or by making him appear in his dreams, or by unbinding himself from his material body to rise to meet the spirit.[11]

Such feats are especially associated with a type of Sufi known as *Uwaysi*, a name derived from a contemporary of Muhammad called Uways Qarani, who lived in Yemen and communicated with the Prophet telepathically.[12] The claim to this kind of knowledge is still alive in contemporary Sufism and is commonplace in the Naqshbandiyya *tariqa*.[13]

Ibn Arabi's biography is primarily a history of his visions and mystical states; his journey from West to East, from the abode of darkness to the abode of light, is as much internal as external. His states (*ahwal*), stations (*maqamat*), and abodes (*manazil*) are so numerous and extraordinary it is possible to give only an indication of them here. For instance, Bukhari tells us (*Iman*, 3) that the Prophet said: "I see behind my back." Ibn Arabi tells us:

> At the *mihrab* my entire essence became one single eye; I could see from every side of myself in just the same way that I could see my *qibla*. Nobody escaped my view: neither the person who was entering nor the person who was leaving, and not even those who were performing the prayer behind me. (*Fut.* 69)

> I obtained this station in 593 at Fez, during the *asr* prayer while I myself was directing the prayers at the al Azhar mosque. . . . It appeared to me in the form of a light that was if anything more

visible than what was in front of me. Also, when I saw this light the status of the direction "behind" [*hukm al khalf*] ceased for me. I no longer had a back or the nape of a neck, and while the vision lasted I could no longer distinguish between the different sides of myself. I was like a sphere; I was no longer aware of myself as having any "side" except as the result of a mental process—not an experienced reality. . . . (*Fut.* 206)[14]

The quality of being a "face without a nape" is a characteristic of the Pole (*qutb*) of the Age, the most elevated spiritual person at any particular time, and a part of the heritage of Muhammadan sainthood (*walaya muhammadiyya*).

In 586/1190 Ibn Arabi was in Cordoba accompanying his father on a visit to a saint of that city named Abu Muhammad Makhluf al Qaba'ili:

One day I left the company of the Shaikh and returned to my house, the Shaikh being in good health when I left him. That same night I dreamt that I was in open country with low-lying clouds overhead. Suddenly I heard the sound of neighing horses and the thundering of their hooves and saw a company of men, both mounted and on foot, descending from the skies in such numbers that they filled the heaven. I had never seen men with such fine faces, resplendent clothing and excellent horses. Then I saw in the midst of them a tall man with a large beard and silvery hair, his hand upon his cheek. I spoke to him and asked him the meaning of it all. He told me that the men I saw were all the prophets from Adam to Muhammad. When I asked him who he was, he replied that he was Hud of the people of Ad. On my asking the purpose of their descent he told me that they had come to visit Abu Muhammad in his sickness. As soon as I awoke, I enquired about Abu Muhammad and learned that he had fallen ill that very night. He lived a few more days and then died.[15]

The real purpose of this gathering of all the prophets, however, as Ibn Arabi revealed to his closest disciples, was to announce to him his office of Seal of Muhammadan Sainthood.[16]

It was while staying in Fez in 594/1197, after the experience of being a "face without a nape," that Ibn Arabi emulated the Prophet's night journey (isra, K.17:1) and ascent to heaven (miraj, K.53:1–18).[17] He made several attempts to describe this event (Kitab al Isra, Risalat al Anwar, Futuhat 167) of which the most accessible is chapter 567 of the Revelations of Mecca.[18]

After purging his bodily nature by passing through the elemental realms of earth, water, air, and fire, Ibn Arabi enters the first heaven, where he meets his "father," the prophet Adam. From Adam he learns many hidden meanings of the Koran and the Hadith, meanings that form the basis of his metaphysical doctrines; this sets the pattern for his passage through the remaining heavens. In the second heaven he meets the prophets Jesus and John the Baptist, in the third heaven Joseph, in the fourth heaven Idris, in the fifth heaven Aaron, in the sixth heaven Moses, and in the seventh heaven Abraham and the Temple of the Heart. The latter is the key to the whole process, since the Temple of the Heart is the celestial Kaaba, the House of Abraham, and marks the transition between the cosmological realm of the heavens and the paradisal realm beyond. It is none other than the heart of the visionary, the site of the whole journey.

Proceeding beyond the Temple of the Heart, Ibn Arabi comes to the Lote Tree of the Limit (K.53:14), which is also the form of the Perfect Man (insan al kamil) that encompasses all the planes of Being:

> Then I "was enveloped by the [divine] lights" until all of me became Light, and a robe of honor was bestowed upon me the likes of which I had never seen. So I said "O my God, the Signs [ayat] are scattered." But then "He sent down upon me" at this moment [His] Saying . . . (K.3:84). Thus he gave me all the Signs in this Sign, clarified the matter [i.e., of the eternal Reality of the Koran] for me, and made this Sign for me the key to all knowledge. Henceforth I knew that I am the totality of those [prophets] who were mentioned to me [in this verse]. Through this [inspiration] I received the good tidings that I had [been

granted] the "Muhammadan station," that I was among the heirs of Muhammad's comprehensiveness. . . . Now when that happened to me I exclaimed: "Enough, enough! [bodily] elements are filled up, and my place cannot contain me!" and through that [inspiration] God removed from me my contingent dimension. Thus I attained in this nocturnal journey the inner realities [ma'ani] of all the Names, and I saw then all returning to One Subject and One Entity: that Subject was what I witnessed, and that Entity was my Being. For my voyage was only in myself and only pointed to myself, and through this I came to know that I was a pure "servant," without a trace of lordship in me at all. Then the treasures of this station were opened up [for me], and among the kinds of knowledge I saw there were . . .[19]

Then follows a list and explanation of some sixty-nine different kinds of knowledge, which together constitute the substance of Ibn Arabi's metaphysics.

By the sacred month of Ramadan in the year 598/1202, Ibn Arabi had reached the East and was in Mecca. It was here that the last act in his accession to Muhammadan sainthood took place, not only at the "navel of the earth," but in "God's Vast Earth" (ard Allah al wasi'a), the Imaginal World (barzakh, alam al mithal). With Jesus, the Seal of Universal Sainthood, in attendance, Ibn Arabi saw himself consecrated by the Prophet himself:

He [the Prophet] saw me behind the Seal [Jesus], a place where I was standing because of the community of status that exists between him and me, and he said to him, "This man is your equal, your son and your friend. Set up for him before me the Throne of tamarisk." Then he made a sign to me, "Rise, oh Muhammad, and ascend to the throne, and celebrate the worship of Him who sent me, and my worship also, for in you there is a fragment of me which can no longer bear to be away from me, and that fragment governs your innermost reality." . . . Then the Seal set up the Throne in that solemn place. On its front was written in blue light: "This is the most pure Muhammadan station! He who ascends into it is its heir, and God sends him to watch over the respect for the divine Law!" At that moment the Gifts of Wisdom were bestowed on me: and it was as though I had been granted the Sum of the Words (*jawami al kalim*).[20]

This event is described in the prologue to the *Revelations of Mecca* and sets the tone for the series of "openings" or "revelations" recorded in the rest of the book, an enormous work consisting of 560 chapters, many of which are themselves of book length.[21]

Following the remarkable experience related in the prologue, the first chapter of the *Futuhat* continues with a description of an equally extraordinary event which occurred to Ibn Arabi at the Kaaba not long after his arrival in Mecca:

As I was carrying out the circumambulations and reciting the formulas of glorification, praise, magnification and Oneness— now kissing the Black Rock, now touching the Yemenite corner, now drawing near to the Wall of Multazam—as I was standing in a state of ecstasy in front of the Black Rock I encountered the Evanescent Youth, the Silent Speaker, He who is neither alive nor dead, the Simple Composite, He who envelops and is enveloped. When I saw him perform the ritual circuits around the Temple, like a living person revolving round a person who has died, I recognized his true reality and his metaphorical form, and I understood that the circuit round the Temple is like the prayer over a corpse. . . . Then God revealed to me the dignity of this Youth and his transcendence with regard to "where" and "when." When I recognized his dignity and his descent [*inzal*], when I saw his rank in existence and his state, I embraced his right side, wiped away the sweat of revelation on his forehead and declared to him: "Look upon him who aspires to your company and desires your intimacy!" He replied to me using signs and enigmas he had created so that he would never have to speak except in symbols: "When you recognize, understand and realize my symbolic language, you know that it can never be grasped either by the most eloquent of orators or by the most competent of rhetoricians." . . . He gestured to me and I understood. The reality of his Beauty unveiled itself to me and I was overcome with love. I became powerless and was instantly overwhelmed. When I recovered from my swoon, my sides shot through with fear, he knew I had realized who he was. . . . He said to me: "Observe the details of my constitution and the disposition of my form! You will find what you ask of me written upon me, because I neither speak nor converse. I have no knowledge apart from the knowledge of Myself; My Essence does not differ from My Names. I am Knowledge, the Known and the Knower; I am Wisdom, the Sapiential Dead and the Sage! I am the ripe orchard and the full harvest! Now lift my veils and read what is contained in my inscriptions. Whatever you observe in me, put it in your book and preach it to all your friends." So I raised his veils and read his inscriptions. The light lodged within him enabled my eyes to see the hidden knowledge which he contains and conceals.The first line I read, and the first secret with which I became acquainted is what I will now record in writing in the second chapter.[22]

Once again, the qualities of this visionary youth are symbolic personifications of many elements of Ibn Arabi's metaphysical doctrines and are not unrelated to the vision of the Lotes Tree of the Boundary, which is also the form of the Perfected Man.

The Kaaba loomed large in Ibn Arabi's life at this time and was the initiator of many other visions and inspirations.[23] On one occasion in 598/1202, while circumambulating the Kaaba at night and composing poems in an ecstatic state, he had a vision of a beautiful girl who interpreted the inner meaning of his verses to him as soon as he spoke them. He later recognized her earthly embodiment in the form of Nizam, the young daughter of his friend in Mecca, Sheikh Abu Shuja Zahir b. Rostem al Isfahani. Nizam was the inspiration for the composition of the mystical-erotic poem *The Interpreter of Desires* (*Tarjuman al Ashwaq*), which contains the famous lines:

My heart has become capable of every form; it is a pasture for
    gazelles and a convent for Christian monks,
And a temple for idols and the pilgrim's Kaaba and the tables of
    the Tora and the book of the Koran.
I follow the religion of Love: whatever way Love's camels take,
    that is my religion and my faith.[24]

For Ibn Arabi, the Kaaba, like every other object in the universe, was a sentient entity that both speaks and listens. On one
occasion it called out to him to perform the circumambulation at
the same time as Zamzam, the sacred well at Mecca, called him to
drink its water. On another occasion, when performing the circumambulation in the dark of a rainy night, the Kaaba appeared
to rise from its foundations and threaten to crush him for his presumption in considering gnostics like himself more excellent than
itself and was appeased only by some hastily composed laudatory
verses. The Kaaba also played a part in yet another vision confirming Ibn Arabi's role as Seal of Muhammadan Sainthood. He
dreamt that the Kaaba was built of bricks that were made alter-
nately of silver and gold. At first it seemed that the structure was
complete, but then he saw that two bricks were missing in the top
two rows between the Yemenite and Syrian corners, in the lower
row a silver and in the top a gold.

> I then saw myself being inserted into the place reserved for the
> two missing bricks. I myself was the two bricks; with them the
> wall was complete and the Kaaba faultless. . . . Interpreting the
> vision I said to myself, "In My category [saints, *awliya*] I am
> among the 'followers' just as the Messenger of God is among the
> prophets, and perhaps it is through me that God has sealed
> sainthood."[25]

These glimpses into Ibn Arabi's visionary inner life could be
extended to fill volumes and stand as exemplification of the inner
life of Sufism as such, albeit at perhaps its highest point. The
importance of these experiences lies in their residue of ideas and

doctrines that have influenced generations of Sufis, and Muslims in general, down to the present day. These ideas form an integrated body, no aspect of which is unrelated to any other, but for reasons of explication this body of doctrine is best approached by focusing on five main ideas that infuse the whole: (1) Oneness of Being (*wahdat al wujud*), (2) the Divine Names (*asma dhatiyah/ asma sifatiyah*), (3) the Imaginal World (*alam al khayal*), (4) the Five Divine Presences (*al hadarat al ilahiyyah al khams*), and (5) the Perfect Man (*al insan al kamil*).

The name of Ibn Arabi has come to be especially associated with the doctrine known as Oneness of Being (*wahdat al wujud*). Although the term does not occur in his works and was only adopted by his followers as descriptive of his point of view, the expression is nevertheless accurate as far as it goes. It is not sufficient, however, since Ibn Arabi affirms the Manyness of being as much as its Oneness so that the fullness of being (*wujud*) is often described as the One/Many (*al wahid al kathir*), the One preceding the Many as light precedes the colors: "Though Being is One Entity, the entities of the possible things have made It many, so it is the One/Many. . . . There is nothing in existence but the One/Many. Within it become manifest the enraptured angels, the Intellect, the Soul, and Nature."[26]

The term *wujud* is usually translated in English as "being" or "existence" and as such has its roots in Islamic philosophy and theology. As used by Ibn Arabi, *wujud* has the additional meaning of "finding" in the sense of both being and perceiving that which is. In other words, he is concerned not just with the mental concept of being, but with its taste (*dhawq*); his ideas are a matter not simply of ratiocination, but of direct religious or metaphysical experience. This is why Ibn Arabi's mystical inner life is an integral part of his philosophy. Finding is as much ontological as epistemological in that nothing can know unless it is, and nothing truly is but God. As the Sufis say: "None knows God but God."[27]

The basic division within *wujud*, that which makes the One into the Many, is between Necessary Being (*wajib al wujud*) and contingent or possible being (*mumkin al wujud*). Necessary

Being is that which cannot not be, God (Allah) or the Real (*al haqq*) in its Essence (*dhat al haqq*); everything else, all that is other than God in this sense (*ma siwa Allah*), is the possible (*al mumkin*). All possibilities (*mumkinat*) have being in that they are not nothing and as such are objects of God's knowledge and immutable entities (*al ayan al thabita*), but they do not have existence in the sense of being manifested outwardly as things (*ashya*) in the cosmos: "If the possible thing were an existent which could not be qualified by nonexistence, then it would be the Real. If it were a nonexistence which could not be qualified by existence, then it would be impossible [*muhal*]."[28]

What brings possible things from the state of possibility or nonexistence to the state of actuality or existence is the desire of the Necessary Being, who gives preponderance (*tarjih*) to existence over nonexistence:

> God gave preponderance to the existence of the possible things over their nonexistence because they sought this preponderance by their very essences. Hence, this was a kind of submission [*inqiyad*] of the Real to this seeking on the part of possibility, and also a gratuitous kindness [*imtinan*]. For God is Independent of the worlds. But He described Himself by saying that He loved to be known by the possible things, since He was not known, and one of the characteristics of the lover is to submit himself to his beloved. But in reality, He only submitted to Himself. The possible thing is a veil over this divine seeking.[29]

The saying "He loved to be known . . ." is a favorite *hadith qudsi* among Sufis in explanation of creation and is usually found in the form "I was a Hidden Treasure, so I loved to be known. Hence I created the creatures that I might be known." It is not accepted by *hadith* scholars as authentic but is accepted by Sufis on the basis of unveiling (*kashf*), or vision of the Prophet in the Imaginal World.

The division within *wujud* is thus in reality twofold. Necessary Being gives rise to Possible Being, and Possible Being is brought into existence, or Actual Being. This Aristotelian ontology, the transformation of things *in potentia* into things *in actu*, in Ibn Arabi's terminology becomes the self-manifestation (*tajalli*) of the One-Absolute-Real, a self-manifestation that is at the same time a self-determination or delimitation (*ta'ayyun*).[30] As we shall see below, this self-delimitation of *wujud* appears further in the hierarchical form of the cosmos (*tartib al alam*) and its several ontological levels (*maratib al wujud*), but another way of conveying the same idea is by likening Being to Light.

The Koran says that God is Light, and Ibn Arabi inherited a long tradition in Sufism of identifying Light (*nur*) with Being (*wujud*). Light/Being is contrasted with Darkness (*zulma*)/Nothingness or the impossible, and the cosmos is seen as a domain of brightness between the two: "Light is perceived, and through it perception takes place. Darkness is perceived, but through it no perception takes place. . . . God is sheer Light, while the impossible is sheer darkness. . . . Creation is the Barzakh [*isthmus*] between Light and darkness. . . ."[31] For Ibn Arabi, Light, like Being, is as once ontological and epistemological, which is conveyed by associating Light with perception and knowledge, hence, knowledge is a "light which God throws into the heart of whomsoever He will." This is the root of Ibn Arabi's mystical ontology in that real knowledge is knowledge of the Real, a matter of opening and unveiling (*futuh al mukashafa*).

The veils (*hujub*) are the secondary causes or forms (*suwar*) that obscure the Light of the First Cause, Necessary Being, or God in his essence. The purpose of a veil is both to hide and to reveal; without the veils the Light of the Real would be blindingly incomprehensible, and with the veils it is comprehensible in all but its naked Reality. What human beings can know of the Real is what the Real in its descents or self-manifestation (*tajalli*) chooses to reveal. For Islam the ultimate unveiling or revelation is the Koran, and it is from the Koran that we know the Divine Names (*al asma al ilahiyah*).

It is well known that the Koran contains ninety-nine names of God, the "most beautiful names" (*al asma al husna*, K.7:179, 17:110, 20:7), and that the Muslim rosary (*subha*) contains ninety-nine beads in three sets of thirty-three, in reference to this fact. These names are often divided into names of essence (*asma dhatiyyah*) and names of quality (*asma sifatiyyah*). Typical names of essence are Allah, the Holy (*al Qaddus*), the Truth (*al Haqq*), the Light (*an Nur*), and the Self-Subsistent (*al Qayyum*). Names of quality are often divided into names of Majesty (*jalal*), such as the Repairer (*al Jabbar*), the Contracter (*al Qabid*), and the Abaser (*al Mudhill*); names of Beauty (*jamal*), such as the Merciful (*ar Rahim*), the Forgiving (*al Ghafur*), and the Provider (*ar Razzaq*); and names of Perfection (*kamal*), such as the Wise (*al Hakim*), the Mighty (*al Azim*), and the Just (*al Adl*). In the writings of the philosophers and theologians the names of God become the attributes of God (*sifat*) chiefly the Knowing (*al Alim*), the Powerful (*al Muqtaddir*), the Living (*al Hayy*), the Willing (*al Iradah*), the Hearing (*al Sama*), the Seeing (*al Bashir*), and the Speaking (*al Mutakallim*).[32]

In the philosophy of Ibn Arabi the names are the *barzakh*, or *isthmus*, between God in his essence (*dhat/Haqq*) and the created world of the cosmos (*khalq*), and certain important points need to be understood about them in this regard. First, the names are really the "names of the names" (*asma al asma*) in that the words employed to designate the names are not the qualities named, not the names in themselves. Second, each name designates both the divine essence and a meaning or quality specific to itself. Third, the names are relationships, not entities or existing things. Each name is a special aspect of the Absolute or divine essence in its self-manifestation, and since the relations that the Absolute can have with its manifestation are infinite, the Divine Names are also infinite. It does not follow from this, however, that all the names are of the same qualitative status; rather, they are ranked according to the degree of being of the things in the hierarchical cosmos.

The names are not existent in the same way that things are existent, but neither are they nonexistent, since they are intelligible qualities that refer to both the divine essence and its effects. The names are not the effects but intelligible qualities recognizable in the effects: "Examples of these intelligible qualities include creation, provision, gain, loss, bringing into existence, specification, strengthening, domination, severity, gentleness, descent, attraction, love, hate, nearness, distance, reverence, and contempt. Every attribute [*sifa*] manifest within the cosmos has a name known to us through the Law [*ash shar*].[33]

Creation is the *barzakh* between light and darkness, and the Divine Names are the *barzakh* between God in his essence and the created world. *Barzakh* is thus a term for conveying the notion of inbetweenness, and the *barzakh par excellence* is the world of imagination (*alam al khayal*) or world of images (*alam al mithal*), that lies between the essence of God and the physical world apprehended by the rational mind. It is no exaggeration to say that this is the most important feature of Ibn Arabi's metaphysics, without some grasp of which it is impossible to understand not only the Sheikh al Akbar but Sufism as such.

According to Ibn Arabi, beyond the divine essence and among the possible things, there are three levels of known things (*ma'lumat*) and three modes of knowing:

(1) A level that belongs to meanings disengaged [*mujarrad*] from the substrata; the characteristic of meanings is that rational faculties perceive them through proofs or a priori [*bi tariq al badaya*].

(2) A level whose characteristic is to be perceived by the senses; these are the sensory things.

(3) A level whose characteristic is to be perceived either by the rational faculty or by the senses. These are imaginal things. They are the meanings that assume shape [*tashakkul*] in sensory forms; they are given form by the form-giving faculty [*al quwwat al musawwira*], which serves the rational faculty.[34]

The third level is that of the imaginal world in which ideas, qualities, and meanings are given form in the shape of personifications and symbols. Ibn Arabi also distinguishes between three different kinds of imagination (*khayal*). First, imagination in its widest sense, "nondelimited imagination" (*al khayal al mutlaq*), which refers to all existence other than the divine essence, all that is He/not He. Second, "discontiguous imagination" (*al khayal al munfasil*), which is the intermediate imaginal world (*alam al khayal*) that Ibn Arabi insists exists independently of its viewer. Third, "contiguous imagination" (*khayal al muttasil*), which is the faculty of imagination in the individual soul.[35]

The type of imagination known to all is the dream, and it is a feature of Islam that dreams can be revelatory keys to the mysteries of existence. Dreams require an interpreter (*mu'abbir*) to reveal the meaning of their sensory forms, and this raises the question of interpretation. How are dreams revelatory of true and divine things to be distinguished from fantasies produced by the ordinary human mind? How are the waking visions of forms in the imaginal world produced by angelic and divine influxes to be distinguished from those produced by devils (*shaitans*) and deluding spirits (*jinn*)? This is the problem of "the discernment of spirits" and was well recognized by Ibn Arabi, for whom it was solved by means of the "mark" (*alama*). This mark is given by God *individually* to the true seer so that he can recognize true visions: "Hence, if he has a mark, he will stand upon a clear sign from his Lord. Otherwise, delusion will occur for him, and there will be a lack of certain knowledge. . . ." The sheikh does not reveal what the mark is since he does not want to licence false claims. Concerning the mark of adepts who have become disengaged from the natural world and have entered among the angels, he says: "We know this mark, having tasted it. But we will not mention it to anyone, lest he make it manifest sometime while being a liar in his claim. That is why God has commanded me and my peers to conceal it."[36] We have already given a variety of examples of Ibn Arabi's experiences of the imaginal world, and it must be supposed that each carried with it its mark of authenticity.

The imaginal world is just one of the Divine Presences (*hadarat*), a term virtually synonymous with level (*martaba*), indicating the ontological hierarchy that makes up the cosmos. A

Presence (*hadra*) is a particular mode in which the Divine Essence manifests and delimits itself, and although Ibn Arabi often employs the term when speaking of the Divine Names, such as the Presence of the Merciful (*hadrat ar Rahman*) and the Presence of the Self-Subsistent (*hadrat al Qayyum*), and various worlds, such as the Presence of the Kingdom (*hadrat al Malakut*), the idea was systematized by his followers. Al Qunawi (d. 673/1274), al Farghani and al Jandi (both d. 700/1300), al Kashani (d. 750/1329) and al Qaysari (d. 751/1329) often speak of the "levels of existence" (*maratib al wujud*), which they consider to be infinite but which are usually reduced to five or six broad categories (*kulliyat*). As used by these followers the term "presence" (*hadra*) is equivalent to the term "world" (*alam*), which as Qaysari points out derives from "knowledge" (*ilm*), from which in turn is derived "mark" (*alama*), referred to above. So the Divine Presences, worlds, or levels are the marks or signs by which the One Being shows itself to those who can see.

Islam, like all religions, makes a fundamental distinction between the "visible" (*ash shahada*) and the "unseen" (*al ghayb*), and to be a Muslim is to necessarily "believe in the unseen" (*yu'min bi l'ghayb*). The imaginal world is a blending of the visible and the unseen in that it is a place where spiritual realities (the unseen) become visible and material things (the visible) become spiritualized or unseen. The unseen, the relative unseen, and the visible are thus the three fundamental presences, worlds, or ontological levels, but this basic scheme is usually elaborated to include five or six presences; if the Divine Essence is included there are said to be six presences, if not, there are said to be five. Of the numerous schemes available,[37] we will illustrate the five Divine Presences according to the explanation given by al Qaysari in his commentary on Ibn Arabi's book *The Bezels of Wisdom* (*Fusus al Hikam*).[38]

The first of the universal Presences is the (1) Presence of the Nondelimited Unseen. Its world is that of the immutable entities in the Presence of Knowledge. Facing it in the opposite position

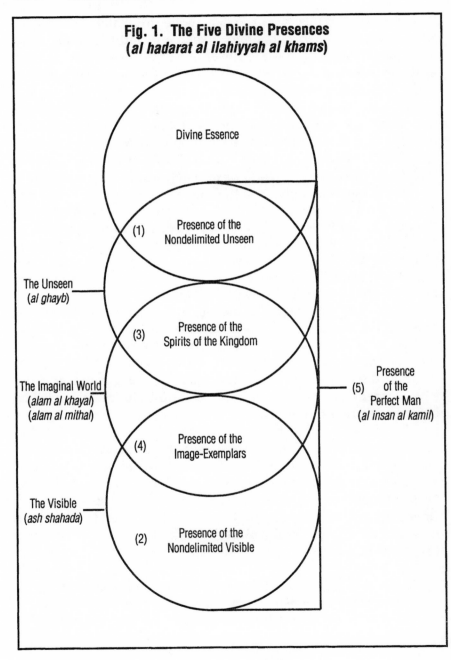

Fig. 1. The Five Divine Presences
(*al hadarat al ilahiyyah al khams*)

Divine Essence

(1) Presence of the Nondelimited Unseen

The Unseen
(*al ghayb*)

(3) Presence of the Spirits of the Kingdom

The Imaginal World
(*alam al khayal*)
(*alam al mithal*)

Presence of the Perfect Man
(*al insan al kamil*)

(5)

(4) Presence of the Image-Exemplars

The Visible
(*ash shahada*)

(2) Presence of the Nondelimited Visible

is the (2) Presence of the Nondelimited Visible, whose world is that of the Dominion [*al mulk*, the World of Sense-Perception]. Then there is the Relative Unseen. It is divided into two parts: the first is (3) that which is nearer to the Nondelimited Unseen. Its world is that of the Spirits of the Kingdom [*al malakut*] and the Invincibility [*al jabarut*], i.e., the world of the disengaged [*mujarrad*] Intellects and Souls. The second part of the Relative Unseen is (4) that which is nearer to the Visible. Its world is that of the Image-Exemplars; the reason the Relative Unseen becomes divided into two parts is that Spirits posses imaginal forms which have an affinity with the World of the Nondelimited Visible, and intellectual, disengaged forms which have an affinity with the Nondelimited Unseen. The fifth is the (5) Presence which comprehends the above four. Its world is the human world, which comprehends all worlds and everything within them.[39]

The fifth presence of the human is also that of the Perfect Man. If the ordinary "animal man" (*al insan al hayawan*) is the microcosm, the cosmos in miniature, he is also virtually the macrocosm, the cosmos at large, the Perfect Man (*al insan al kamil*) who encompasses all the Divine Presences: "God only created the cosmos outside of man to strike an example for him and so that he might know that everything manifest in the world is inside himself, while he is the goal. . . . In him all the Divine Names and their effects are displayed."[40] Ibn Arabi calls these perfect men the Muhammadan friends of God, in that they have inherited all the perfections of Muhammad and occupy the highest of all human states, the Station of No Station; they are the actualization of all the perfections of being, the prophets and saints, guides for all humankind, the fulfilment and exemplification of every virtue and wisdom. Metaphysically speaking, the Perfect Man is the embodiment of the Muhammadan Logos, the creative principle immanent in the cosmos. Ibn Arabi employs twenty-two terms, derived from philosophy and Islamic tradition, to indicate this principle, such as the Spirit of Muhammad (*Ruh Muhammad*), the Reality of Realities (*Haqiqat 'l Haqa'iq*), the Throne (*al Arsh*), the Most

Exalted Pen (*al alarmu 'i A'la*), the Real who is the instrument of creation (*al Haqqu 'l makhluqu bihi*), the Origin of the Universe (*Aslu 'l Alam*), and the First Intellect (*al Aqlu 'l Awwal*).[41]

There are two further features of Ibn Arabi's thought that are necessary for a complete picture of his philosophy and that have had an influence on certain Western "esoterists" in the twentieth century. The first is the idea of the transcendent unity of religions, and the second is the type of epistemology on which the whole edifice of Ibn Arabi's metaphysics rests.

There is a *hadith* in the *Sahih* of Muslim (*Iman*, 302) that describes the scene on the day of Resurrection. God discloses himself to the various groups of the resurrected, but they deny him. Then he says to them: "Is there a sign [*aya*] by which you will recognize God?" They reply that there is, and he shows it to them, whereupon they recognize him as their Lord. This sign is what Ibn Arabi calls the "mark" (*alama*), which he associates with God's capacity for self-transmutation (*tahawwul*) and the divine self-disclosure in the forms of beliefs: "Every group have believed something about God. If he discloses Himself in other than that something, they will deny Him. But when He discloses Himself in the mark which this group have established with God in themselves, then they will acknowledge Him."[42]

Perhaps the most remarkable explication of this idea in the works of Ibn Arabi is to be found in the chapter of the *Fusus al Hikam* on the Word of Muhammad:

> The believer . . . only praises the Divinity comprised within his belief (such as it is comprised therein) and it is to this that he is attached; he cannot perform any act that does not revert to him (its author) and likewise he cannot praise anything without thereby (in effect) praising himself. For without doubt, to praise the work is only to praise its author; beauty, like the lack of beauty, reverts to the author (of the work). The divinity in whom one believes is (so to speak) fashioned by he who conceives [*nadhir*], it is therefore (in this respect) his work; the praise addressed to what he believes is praise addressed (indirectly and

with regard to conceptualization) to himself. And this is why he (the believer insofar as he limits God) condemns every belief except his own: if he were just, he would not do this but he does it because, fixed on a particular object of worship [al ma'bud al khass], he is beyond all doubt in ignorance; and this is why his belief in God implies the negation of everything that is other than it. If he knew what Junayd said—that the color of the water is the color of the vessel—he would allow every believer (whose belief is other than his own) to believe what he (the other believer) believes; he would know God in every form and in every object of belief. But he (the man limited by his belief) follows his opinions without having (total) knowledge and that is why God said (through a *hadith qudsi*): I conform to the opinion that my servant forms of Me [*'inda dhanni 'abdi bi*]. That is to say, I only appear to him in the form of his belief; if he will, let him expand [*atlaga*] (his conception of Me), and if he will, let him constrict it [*qayyada*]. The Divinity in which one believes assumes the limits (of the belief), and this is the Divinity which (according to a *hadith qudsi*) the heart of the slave contains; the absolute Divinity not being contained in anything since it is the essence of things as well as its own essence. . . .[43]

Such ideas did not bear fruit until the twentieth century in the works of the translator of this passage.

The divine self-disclosure in the different religions, the Oneness of Being, the Divine Names, the Divine Presences, the Perfect Man, are all known by means of the Imaginal World, and access to the Imaginal World is only by means of spiritual practice (*dhikr, salat*), divine descent (*tajalli*), and disclosure, unveiling (*kashf*), tasting (*dhawq*), opening (*fath*), insight (*basira*), witnessing (*shuhud, mushahada*). This is a gnosis above and beyond the rational faculty (*al aql*), a gnosis without which Ibn Arabi's teachings would be little more than a compendium of all the philosophical, religious, and mystical ideas that the Sufism of his day had inherited from former times. This mode of knowing is the essential element in any expression or advocacy of Ibn Arabi's thought, whether in the twelfth or the twentieth century.

This short sketch of Ibn Arabi's life and works has only skimmed across a small part of the surface of an ocean of vast expanse and depth. Although Sheikh al Akbar did not found a Sufi brotherhood (*tariqa*) that bears his name, there was, and is, undoubtedly an Akbarian mantle (*khirqa akbariyya*) that conveys his spiritual presence (*baraka*) down through the generations and that still circulates to this day.[44] The heart of Islam is sheltered by it, and only a reckless unbeliever would call it in question.

Notes

1. Kalabadhi, *Kitab at ta'arruf* (*The Doctrine of the Sufis*), trans. A. J. Arberry (Cambridge: Cambridge University Press, 1935), p. 9.

2. See T. Burckhardt, *An Introduction to Sufism* (London: Thorsons, 1995), p. 15, n. 1.

3. See V. Danner, "The Necessity for the Rise of the Term Sufi," *Studies in Comparative Religion* 6, no. 2 (spring 1972): 71–72.

4. See chap. 3, pp. 73f.

5. Kalabadhi, *Kitab*, pp. 15–16.

6. See R. McCarthy, *Freedom and Fulfillment* (Boston: Twayne, 1980).

7. Quoted in W. C. Chittick, "Ibn Arabi and His School," in *Islamic Spirituality*, ed. Nasr (London: SPCK, 1989–91) vol. 2, p. 52.

8. See C. Addas, *Quest for the Red Sulphur* (Cambridge: Islamic Texts Society, 1993), pp. 18–27.

9. Ibid., pp. 36–37.

10. Ibid., pp. 39–43.

11. H. Corbin, *Creative Imagination in the Sufism of Ibn Arabi* (Princeton: Bollinger, 1969), p. 224.

12. See A. Hussaini, "Uways al Qarani and the Uwaysi Sufis," *Muslim World* 57 (1967): 103–13.

13. See M. Kabbani, *The Naqshbandi Sufi Way* (Chicago: Kazi Publicaitons, 1995), pp. 9–14.

14. Quoted in Addas, *Quest*, p. 149.

15. R. Austin *Sufis of Andalusia*, trans. of Ibn Arabi's *Ruh al Quds* (Sherborne: Beshara Publications, 1988), p. 124.

16. See M. Chodkiewicz, *Seal of the Saints* (Cambridge: Islamic Texts Society, 1993), chap. 9.

17. See A. Guillaume, *The Life of Muhammad*, trans. of Ibn Ishaq *Sirat Rasul Allah* (Oxford: Oxford University Press, 1955), pp. 181–87.

18. See J. Morris, "Ibn Arabi's Spiritual Ascension," in *Les Illuminations de la Mecque*, ed. M. Chodkiewicz (Paris: Sinbad, 1988), pp. 349–81; also J. Morris, "The Spiritual Ascension," *Journal of the American Oriental Society* 107 (1987): 629–52; 108 (1988): 63–77.

19. Chodkiewicz, *Les Illuminations*, pp. 378–81.

20. Chodkiewicz, *Seal of the Saints*, pp. 130–31, cf. L. Shamash and S. Hirtenstein, "From the Preface to the *Futuhat Al-Makkiya* by Ibn Arabi," *Journal of the Muhyiddin Ibn Arabi Society*, vol. 4 (1985): pp. 4–6.

21. It has been estimated that the projected critical edition of the *Futuhat al Makkiyya* will contain some seventeen thousand pages. See W. C. Chittick, *The Sufi Path of Knowledge* (New York: SUNY Press, 1989), pp. x–xv.

22. *Fut.* 1, quoted in Addas, *Quest*, pp. 201–3, cf. Corbin, *Creative Imagination*, pp. 279–81, and F. Meier, "The Mystery of the Kaaba," in *The Mysteries* (Princeton: Bollinger, 1971), pp. 149–68.

23. See Addas, *Quest*, pp. 193–216.

24. R. Nicholson, *Interpreter of Desires*, trans. of Ibn Arabi's *Tarjuman al Ashwaq*, (London: Theosophical Publishing House, 1978), XI, 13–15, p. 67.

25. *Fut.* 1, quoted by Addas, *Quest*, p. 213.

26. *Fut.* chs. 360 and 371, quoted in Chittick, *The Sufi Path of Knowledge*, pp. 214, 140.

27. Ibid., p. 4.

28. *Fut.*, ch. 360, ibid., p. 82.

29. *Fut.*, ch. 351, ibid.

30. See T. Izutsu, *Sufism and Taoism* (Los Angeles: University of California Press, 1984), chap. 11.

31. *Fut.*, ch. 360, Chittick, *The Sufi Path of Knowledge*, pp. 213–14.

32. See R. Stade, *The Ninety-Nine Names of God*, trans. of Ghazali's *al maqsad al asma* (Ibadan: Daystar Press, 1970); and Abd ar Rahman Abu Zayd, *Al Ghazali on Divine Predicates*, trans. of Ghazali's *Al Iqtisad fil I'tiqad* (Lahore: S. H. Muhammad Ashraf, 1970); also H. Wolfson, *The*

Philosophy of the Kalam (Harvard: Harvard University Press, 1976), chap. 2.

33. *Fut.*, chap. 371, Chittick, *The Sufi Path of Knowledge*, p. 35.

34. *Fut.*, chap. 73, ibid., p. 115.

35. Ibid., p. 117. Cf. Corbin, *Creative Imagination*, pp. 219–20.

36. *Fut.*, chaps. 283 and 375, quoted in Chittick, *Imaginal Worlds*, chap. 6. Cf. Corbin, *Creative Imagination*, pp. 150, 331.

37. See W. C. Chittick, "The Five Divine Presences: From Al Qunawi to Al Qaysari," *Muslim World* 80 (1982): 107–28.

38. After the *Futuhat al Makkkiya*, the *Fusus al Hikam* is probably the most important and influential of Ibn Arabi's works. It was shown to him in a vision by the Prophet. See Addas, *Quest*, p. 277

39. Chittick, "Five Divine Presences," p. 123. Cf. Corbin, *Creative Imagination*, pp. 360–62, and T. Burckhardt, *The Wisdom of the Prophets*, trans. of excerpts from Ibn Arabi's *Fusus al Hikam* (Aldsworth: Beshara Publications, 1975), pp. 30–31.

40. *Fut.* III, p. 417. Quoted in Chittick, "Ibn Arabi and His School," in Nasr ed., *Islamic Spirituality*, vol. 1, p. 66.

41. See A. Affifi, *The Mystical Philosophy of Muhyid Din Ibnul-'Arabi* (Cambridge: Cambridge University Press, 1936), chap. 2; also Izutsu, *Sufism and Taoism*, chs. 14–17; R. Nicholson, *Studies in Islamic Mysticism* (Cambridge: Cambridge University Press, 1978), chap. 2; T. Burkhardt, *Universal Man*, trans. of Abd al Karim al Jili's *Al Insan al Kamil* (Sherborne: Beshara Publications, 1983).

42. *Fut.*, chap. 48, Chittick, *The Sufi Path of Knowledge*, p. 336.

43. Quoted in F. Schuon, *Sufism: Veil and Quintessence* (Bloomington: World Wisdom Books, 1981), pp. 53–54. Cf. Burckhardt, *Universal Man*, pp. 132–33, and R. Austin, trans. *The Bezels of Wisdom*, trans. of Ibn Arabi's *Fusus al hikam* (London: SPCK, 1980), pp. 283–84.

44. See M. Chodkiewicz, *An Ocean Without Shore* (New York: SUNY, 1993), pp. 15-16, and the introduction to Chodkiewicz, *The Spiritual Writings of Amir Abd al Kader* (New York: SUNY Press, 1995). Also G. Elmore, "Ibn al-'Arabi's Testament on the Mantle of Initiation (al-Khirqah)," *Journal of the Muhyiddin Ibn 'Arabi Society* 26 (1999): 1–33.

Chapter 6

Sufism: A Secular Perspective

There is a clear parallel between the doctrine of irrationalism, which entitles its advocates to get away without providing arguments, and the doctrine of esotericism, which entitles its advocates to get away without providing evidence. The many different views of mystics on mysticism are not consistent with each other; and most of them result from prior convictions and are mere dogmatic assertions. One may turn out to be the correct; or all may be wrong; but, since they differ, they cannot all be right.
—Fritz Staal

Ｆrom a secular perspective the problem with Sufism is the same as the problem with Islam, a problem with three aspects—historical, rational, and experiential. Historically, insofar as Sufism identifies itself with the traditional account of the origin of Islam outlined in chapter 1, it suffers from all the problems with that account discussed in chapter 2. Rationally, insofar as it assumes the beliefs of Islam outlined in chapter 3, it is subject to the objections to those beliefs raised in chapter 4, not to mention all the objections that can be raised to any form of theism. If the special sphere of Sufism is religious experience, it is susceptible to the analysis to which such experience has been subjected in contemporary philosophy and religious studies.

First, something must be said about the origin of Sufism in its relation to early Islam. It is the contention of apologists for Sufism that what exists today under that name existed from the beginning, even if the name did not. Indeed, it existed in the beginning in its purest form, as the old Sufi saying has it: "In the beginning Sufism was a reality without a name, today it is a name without a reality."[1] There is, of course, no more evidence for this assertion than there is for any other that traditional Islam makes about its origins.

In order to counter accusations that Sufism was heterodox and not an integral feature of Islam, Sufis have always been eager to derive their doctrines from the Koran and the Hadith; this was an early feature of Sufi apologetics and is still going on today.[2] This apologetic device depends upon the traditional account of the origin of the Koran and the Hadith. If this account is wrong, as we have given good reason to think that it is, then Sufism is as much a late construct resulting from the Arabs' acquiring an empire as Islam itself. The chains of descent (silsila) of the Sufi brotherhoods, which include Muhammad and Ali, are simply one more fantasy on top of all the other fantasies that pass for history in Islam.

However, if the Koran and the Hadith were not there from the beginning, it can still be claimed that certain texts that were later incorporated in them were in existence from early times, and it is these that form the literary evidence for the early existence of Sufism. This would fit the fact that Sufism has, in effect, its own Koran and Hadith, in that there are certain texts that are repeatedly cited in Sufi literature and others that are hardly cited at all.[3] The favorite texts, not surprisingly, are those that lend themselves to a mystical interpretation.

Sufism is heavily dependent on the *hadith qudsi*, supposedly direct sayings of God not included in the Koran. Beside the ubiquitous "I was a hidden treasure . . ." favorites are "My Heaven cannot contain Me, nor can my earth, but the heart of my believing servant contains Me"; "God is beautiful, and He loves beauty"; "The heart of man is the throne of God"; and "Whoso knoweth himself knoweth his Lord." There are many similar texts scattered throughout the Koran, such as: "He [God] is the first and the last, the outwardly manifest and the inwardly hidden" (K.57:3); "Wheresoever you turn, there is the face of God" (K.2:115); and "We [God] are nearer to him [man] than his jugular vein" (K.50:16). Most popular of all is the following from the *sura* "Light," a text that has licensed whole schools of mystical philosophy:

> God is the Light of the heavens and the earth; the likeness of His Light is as a niche wherein is a lamp (the lamp in a glass, the glass as it were a glittering star) kindled from a Blessed Tree, an olive that is neither of the East nor of the West whose oil wellnigh would shine, even if no fire touched it; Light upon Light; (God guides to His Light whom He will.) (And God strikes similitudes for men, and God has knowledge of everything.) . . . And to whomsoever God assigns no light, no light has he. (K.24:35–40)

A favorite text for those who subscribe to the transcendent unity of religions idea is K.5:48: "To every one of you we have appointed a right way and an open road. If God had willed, He would have made you one nation; but that He may try you in what has come to you. So be you forward in good works; unto God shall you return, all together; and He will tell you of that whereon you were at variance." Although set wholly within the context of the Semitic religions and only intended to refer to such, this text has been taken, perhaps by Ibn Arabi and certainly by his latter-day followers, to refer to all "orthodox" religions.

Such texts as these are undoubtedly mystical, or at least capable of being so interpreted, but they are not distinctly Islamic. They could have been uttered by anyone, anywhere, at any time. That they have found their way into texts that are distinctly Islamic in other respects demonstrates that mysticism is a common feature of human nature and can raise its head in any context, thereafter taking on the color of its milieu, in this case by adding references to Muhammad and the Koran; we know of similar sentiments expressed in adjacent communities adorned with the appropriate Jewish and Christian references.

The way that Islam drew its mystical as well as its religious elements from the common culture of the Middle East has been well documented in the pioneering works of Margaret Smith.[4] More recently, Julian Baldick has reinforced her conclusions by drawing on the revolution in the study of Islamic origins brought about by the British academics quoted at length in chapters 2 and 4. Baldick maintains: "The Islamic historical tradition, in its presentation of the religion's beginnings, has to be seen as reflecting subsequent political and doctrinal bias" and that the biography of the Prophet is "the result of long regional rivalries; of the projection into one man's life of developments which must have taken place much later; and of the transposition into an Arabian setting of processes which belong to the Fertile Crescent in the north." As for the manufacture of Hadith:

> Most probably, as the new religion of Islam was gradually built up from its Jewish-Christian base . . . it produced on the one hand legal Traditions out of Jewish materials in the Babylonian Jewish community in Iraq; and on the other mystical Traditions out of Christian materials in the Nestorian Church in Iraq.[5]

Baldick demonstrates how Sufi stories about the pious ascetics of early Islam, who are pictured as achieving massive feats of self-mortification, are mostly repetitions of stories about Christian monks. The pattern for this cultural transfer from Christianity to Islam is set by the legends of two women, both named Rabi'a, one of whom, Rabi'a of Basra (d. 801), in Iraq, is the most famous woman in Islamic mysticism, while the other is supposed to have lived in Syria in the early ninth century. It turns out that the models for the lives of these two exemplary Islamic women are two Christian Marys, Mary Magdalen of the Gospels and Mary of Egypt, who is supposed to have repented of a life of promiscuity after the intervention of Mary the mother of Jesus.[6]

Baldick is equally dismissive of many other figures claimed for Sufism: "One can exclude Muhasibi as neither Sufi nor mystic; Dhu 'l Nun as a legend; Abu Yazid as a representative of Indian ideas with no real impact; Tirmidhi as an independent, tutorless figure separated from the mainstream; and Hallaj as someone who cut himself off from the Sufis and was largely rejected by them in his own time."[7] The renowned figure of Muhammad Ghazali (d. 1111) is also dismissed as an unoriginal establishment figure whose biography is not to be taken at face value; he is altogether less worthy of respect than his less famous "drunken" brother Ahmad (d. 1126).[8] As for the real Sufis, they had simply "taken over the Christian mystic's path, with repentance leading through other stages, to 'what no eye has seen.' They had also inherited the ideas of the Covenant and God's friends. To all this they tacked on Gnostic teachings about primordial lights and their own development, presumably from Christian and neo-Platonist sources, of the theme of 'passing away and survival.' " Moreover, some of them "had assumed that they were the most important people in the universe, with the exception of the prophets, and indispensable to it. Others had uttered what seemed to be blasphemous expressions of self-identification with God."[9] Baldick's judgments are a breath of fresh air in the study of Sufism, which is plagued by writers of the mystical-romatic school, in love with their subject and blinded as a result.

By the beginning of the tenth century, Sufism's principal doctrines had been formulated, and by the end of that century they had been set out in several manuals of doctrine by Kalabadhi, Abu Talib (Makki) and others. The main feature of those doctrines additional to those of mainstream Islam are numerous states (*ahwal*) and stations (*maqamat*), which culminate in a "passing away" (*fana*) of the mystic's human attributes and subsequent "survival" (*baqa*) in the attributes of God.

There is much variation among Sufi authors on the order and significance of the various states and stations; what some call states, others call stations, and vice versa. Generally speaking, however, states are considered to be transient and the gift of God, whereas stations are considered to be permanent and the result, to some extent at least, of human effort. The main sequence of stations was as follows: repentance (*tawba*), trust in God (*tawwakul*), poverty (*faqr*), and contentment (*rida*), leading to the different degrees of love (*mahabba*), or gnosis (*ma'arifa*), according to the temperament of the wayfarer (*salik*). Important states that correspond to the stations of fear (*khauf*) and hope (*raja'*) are expansion (*bast*) and contraction (*qabd*).[10]

The methods by which the stations are achieved, and Islamic doctrine in general made alive in the experience of the believer, are subsumed under the heading of remembrance of God (*dhikr Allah*). The relation between doctrine and method is a crucial matter, not only in Islam and Sufism, but in religion in general. All the monotheistic religions have a mystical dimension, and figures who had saintly lives and exalted experiences exemplify and validate the truth of the tradition. The methods or practices of the religions are thus the means by which the doctrines are, supposedly, proved true to the believers. In Islam and Sufism, in addition to *salat,* which is incumbent on all, the methods are remembering God by repetition of his names (*dhikr*), and meditation (*fikr*).

When entering a Sufi brotherhood (*tariqa*), the aspirant (*murid*) takes an oath of allegiance (*bay'a*) to the head of the order (*sheikh*),[11] whereupon he is given his personal *dhikr*, usually consisting of a particular name of God and other short formulae to be repeated a certain number of times per day. In addition, there will be another *dhikr* incumbent on all beginners, such as the following from the Naqshbandiyya *tariqa*:

Shahada—ash-hadu an la ilaha ill-Allah wa ash-hadu anna Muhammadan abduhu wa rasuluh	3 times daily
astaghfirullah	25 times daily
Surah Fatiha	1 time daily
Surah Ikhlas	11 times daily

Surah Falaq	1 time daily
Surah Nas	1 time daily
la ilaha ill-Allah	9 times daily
la ilaha ill-Allah Muhammadun Rasul Allah Allahumma salli ala Muhammadin wa ala ali	1 time daily
Muhammadin wa sallim	10 times daily
Gift the reward of the above recitation to the Prophet and the sheikhs of the Naqshbandi Order	1 time daily
Surah Fatiha	1 time daily
Allah, Allah	1,500 times daily
Allahumma salli ala Muhammadan wa ala ali Muhammadin wa sallim	100 times daily
One thirtieth of the Koran or *Surah Ikhlas*	100 times daily
One chapter of *Dalail al Khairat*[12] or *Allahumma salli ala Muhammadin wa ala ali Muhammadin wa sallim*	100 times daily

This *dhikr* can be increased in stages, at the discretion of the sheikh and according to the capacity of the *murid*, until "Those Who Have Determination" will be reciting *Allah* five thousand times per day aloud and five thousand times per day in the heart (silently), plus corresponding increases in the repetitions of the other formulae.[13]

In addition to this personal *dhikr* performed by the *murid* in his own time, every week on a Thursday or Friday evening, there will be a communal *dhikr* of a different form, chanted rhythmically, led by the *sheikh* or a deputy and attended by as many *murids* as possible.[14] This regime of *dhikr* means, in effect, that practically every waking moment the *murid* will be remembering

God by repeating his names, invoking blessings on the Prophet, and reciting the Koran. Combined with the performance of all possible supererogatory prayers, including rising during the night to pray, the fullest forms of the five obligatory daily prayers, fasting (*sawm*), and seclusion (*khalwa*), *dhikr Allah* is a formidable recipe for the derangement of the senses in a particular direction, practically guaranteed to produce unusual experiences. Meditation (*fikr*) is both the enablement and the reinforcement of these effects by focusing the mind on such Koranic themes as fear (*makhafa*), love (*mahabba*), and knowledge (*ma'rifa*).[15]

All of this takes place in an atmosphere of unquestioning belief in the Koran as the verbatim record of God's speech, the final revelation for all humankind; the Hadith as a trustworthy record of the sayings and doings of the final Prophet; the Prophet as the most perfect man who ever lived, whose life we know in the greatest possible detail; and the *sharia* as the perfect law for all humankind composed by God himself. In such circumstances, it is hardly surprising that experiences that appear to confirm the truth of Islam become commonplace. The method, in Islam as in other religions, is a means for inducing experiences in conformity with the doctrine, a form of pious brainwashing, for the most part voluntarily entered into and gratefully received, the practical implementation of the highest virtue—sincerity (*ikhlas*). Against this background of practice and belief the seemingly extraordinary experiences of Ibn Arabi, cited in chapter 5, become accountable, especially when allied with his highly developed hypnagogic imagination.[16]

Some of the most important distinctions in the study of mystical experience were made by the philosopher W. T. Stace in his groundbreaking work *Mysticism and Philosophy*. Most relevant to Sufism and the experiences of Ibn Arabi is the stipulation that visions and voices are not true mystical phenomena; neither are raptures, trances, and hyperemotionalism.[17] This distinction is often made by mystics themselves and equally often ignored, since the distinction is not absolute, and one kind of phenomena often leads to the other. If rigidly adhered to in the case of Islam, it would at a stroke eliminate 90 percent of the experiences undergone by members of Sufi orders, including their most illustrious and revered representatives. All the visions of the Prophet and the prophets, the angels, the saints, and the *jinn*, plus the Uwaysi experience of being taught by dead sheikhs[18] become so much fantasy and dross and psychological aberration, wholly explicable in terms of cultural conditioning and the ingrained susceptibility of human beings to succumb to the products of their own imaginings.

The isthmus or *barzakh*, the world of imagination (*alam al khayal*) in which Sufism theorizes that these events take place, is in fact the Islamic equivalent of the astral plane, familiar in Western occultism. There are certain techniques, which since the foundation of the Theosophical Society in 1875 have been more or less public knowledge, for gaining access to this world of the imagination. The Hermetic Order of the Golden Dawn, founded in England in 1888, taught these techniques as part of the knowledge lectures accompanying its grades of initiation.[19] The occultist Aleister Crowley (1875–1947) has also given precise instructions[20] together with salutary warnings: "The student, if he attains any success in the following practises will find himself confronted by things (ideas or beings) too glorious or too dreadful to be described. It is essential that he remain the master of all that he beholds, hears or conceives; otherwise he will be the slave of illusion, and the prey of madness."[21] He also notes, when describing the different realms of the astral, that "[t]here are also planes corresponding to various religions past and present, all of which have their peculiar unity."[22]

The trained explorer in such imaginal realms is equipped with a critical mind and an awareness of their delusory nature. The religious believer is at their mercy and pleased to be so, since they appear to confirm whatever he wants, consciously or unconsciously, to be true. Ibn Arabi's distinction between a subjective, personal, "contiguous" imagination (*khayal al muttasil*) and an objective "discontiguous" imaginal world (*khayal al munfasil*) is simply a self-serving distinction in favor of his Islamic astral visions. The Islamic astral plane may be "there" in some sense or other, but so are the astral planes of every other religion and cult that has ever existed, and they are all at the same level of delusion. Ibn Arabi's further claim that he and his fellow Sufi gnostics have a special dispensation from God whereby they can distinguish false from veridical visions by reans of a "mark" (alama) disclosed to them alone is the ultimate self-serving device. It can be dispelled by asking simply: How is it known that the mark is the true mark?

The ascent to heaven (miraj) attributed to Muhammad and emulated by Ibn Arabi is an Islamized version of initiatory visionary ascents to be found in Judaism, Gnosticism, and the Hellenistic mystery religions[23] that are themselves "civilized" versions of shamanistic visionary ascents found worldwide.[24] The methodology of such ascents is also an integral feature of Western occultism, where it is known as "Rising on the Planes" and "Path Working." Here the Lote Tree of the Boundary (K.53:14) becomes the "Tree of Life" of the Qabalah, and the Perfect Man (al insan al kamil) becomes Adam Kadmon.[25] Rising on the Planes is a direct ascent toward heaven by means of the middle pillar of the Tree and the spheres of the moon and sun, while Path Working utilizes the left- and right-hand pillars and each of the spheres attributed to the seven planets and the celestial spheres beyond (see figure 2). These ascents, in which all kinds of symbolic and mythological entities are encountered, have much in common with the technique known as active imagination used by psychologist C. G. Jung, which he may have acquired from occult sources.[26]

The apparent objectivity of these experiences has deluded many, particularly those already inclined to a sense of special election. The reason for this has been pointed out by Merkur: "The unconscious production of autonomous images that conform with learned motifs may happen spontaneously. Conformity may even occur in the absence of conscious belief in the motifs. For some imagers, the apparent confirmation of received tradition by personal experience may have profound religious consequences."[27] This is certainly true of Ibn Arabi. The greatest sheikh (Sheikh al Akbar) turns out, when looked at closely, to be little

Fig. 2. The Qabalistic Tree of Life

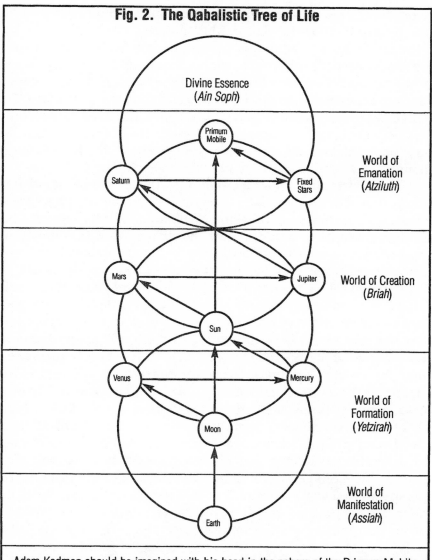

Adam Kadmon should be imagined with his head in the sphere of the Primum Mobile and his feet on the sphere of Earth. Note the resemblance to the diagram of the Five Divine Presences in chapter 5.

more than a rather pedestrian fundamentalist, wholly taken in by the Koran, Hadith, and Sharia while given to claiming a superior visionary backing for his more unconventional and egocentric opinions. As with other mystics, his career and experiences are wholly explicable in psychological and sociological terms, without the need to resort to anything transcendental.[28] In this regard the judgment of Affifi stands: "Ibn al Arabi often deceives himself into the belief that he is a mystic and a saint. He believes all that he says about himself, and he is quite sincere about it, but there is no doubt that he is the victim of his own imagination."[29]

These strictures apply especially to those statements of Ibn Arabi that some would claim as endorsements of the idea of the transcendent unity of religions. William Chittick says of Ibn Arabi's attempts to describe how the divine Word becomes pluralized as it enters the cosmos, that: ". . . he explains all this not through a theory that he has concocted, but on the basis of having seen the revelatory process in action and tasted it himself. This tasting [dhawq] belongs to him not as a prophet, of course, but as an inheritor of the sciences revealed to the prophets."[30] But the idea of God's Word coming through various prophets is Koranic, so he has no need to "concoct" it. It is hardly surprising that an ardent Muslim induces in himself, to the extent of "tasting," the truth of an idea he already takes for granted. In any case, whoever "concocted" those passages of the Koran in which this idea occurs almost certainly had nothing more in mind than the diversity of the Semitic "religions of the Book." In this matter of different revelations and diverse perspectives Chittick also claims: "The Shaykh never denies the relative validity of limited perspectives, even the schools of thought he criticizes. What he does deny is that any specific position can embrace the position of no position, or the Station of No Station, which is available only through divine bestowal and unveiling."[31] In other words, it is available only to him—another instance of Ibn Arabi making an exception in his own favor. He alone can see the truth of every matter because he has a special dispensation from God. These sentiments have been inherited in our own day by exponents of the "perennial philosophy" and "traditionalism," with which Chittick is in sympathy.

It could be claimed, however, in defense of Ibn Arabi, that not all his experiences are of the self-serving and visionary kind and that this is true of Islamic mysticism in general in the experiences of *fana* and *baqa*. Chittick has argued against Henry Corbin's emphasis on the visionary aspects of Ibn Arabi's mysticism: ". . . in his zeal to revive the honor due to the imaginal realm, Corbin tended to de-emphasize the cornerstone of Islamic teachings, *tawhid*, the 'declaration of God's Unity.' It is as if Corbin was so entranced by the recovery of the imaginal that he had difficulty seeing beyond it."[32] Beyond the imaginal realm of visionary experiences lies the realm of pure mysticism, experiences that may be devoid of all sensory imagery yet infused with a sense of Oneness and Unity. This is, indeed, what Islam calls *tawhid* and makes the epitome of its worldview. It is also the universal core of mysticism as defined by W. T. Stace.

In seeking out the core or essence of true mystical experience, Stace finds that it can be classified under two main headings, the extrovertive and the introvertive, both of which are experiences of Unity or Oneness:

> The essential difference between them is that the extrovertive experience looks outward through the senses, while the introvertive looks inward into the mind. Both culminate in the perception of an ultimate Unity—what Plotinus called the One— with which the perceiver realizes his own union or even identity. But the extrovertive mystic, using his physical senses, perceives the multiplicity of external material objects—the sea, the sky, the houses, the trees—mystically transfigured so that the One, or the Unity, shines through them. The introvertive mystic, on the contrary, seeks by deliberately shutting off the senses, by obliterating from consciousness the entire multiplicity of sensations, images, and thoughts, to plunge into the depths of his own ego. There, in that darkness and silence, he alleges that he perceives the One—and is united with it—not as a Unity seen

through a multiplicity (as in the extrovertive experience), but as the wholly naked One devoid of any plurality whatever.[33]

These two types of mystical experience are two species of one genus, and Stace summarizes their characteristics as follows:

Common Characteristics of Extrovertive Mystical Experience	Common Characteristics of Introvertive Mystical Experience
1. The Unifying Vision— all things are One	1. The Unitary Consciousness; the One; the Void; pure consciousness
2. The more concrete apprehension of the One as an inner subjectivity, or life, in all things	2. Nonspatial, nontemporal
3. Sense of objectivity or reality	3. Sense of objectivity or reality
4. Blessedness, peace, etc.	4. Blessedness, peace, etc.
5. Feeling of the holy, sacred, or divine	5. Feeling of the holy, sacred, or divine
6. Paradoxicality	6. Paradoxicality
7. Alleged by mystics to be ineffable	7. Alleged by mystics to be ineffable[34]

The characteristics from 3 to 7 are the same in both cases, and Stace identifies them as the:

universal common characteristics of mysticism in all cultures, ages, religions, and civilizations of the world. . . . By far the most significant characteristics are 1 and 2 in the extrovertive list and 1 in the introvertive. In this general experience of a unity which the mystic believes to be in some sense ultimate and basic to the world, we have the very inner essence of all mystical experience.[35]

More recently, Richard Jones has attempted to refine Stace's definitions by distinguishing between mystical experiences resulting from concentrative techniques that focus attention and receptive techniques that destructure our normal conceptual frameworks. This results in a distinction between "experiences totally free of all conceptual and sensory content ['depth-mystical experiences'] and others having some conceptual differentiation regardless of whether thought content or sensory stimuli are involved ['nature-mystical experiences'].[36] This emphasis on techniques, however, obscures the fact that such experiences may occur spontaneously.

It is the idea and experience of Oneness or Unity (*tawhid*), whether extrovertive or introvertive, that Islam claims for itself as its characteristic doctrine, delivered by God himself in a special revelation as if the world would otherwise have no knowledge of it. Seen against its original Semitic background, the Islamic doctrine of the one God and Oneness as ultimate truth is a reaction to the apparent splitting of divinity in Christianity. In the hands of its latter-day apologists, *tawhid* becomes the means of demonstrating the universality of the Islamic revelation, the evidence for its providential finality. This can be done on the basis of the claim that Islam simply confirms all that has gone before in all the other revelations, even the primordial state of Adam in paradise. Looked at from the secular perspective, in which none of the religions are revelations but merely human constructs, the doctrine of Oneness is not the result of divine revelation, rather, the "revelation" is the result of the experience of Oneness.

This brings us to the third and most important distinction made by Stace in his study of mysticism, that between an experience and its interpretation.[37] This distinction is crucial in that it raises the question of the objectivity and cognitive status of mystical experiences. There is a difference between a sense experience and its interpretation; the American visitor to Madame Tussaud's who tried to shake hands with a waxwork policeman is the classic example. Stace contends that this distinction also applies to mystical experience and that we should not accept without question the interpretations that mystics themselves give to their experiences. It is probably true that in neither sensory nor nonsensory experience is it possible to isolate a pure experience perfectly free from all interpretation, but that there can be successive interpretations of the same experience is enough to validate the distinction.

However, in a seminal essay,[38] Steven Katz criticizes Stace for failing to recognize the full import of the experience-interpretation distinction. While agreeing that "[t]here are NO pure (i.e., unmediated) experiences,"[39] he objects that "[t]he focus of Stace's remarks is on the relation between the mystics' experience and 'the beliefs which the mystics based upon their experiences.' Here the symmetry is always one-directional: from 'experience' to 'beliefs.' There is no recognition that this relationship contains a two-directional symmetry: beliefs shape experience, just as experience shapes belief."[40] Failure to recognize this two-way influence between experiences and beliefs leads to an oversimplification, which in Stace's case means that he fails to acknowledge the possible variety of mystical experiences. Like the advocates of the perennial philosophy, Stace has a bias in favor of a nonpersonal monism, and he identifies this as the highest form and universal core of mysticism. On the other hand, the Catholic scholar R. C. Zaehner, not surprisingly, finds the truest mystical experience to be that of union, not identity, with a personal God.[41] The conceptual bias that mystics bring to and read out of their experiences is thus compounded by that of the scholars who attempt to classify and account for them.

It may be true, as Stace claims, that accounts of experiences of Oneness and Unity can be found worldwide, in all cultures and all times, but it does not follow from this that these accounts all refer to identical experiences or that they are the only experiences that should be allowed to count as the universal core of mysticism. Nor should it be assumed that the experience of Oneness is simply "found" and then accurately described in neutral language, rather than induced by cultural and conceptual expectation and then reported in formulae prescribed by the tradition into which the mystic happens to have been born. As Steven Katz says elsewhere

The metaphysical naivete that seeks for, or worse, asserts, the truth of some meta-ontological schema in which either the mystic or the student of mysticism is said to have reached some phenomenological "pure land" in which he grasps transcendent reality in its pristine pre-predicative state is to be avoided. Given the epistemic elements involved in arriving at a comprehensive phenomenology of mysticism it is wiser to stand on its head the traditional, though arbitrary, analysis of mystical experience, which contends for separable components of "experience" and "description," and argue that ontological structures inherent in language and judgement pre-create the contours of experience and thus make "pure experience" a chimera.[42]

The idea that there is a unique mode of mystical consciousness that discloses the true nature of Ultimate Reality is the perennial fantasy of the perennial philosophy. Ibn Arabi said, "None knows God but God." This statement is the key to both the doctrine of *wahdat al wujud*, and its prolongation among present-day apologists for Islam, Sufism, and the transcendent unity of religions.

William Chittick tells us that the term *wujud* as used by Ibn Arabi "signifies not only Being/existence but also the 'finding' of God by God himself or by the servant; as such it is a synonym for *kashf*, and the great Sufis are the 'People of kashf and wujud.'"[43] *Kashf* is usually translated as "unveiling" and defined along the lines of "knowledge given . . . by God without the interference of that rational ['*aqli*] or considerative [*nazari*] faculty known as reflection,"[44] while it is also admitted that "[f]or the most part unveiling takes a visionary form."[45] Martin Lings makes the same point by quoting the *hadith qudsi*: "My slave seeketh unremittingly to draw nigh unto Me with devotions of his free will until I love him; and when I love him, I am the Hearing wherewith he heareth and the Sight wherewith he seeth and the Hand wherewith he smiteth and the foot whereon he walketh." To which he adds the comment "It cannot be concluded from this Tradition that this identity was not already there, for the Divinity is not subject to change. The 'change' in question is simply that what was not perceived has now been perceived." And in case the point is not clear, he appends a footnote: "It has been perceived only because the agent of perception is God, not the mystic. 'I am . . . his Sight,' or to use the Koranic phrase: *The sight overtaketh Him not, but He overtaketh the sight* (K.6:103)."[46]

This is in fact the Hindu doctrine of "Thou art That" (*tat tvam asi*), the idea that the true Self (*atman*) of the human individual (not the empirical ego) is identical to the divine Absolute Self (*brahman*). That this notion can be legitimately read out of Islamic texts is highly controversial and can be cogently argued against by Muslims who feel that it betrays the fundamental Koranic idea of the transcendence of God.[47] The only way to outface such criticisms is to claim an infallible knowledge, an unveiling (*kashf*) that reveals the true meaning of the texts, a knowledge at once indubitable and self-authenticating. That any such knowlege is possible, in view of the observations of Stace, Katz, and others outlined above, appears highly unlikely, since it collapses the distinction between an experience and its interpretation. It is, however, the claim made by gnostics, by Ibn Arabi, and by those who would defend his ideas and extend them to include all religion. *Atman* is renamed "Intellect" and regarded as God knowing himself in the sanctified man.

What God knows when he knows himself in the gnostic or sanctified man is, according to the school of Ibn Arabi, the Oneness of Being (*wahdat al wujud*), a mystical and metaphysical version of the Koranic theme of the Oneness (*tawhid*) of God. It is interesting to note that despite the fact that the notion of *tawhid* has become the ideological slogan of Islam, wielded by both its fundamentalist and its mystical parties, the word *tawhid* is not to be found in either the Koran or the Hadith.[48] The idea of *tawhid* has in fact two opposed meanings as used by these two groups. For fundamentalists, mainly the Wahhabis, *tawhid* is an exclusivist idea, denying any analogy or similarity between the world and God, who is always utterly transcendent. For Sufis, today chiefly the exponents of traditionalism and the perennial philosophy, *tawhid* is an inclusivist idea: nothing is considered to be outside God.

If God is utterly transcendent and unlike anything in the world, it is hard to understand how anything could be known of such an entity. The apparent solution is to say that all that can be known of God is what God chooses to tell. For fundamentalists this telling is confined to revelation in the Koran and Hadith. For Sufis there is also *kashf*, the unveiling that takes place in the experience of the mystic. For both parties there is always God's essence, how he is in himself, which remains forever unknown by definition. Saying that God is known only by means of revelation raises the question of how a "revelation" is known to be a revelation. If God is unknown apart from what he says of himself in the Koran, how is it known that what is said in the Koran is from God? On the fundamentalist definition, the Koran can never be got behind to see if it is really God who is speaking. The mystic is hardly in a better position, since he can be sure that his unveilings are from God only by checking them against the Koran. In this regard, the problems of transcendence are compounded for fundamentalists since they have to make an exception in the case of the Koran in order to boost its sacrality and authority. Like God himself, the Koran is said to be eternal and uncreated, not only in its essence but even, according to Ibn Hanbal, in its letters and sounds. If divinity can descend and "incarnate" to this extent in the Koran, why not in other ways also?

The inclusivist definition of *tawhid*, the idea that nothing is outside God, has to counter the charge of pantheism. Chittick tells us that *wahdat al wujud*, simply stated, is the idea that "there is only one Being, and all existence is nothing but the manifestation or outward radiance of that One Being. Hence 'everything other than the One Being'—that is, the whole cosmos in all its spatial and temporal extension—is nonexistent in itself, though it may be considered to exist through Being." This apparently contradictory statement does not amount to pantheism, because: "When the Shaykh himself explains what he means by the statement that Being is one, he provides one of the most sophisticated and nuanced expressions of the 'profession of God's unity' [*tawhid*] to be found in Islamic thought."[49] In other words, it is not pantheism, because for every statement that might appear to amount to such, another statement can always be found elsewhere in his works that appears to deny it. Any accusations of pantheism can always be blunted by pointing out the size and subtlety of the sheikhs writings and how the accuser has not rightly understood what is being said. Moreover, there is always the trump card that the sheikh's mystical experiences are a validation of his formulations to which the critic has no access and therefore no right to pass an opinion. The same goes, of course, for the expressions of his present-day defenders.

According to Titus Burckhardt, pantheism is found only among European philosophers and Easterners influenced by ninetenth-century Western thought: "Pantheism arose from the same mental tendency which produced, first, naturalism and then materialism. Pantheism only conceives of the relationship between the Divine Principle and things from the one point of view of view of substantial or existential continuity, and this is an error explicitly rejected by every traditional doctrine." However, ". . . all beings are God, if considered in their essential reality, but God is not these beings and this, not in the sense that his reality excludes them; but because in face of His infinity their reality is nil."[50] This denial of pantheism rests on stipulative definitions of such slippery terms as "substance," "essence," and "infinity," deriving from distinctions originally made by Frithjof Schuon.

In his first book, Schuon made the distinction between "substantial" identity and "essential" identity but did not define the terms.[51] Subsequently, definitions are offered along the following lines:

> We speak of "Substance" in order to illustrate the gulf separating that which subsists by itself and that which exists only secondarily and whose profound cause lies in a greater and higher reality. The term is used here in preference to the term "Essence" inasmuch as it is allowable to conceive of a sort of continuity between Substance and accident—"all things are

Atma"—whereas between Essence and forms there is none. This being so the relationship between Substance and accident may be compared to that between water and drops of water and the relationship between Essence and form to that between the fruit-stone and the fruit, or between fire and the wood it consumes; 'Brahma is not in the world.'

Yet it is admitted that: "If this is a kind of pantheism, then we are obliged to admit that pantheism is not entirely without justification when it is considered from a particular standpoint, namely that of the metaphysical homogeneity or solidarity of not-nothingness, nonunreality, or nonimpossibility. In a certain sense all that is not nothing is God, not in its particularity, but in and through ontological Substance."[52] While after another exposition of the same set of ideas we are told that "[a]ll this is a question of emphasis for, in fact, the notions of 'Essence' and 'Substance,' or 'form' and 'accident' are broadly interchangeable."[53] These definitional contortions are what passes for discernment in traditionalist circles. From the secular point of view they appear as quibbles over matters inherently incapable of being settled and in any case without consequence. What, it might be asked, is *wrong* with pantheism that it needs to be denied.

Many of the problems faced by the Oneness of Being doctrine are similar to those that beset the One of Plotinus, which is hardly surprising, since Neoplatonism had saturated Islamic philosophy and mysticism long before the time of Ibn Arabi.[54] Perhaps the most fundamental of these problems is why and how the One becomes Many, a problem that takes many related forms—if the Good, why and how Evil; if the Immaterial (Mind), why and how the Material (Matter); if the Absolute, why and how the Relative; if the Infinite, why and how the Finite; if Light, why and how Darkness. The solution favored by Plotinus and taken up by Ibn Arabi and his latter-day followers is a set of variations on the theme of an analogy based on the sun and its radiations. This analogy fails as a defense of the Oneness of Being doctrine since it requires the existence of an independent and opposed principle.

According to Ibn Arabi: "The Real is sheer Light, while the impossible [al muhal] is sheer darkness [zulma]. *Darkness never turns into Light, nor does Light turn into darkness.* Creation is the Barzakh between Light and darkness."[55]

If this is true, and not just a piece of metaphysical rhetoric, "The Real" is not the sole principle upon which "reality" is based. There is "the Real" and "darkness," and the world is a mixture of the two. The sun's light does not dissipate and become less for reasons in itself but because it is obstructed by an independent and opposed entity, darkness. If the sun, or Light, were the only ultimate reality, it would never fail or become less for any reason whatever. Perfect Reality/Light cannot "overflow" into anything other than itself since there is nothing other than itself. By definition the One and only Perfect Reality must fill all dimensions of Reality, otherwise it is imperfect. The Real (Light) does not produce darkness but needs darkness in order to produce the world. The Oneness of Being doctrine is thus revealed as a sham. In truth it is a twoness of Being doctrine: One/Many, Light/Darkness, Being/Non-Being, Existence/Non-Existence, Good/Evil, never one without the other, yet no way that the second item can ever be derived from the first.[56]

Tawhid, whatever form it takes, turns out to be a slogan incapable of coherent explication. Its only plausible basis is to be found in the extrovertive and introvertive mystical experiences identified by Stace, and these, when critically examined, do not require any ontological or supra-ontological interpretation. As for mysticism in general as revelatory of anything divine it is hard to disagree with the verdict of Fritz Staal: "It seems likely that the belief in gods is a special outcome of mystical experiences, interpreted as divine, and is in turn a device that facilitates the attainment of such experiences."[57]

What, then, is left of Sufism after this analysis? The final word for the defense may be left to one of Islam's most able apologists: ". . . Sufi explanations of Islamic teachings are not made to subvert the dogma but to support it and to open the way to faith for those individuals who find the unidimensional explanations offered by theologians and jurists intellectually and spiritually stultifying."[58] In other words, Sufism is a form of sophisticated apologetics designed to make implausible ideas appear slightly less implausible. This is combined with a method, basically *dhikr*, designed to induce experiences in conformity with the doctrine, thus rendering them worthless as evidence for anything objective and independent of the effect that a dogmatic milieu can have on the mind of a willing subject.

Notes

1. Abu al Hasan Bushanji, 3rd Muslim century.

2. See A. J. Arberry, *The Doctrine of the Sufis*, trans. of Kalabadhi's *Kitab at ta'arruf* (Cambridge: Cambridge University Press, 1935); and M. Valiuddin, *The Quranic Sufism* (Delhi: Motilal Banarsidas, 1959).

3. A handy collection of favorite Sufi texts from the Koran and Hadith can be found in W. Stoddart, *Sufism* (Wellingborough: Aquarian Press, 1984), pp. 77–82. Samples of the *other* Koran and Hadith, which apologists for Islam would rather forget, can be found in R. Burns, *The Wrath of Allah* (Houston: A. Ghosh, 1994), pp. 1–60, 155–65; and W. Harwood, *Mythology's Last Gods* (New York: Prometheus, 1992), pp. 371–74.

4. See esp. M. Smith, *Studies in Early Mysticism in the Near and Middle East*, reprinted as *The Way of the Mystics: The Early Christian Mystics and the Rise of the Sufis* (London: Sheldon Press, 1976).

5. Baldick, *Mystical Islam* (London: I. B. Tauris, 1989), pp. 14, 27.

6. Ibid., pp. 29–30; see also Baldick, "The Legend of Rabia of Basra: Christian Antecedents, Muslim Counterparts," *Religion* 20 (1990): 233–47.

7. Baldick, *Mystical Islam*, p. 49.

8. Ibid., pp. 65–67.

9. Ibid., p. 49.

10. See A. Schimmel, *Mystical Dimensions of Islam* (Chapel Hill: University of North Carolina Press, 1975), pp. 98–148.

11. Also, by implication, to all the previous sheikhs of the *tariqa* back to Muhammad, thence to Allah.

12. A book of prayers on the Prophet by Muhammad al-Jazuli (d. 869/1465, or 875/1470).

13. See M. Kabbani, *The Naqshbandi Sufi Way* (Chicago: Kazi Press, 1995), pp. 417–22; cf. J. Bennett, *Sufi Spiritual Techniques* (High Burton: Coombe Springs Press, 1984); M. Valiuddin, *Contemplative Disciplines in Sufism* (London: East West Publications, 1980), chaps. 4 and 7; J. Trimingham, *The Sufi Orders in Islam* (Oxford: Oxford University Presss, 1971), chap. 7.

14. See Kabbani, *The Naqshbandi Sufi Way*, pp. 423–26.

15. See N. Lings, *What is Sufism?* (London: George, Allen and Unwin, 1981), pp. 88–91.

16. See C. Tart, *Altered States of Consciousness* (San Francisco: HarperCollins, 1990), pp. 91–136.

17. See W. Stace, *Mysticism and Philosophy* (London: Macmillan, 1960), pp. 47–55.

18. See J. Baldick, *Imaginary Muslims* (London: I. B. Tauris, 1993).

19. See I. Regardie, *The Complete Golden Dawn System of Magic* (Phoenix: Falcon Press, 1985), vol. 5, pp. 84–109; also F. King, ed., *Astral Projection, Ritual Magic, and Alchemy* (Wellingborough: Aquarian Press, 1987), pp. 47–101.

20. See A. Crowley, *Magick* (York Beach: Weiser, 1994), pp. 241–49, 602–15.

21. Ibid., p. 602.

22. Ibid., p. 246.

23. See D. Merkur, *Gnosis: An Esoteric Tradition of Mystical Visions and Unions* (New York: SUNY Press, 1993), esp. chap. 9.

24. See M. Eliade, *Shamanism* (Princeton, N.J.: Bollinger, 1972), ch. 4 & passim, also J. Halifax, *Shaman* (London: Thames and Hudson, 1982).

25. See L. Schaya, *The Universal Meaning of the Kabbalah* (London: George, Allen, and Unwin, 1971), pp. 83, 126. Also G. Scholem, *On the Kabbalah and Its Symbolism* (London: Routledge and Kegan Paul, 1965), pp. 104f, 112–15, 128.

26. See Merkur, *Gnosis*, chap. 2, and R. Noll, *The Jung Cult* (Princeton: Princeton University Press, 1996), chaps. 10 and 11.

27. Merkur, *Gnosis*, p. 45.

28. See E. Fales, "Scientific Explanations of Mystical Experiences," *Religious Studies*, vol. 32, nos.1 & 2 (1996), and "Mystical Experience as

Evidence," *International Journal for the Philosophy of Religion* 40 (1996): 19–46.

29. A. Affifi, *The Mystical Philosophy of Muhvid'Din Ibnul-'Arabi* (Cambridge: Cambridge University Press, 1936), p. 113.

30. W. C. Chittick, *Imaginal Worlds* (New York: SUNY Press, 1994), p. 75.

31. Ibid., p. 183, n. 1.

32. Chittick, *The Sufi Path of Knowledge*, p. x.

33. W. T. Stace, *Mysticism and Philosophy* (London: Macmillan, 1960), pp. 61–62.

34. Ibid., pp. 131–32.

35. Ibid., p. 132.

36. R. Jones, *Mysticism Examined* (New York: SUNY Press, 1993), p. 19.

37. Stace, *Mysticism and Philosophy*, pp. 31–38.

38. See S. Katz, "Language, Epistemology, and Mysticism," in *Mysticism and Philosophical Analysis*, ed. Katz (London: Sheldon Press, 1978), pp. 22–74.

39. Ibid., p. 26.

40. Ibid., p. 30.

41. See R. Zaehner, *Mysticism Sacred and Profane* (Oxford: Oxford University Press, 1957), p. 204.

42. S. Katz, ed., *Mysticism and Religious Traditions* (Oxford: Oxford University Press, 1983), p. 41.

43. Chittick, *The Sufi Path of Knowledge*, p.226.

44. Ibid., p. 63.

45. Ibid., p. 220.

46. M. Lings, *A Sufi Saint of the Twentieth Century* (London: George, Allen and Unwin, 1971), p. 129.

47. See M. Raschid, *Iqbal's Concept of God* (London: KPI, 1981), pp. 64–105.

48. See A. Philips, *Fundamentals of Tawhid* (Riyadh: Tawheed Publications, 1990), p. l.

49. Chittick, *The Sufi Path of Knowledge*, p. 79.

50. Burckhardt, *Introduction to Sufism*, p. 21.

51. See F. Schuon, *The Transcendent Unity of Religions* (London: Faber & Faber, 1953; rev. ed. New York: Harper & Row, 1974), 1st ed.,

pp. 53–56, and the critique by Raschid, *Iqbal's Concept of God*, pp. 64–67.

52. F. Schuon, *Logic and Transcendence* (New York: Harper Torchbooks, 1975), pp. 76–77.

53. F. Schuon, *Islam and the Perennial Philosophy* (London: World of Islam, 1976), p. 177.

54. See I. Netton, *Muslim Neoplatonists* (London: George, Allen and Unwin, 1982), and P. Morewedge, ed., *Neoplatonism and Islamic Thought* (New York: SUNY Press, 1992).

55. *Fut.*, ch. 360, trans. Chittick, *The Sufi Path of Knowledge*, p. 362.

56. For a masterly discussion of these problems in Plotinian metaphysics, see B. Fuller, *The Problem of Evil in Plotinus* (Cambridge: Cambridge University Press, 1912).

57. J. F. Staal, *Exploring Mysticism* (Harmondsworth: Penguin, 1980), p. 179.

58. Chittick, *Imaginal Worlds*, p. 97.

Part IV
Islam in the Modern World

Chapter 7

Islam's View of Itself in the Modern World

Could anyone say that Intellect, the true and real Intellect, will ever be in error and believe the unreal? Certainly not. For how could it still be Intellect when it was being unintelligent? It must, then, always know and not ever forget anything, and its knowing must not be that of a guesser, or ambiguous, or like that of someone who has heard what he knows from someone else.

—Plotinus

It is axiomatic that if Islam is true, the modern world is in error. If Muhammad was the final Prophet and the Koran God's final Word to mankind, a world that ignores those facts is fundamentally astray. A world that puts doubt before belief, freedom before submission, and innovation before tradition, can be nothing other than a satanic inversion, a willful turning away from God's providence and mercy. A sign of that providence and mercy is that Islam reaches from East to West and still contains, despite an inevitable falling away, fully qualified witnesses to the One Truth that it is its mission to proclaim: *La ilaha illa Llah, Muhammadun Rasul Allah.*

This formula of bearing witness (*shahada*) contains not only the message of Islam, but the essence of religion as such. Chapter 3 pointed out how the *shahada* comprises two parts, the first referring to Islam in the universal sense of submission to God, and the second to the particular form of that submission brought by the Prophet Muhammad. Chapter 3 also indicated that the first half of the *shahada* itself has two parts based on the words *ilah* (god) and *Allah* (God). This analysis can be carried further to express the highest metaphysical truth.

The four words *La ilaha illa Llah* fall naturally into two halves, the first negative and the second affirmative. The negation (*nafy*) refers to manifestation as a whole: *La* to peripheral manifestation and *ilaha* to central or principial manifestation. The affirmation (*ithbat*) refers to the principle in itself, *illa* being the Principle manifest *in divinis*. In other terms, the "Principle in itself" is Beyond-Being, and the "Principle in divinis" is Beyond-Being in Being, in other words, the Logos. This division *in divinis* is that which prefigures and gives rise to the world or "peripheral manifestation." The first half of the *shahada* taken as a whole is the formula of abstraction or transcendence (*tanzih*), whereas the second half is the formula of analogy or immanence (*tashbih*), transcendence/immanence being the inner dimensions of Oneness (*tawhid*). These truths are the Truth at the heart of Islam. They are known to all and all that needs to be known. They are known to all by means of man's primordial nature (*al fitra*), which is obscured but not destroyed. They are all that needs to be known, since their realized truth is salvific in itself.

Opposed to these truths is the world (*dunya*), the objectification of the empirical ego (*nafs*), which is itself opposed to the awareness of the observing self or heart-intellect (*qalb-'aql*), that which knows the *shahada* as true. The function of Islam as an all-encompassing revelation is to reabsorb the world into the axis of its descent, to bring it under a sacred canopy that leaves no fissure for the entry of dispersive worldliness by sacralizing the whole of human life; prayer (*salat*), and the remembrance of God (*dhikr Allah*) are the subjective face of the sacred canopy objectified as law (*sharia*). A worldview that takes God and revelation as obvious and indubitable truths can have no dialogue as between equals with a worldview that makes no such assumption. Indeed, to assume an equality would be tantamount to surrender, a culpable giving over of the realm of faith and submission (*dar al Islam*) to the realm of doubt and unbelief (*dar al kufr*). There can be no compromise between Truth and error; as the maxim of the Maharajahs of Benares puts it: *There is no right superior to that of Truth*. Truth has an intrinsic ineluctable quality that absorbs, dissolves, and ultimately transmutes error, hence the death penalty for apostasy (*irtidad*). A world that finds this monstrous is itself monstrous in its rejection of Truth.

If the world as such is distraction, dispersion, and lack of center, the modern world raises these negative qualities to the status of principles and ways of life. From the point of view of that world, Islam can only appear a case of arrested development, a virtual stopping of history that traps a whole section of humanity in a "biblical" mentality. From the point of view of Islam, this is the best thing that it could possibly do and further evidence of its providential nature. If Islam did not produce a Renaissance or a Reformation, much less an Industrial Revolution or a French Revolution, it is because of its holy finality, its role as witness to the adamantine Truth that saves until the end of time. The events that produced the modern world are not signs of life in contrast to the cadaverous rigidity of Islam but signs of a Promethean betrayal that refuses the demands of heaven. If certain sections of humanity have ceased to see the truth in scripture and have become blind to the metaphysical transparency of phenomena, it is not through any newly acquired objectivity or outgrowing of naivete but through an obscuring of vision that ceases to see anything beyond the material.

It hardly needs to be said that the Koran is not a philosophical document; it is a call from beyond the world to recognize the world for what it is: a sign (*ayat*) of its transcendent origin, yet this "argument" of the Koran is the only argument that retains any credibility in philosophy of religion. The teleological argument, the argument from or to design, especially in its newer forms, calls attention to the fact that the universe does not contain its own explanation; it bears signs of intelligent design in its cosmological constants without which it could not exist at all, much less produce conscious, intelligent life. In short, it appears like a put-up job. The call of the Koran to recognize the transcendent origin of the universe is the essence of all religion embedded in the *shahada*, and the ubiquity of Islam's insisting on this truth above all in a world that in effect denies it is another sign of its providential presence at the end of time.

Likewise, it is the claim of Islam that humanity is not an accidental product of blind natural forces that just happened to produce a rational animal that can contemplate its own origin. Instead, quite literally, humans were a special creation, God's vicegerent (*khalifa*) on earth. Humankind alone was made in the image of God and is thereby distinguished from the animals by transcendent intelligence, free will, and speech, the proper use of which is to know Truth and act and pray in accordance therewith (*Islam, Iman, Ihsan*). For Islam, the descent of humankind can be only vertical, not horizontal. It is the descent of an eternal archetype from proximity to God in the heaven of all possibility through the degrees of informal and formal manifestation to crystallization in a quasi material form on earth—Adam in paradise solidified in time through the descending ages of the world.

As vicegerent of God on earth, man cannot not contain something of that from which in his essence he derives, which is to say immateriality, subjectivity, consciousness, intelligence. The fact of consciousness and subjectivity is living proof of the fallacy of transformist evolution, since the greater cannot arise from the less, the Spirit from rocks and stones. Since humanity's subjective intelligence derives from the Intelligence that is the source and foundation of the world, it cannot not be adequate to its origin, hence the medieval saying *adequatio rei et intellectus*. It is this insistence on the capacity of humans to know God that makes Islam above all a religion of gnosis. Al Ghazali said, ". . . [M]en will reach a higher degree of nearness [*qurb*] to God only in proportion to their intelligence [*'aql*]," a term that includes both the rational faculty and the immediate knowing, which is Intellectual intuition. It is by means of this capacity for indubitable knowledge that humans know that God exists and what leads to salvation and perdition.

If all people are endowed with intelligence, that intelligence is not necessarily always manifested to its fullest extent. It may be obscured by passion and attachment to the senses, and in such cases it must be forced to yield to its higher forms, whether in the case of the individual striving (*jihad*) against his lower soul (*nafs*) or in the government's ordering of the state. It is the common experience of humankind that it is sometimes necessary to do violence to irresponsible people in their own interest, and this forms the warrant for the coercion sometimes exercised by principled authority. All legitimate authority derives from God on the basis of revelation or Intellection so that his hand is above their hands in both the public and the private spheres, hence the caliph (*Khalifa*) and the sheikh. Needless to say, democracy is foreign to Islam, since it places power in the hands of impious and passional men whose only interest is their own self-interest, not the interest of God and God's realm on earth.

If humanity (*insaniyyun*) as such is theomorphic in its highest nature, it is so while being both male and female. Nevertheless: "The men have a degree above them [women]" (K.2:228). Although the sense in which this is true has numerous social and psychological consequences elaborated upon at length in the Sharia and Koranic commentaries, it is rooted in a metaphysical reality reflected directly in the *Bismillah*: In the Name of God, the Beneficent, the Merciful (*Bismillah ar Rahman ar Rahim*). According to the Koran, the names Allah and *Rahman* are quasi equivalent (K.17:110), while *Rahim* is clearly a prolongation of *Rahman* toward creation and the creatures. The word *rahma*, which intrinsically comprises goodness, beauty, and beatitude, derives from the root *rahim*, meaning "womb" and signifying the feminine in the divine.

Just as it is said that the whole Koran is contained in the first chapter (the *Fatihah*) and that the whole of that chapter in its first verse (the *Bismillah*) and the whole of that verse in the dia-critical point beneath the initial *ba*, so it can be said that the quin-tessence of Islam can be found in the name Allah. The first syl-lable is short, contracted, and absolute, while the second syllable is long, expanded, and infinite. The name thus contains the two dimensions *in divinis* that prefigure gender and foreshadow man-ifestation. In the *Bismillah*, this contracted formula is spelled out further: Allah being the Absolute Principle Beyond-Being and *Rahman* the Infinite womb of All-Possibility, or Being, extended extrinsically toward manifestation as *Rahim*, the Mercy of cre-ation that is Good. The similarity of this formula to those of other traditional doctrines—Brahman/Shiva/Shakti, Tao/Yin/Yang—hardly needs pointing out.

It is in these discernments that the Truth of Islam is to be found, a Truth beyond all denominations and particularities of time and place. It is because all this and more is in the name Allah that the remembrance of God (*dhikr Allah*) by means of his supreme name is the instrument of discernment, and the enemies of that remembrance are the empirical ego (*nafs*) and the secular world (*dunya*). The submission that is Islam is submission to the Truth contained in the name Allah, and the invocation (*dhikr*) of that name is the rite by means of which the invoked (*madhkur*) is brought to birth in the invoker (*dhakir*). Islam in the modern world is the invoker for that world, the faithful witness (*shahada*) to the Truth that is Allah and the life that is Muslim.

Chapter 8

Islam in the Modern World: A Secular Perspective

The originating cause of Scepticism is, we say, the hope of attaining quietude. Men of talent, who were perturbed by the contradictions in things and in doubt as to which of the alternatives they ought to accept, were led on to inquire what is true in things and what false, hoping by the settlement of this to attain quietude. The main basic principle of the Sceptic system is that of opposing to every proposition an equal proposition; for we believe that as a consequence of this we end by ceasing to dogmatize.

—Sextus Empiricus

The problem with depicting Islam in the modern world is the multiplicity of its voices and faces; to an extent this is simply a continuation into modern times of what has always been the case. Despite how it may have appeared to non-Muslim outsiders, Islam has never been a homogeneous phenomenon but has always taken on the color of its environment; Islam in the Far East having a different flavor from Islam in the Middle East, India, North Africa, or Europe. In addition to the influence that its cultural and ethnic environment has had on Islam, there are also the internal differences between Sunni and Shia, the regional schools of law, and the various Sufi *tariqas*. Perhaps most important is the general distinction between an outer, exoteric (*zahir*), formalistic Islam, which emphasizes a punctilious adherence to the Sharia and the literal sense of the Koran and the Hadith, and an inner, esoteric (*batin*), mystical Islam, which finds expression in poetry and art and inner vision.

There is no doubt, however, that all these differences within Islam, especially the latter, have been brought into sharper focus by having to confront the phenomenon that is the modern world, a world that from the Muslim point of view appears not simply non-Muslim in origin and nature, but positively anti-Islamic. It is not just that the modern world was born in a Christian culture and was until recently carried abroad in company with Christian evangelism and colonial exploitation, but, as has become increasingly apparent in the twentieth century, that world is a challenge to any traditional religious worldview, be it Christian, Islamic, or any other. A view of the world that takes scientific methods as its model for acquiring knowledge has no room for revelation, and without revelation, no religion can claim the mandate of heaven. This situation has polarized the inherent differences within Islam between its exoteric and esoteric aspects, making the exoterics even more exoteric, strident, and fundamentalist, and the esoterics so esoteric that they leave behind all but a handful of their fellow Muslims.

The situation confronting Islam in the modern world is the unparalleled power and dominance achieved by the West by ignoring all the precepts Islam holds most dear. This is not how things should be, according to the Koran. By not believing, by doubting and questioning everything, including religion and revelation, the West has achieved the most glittering success the world has ever seen. The Muslim response of sneering at this material success by emphasizing its price in social disintegration can only appear as sour grapes, especially when, in trying to boost pride in the Islamic past, Muslims point to their own material success and scientific progress in the Islamic Middle Ages. The truth is that whatever material success the Muslim world ever achieved was despite Islam, not because of it; it may have occurred within the orbit of Islam, but only because that orbit included the richest vein of pre-Islamic culture.

When not disparaging the deleterious effects of Western science, exoteric Muslims are intent on Islamizing it so that it can become something called "Islamic Science," the first postulate of which would be "Faith in revelation," rather than "Faith in rationality,"[1] a notion that emasculates science as free enquiry from the outset. By "revelation," of course, Muslims mean the Koran, just as Christians pursuing the same line of argument would mean the Bible, Hindus the Vedas, and so on for every group that considers itself to be in possession of a divinely inspired text. This ghettoizing of science is at once sinister and pathetic, as Daniel Easterman has observed: "The whole concept of ideologically predetermined sciences is, at heart, a nonsense, and I cannot see that any good is served, for Muslims or anyone else, by its perpetuation."[2]

Along with science, the other feature of the modern West that sets it apart from traditional societies is democracy. Groups that feel oppressed within Islam have an ambiguous attitude toward democracy, realizing that it is not an Islamic concept. They nevertheless look toward the idea in hope of alleviating their plight. The most obvious oppressed group to whom this applies is women. In a study of Islam and democracy that is more honest than most, the Moroccan sociologist Fatima Mernissi has addressed the fears of Islam vis-à-vis the modern democratic West. While criticizing much of Islamic history and the way Islamic society has developed in an authoritarian fashion, when seeking means of redressing these features her only resource is to turn to an Islamic past in the Koran and the life of the Prophet, which conforms to her chosen ideal, just as any fundamentalist would. "Our liberation will come through a rereading of our past and a reappropriation of all that has structured our civilization. The mosque and the Koran belong to women as much as do the heavenly bodies. We have a right to all of that, to all its riches for constructing our modern identity."³ To which the secular response can only be: Why want "all of that"? Why not to hell with "the mosque and the Koran" and be done with it?

Mernissi well illustrates how beholden even the most sophisticated Muslim intellectuals can be to their cultural inheritance. No matter how critical they dare to be of the way Islam has developed, there is hardly ever a suggestion of rejecting Islam as such. There always remains the fantasy of uncovering a real Islam that meets whatever ideal is entertained. The truth that Muslims have to face is that we do not know, and most likely will never know, how things were in early Islam, and to fool ourselves that we do is the biggest and most debilitating illusion of all. Until Muslims can face this fact and find the courage to cast themselves adrift on the sea of taking responsibility for their own decisions, rather than seeking some phantom of divine sanction, the Islamic world will remain in the parlous state it is at present.

These exoteric voices of Islam in the modern world are ambivalent in their attitude toward that world. Recognizing its unavoidable presence and overwhelming power, they seek to accommodate Islam to it in some fashion, if only by Islamization of its sciences or seeking something similar in the Islamic past. An alternative approach is that of esoteric Islam, the foremost representative of which is Seyyed Hossein Nasr.

Nasr was born in Iran in 1933 and received a traditional Islamic education before going to America to acquire an education in the natural sciences and the history of science at MIT and Harvard. The result of these studies was *Science and Civilization in Islam*, in which he argues that Islamic science has a special genius of its own and was not simply a passive means for the transmission of Greek science to the West. Nasr eventually returned to Iran and was a professor at Tehran University until the revolution of 1979, when he returned to America and became professor of Islamic studies at Washington University. Nasr is the most public proponent of what was identified in chapter 4 as the mystical-romantic school of Islamic studies. By the sheer volume of his output, some thirty books written or edited, he is probably the major influence on the way Islam is presented in the West, especially in academic circles in the United States. Many other prominent writers on Islam in North America, such as William Chittick, Sachiko Murata, and Cyril Glasse, have come under the same set of influences as Nasr and promote the same point of view.

In contrast to the exoterics, far from seeking to accommodate itself to the modern world, the esoteric Islam of Nasr and his associates adopts a combative stance, refusing to admit that that world has any redeeming features whatever. Since this view is promoted from the heart of that world, taking full advantage of its freedoms and facilities, it appears immediately as both extreme and churlish, no matter how civilly it might be argued. In regard to Nasr and those who share his viewpoint, it is important to understand that despite the number of plush publications and high-profile academic posts from which it emanates, it is shared by only a minute minority within the vast body of Islam. Acknowledging this, the esoterics would claim that they may represent only a minority view, but that is without consequence, since numbers do not count in such matters. All that matters is that it is the view of the intellectual and spiritual elite who alone are capable of realizing the full import and true significance of the Islamic tradition. This situation represents the problem of who speaks for "real" Islam in a nutshell: is it the esoteric elite, or the exoteric majority?

Despite Nasr's prestige in certain circles, his works have been subjected to fierce criticism by both Muslims and non-Muslims who specialize in the same fields of study. Reviewing the impressive-looking *Islamic Science: An Illustrated Study*, produced for the 1976 Festival of Islam, David King says,

> Nasr's survey, which contains no "study and analysis" of any texts, is further marred by an inordinately large number of inadequately documented claims and outright errors. Most of Nasr's statements referring to an individual, or a work, or a discovery, contain some kind of distortion or exaggeration resulting from the author's lack of familiarity with the original sources, or his innocence of the mathematics or astronomy involved. . . . [H]e

seems to be quite out of touch with much recent scholarship in
the field of Islamic science.

Then follows some seven pages detailing Nasr's errors, which
end: "The above quotations by no means exhaust the factual
errors and misinterpretations even in the few pages singled out for
discussion in this review. By these inaccuracies Nasr has uninten-
tionally failed to do justice to a scientific tradition which knew no
rival from the eighth to perhaps the fifteenth century."[4]

Ziauddin Sardar, whose first postulate of Islamic science was
quoted above, has his own (exoteric) views of what Islamic science is, or should be, and criticizes Nasr's views for being domi-
nated by Ismaili thought and the non-Islamic perennial philosophy.[5] Nasr belongs to a branch of Shia Islam known as
Ismailism, deriving from Ismail, son of the sixth Shia Imam Jafar
Sadiq, who some Shias believe should have become the seventh
Imam. Ismailis emphasize the supposed inner (batin), esoteric
meanings of the Koran and combine this with elements of Greek
philosophy, Hinduism, Zoroastrianism, alchemy, astrology,
numerology, and angelology. For an exoteric Muslim like Sardar,
this is simply occultism and "the lethal religion of gnosis,"[6] little
better than straightforward heresy. Regardless of whether or not
these things are truly Islamic, Nasr's emphasis on the symbolic
and occult aspects of Islamic science, practically to the exclusion of everything else, certainly seems to sell short its real
achievements in terms of discoveries about the nature of the
physical world. As Sardar says, anyone plowing through Nasr's
An Annotated Bibliography of Islamic Science would be forgiven
thinking that Islamic science was simply "another name for
Ismaili gnosis, Greek mystery religions and the occult."[7] The
same could also be said of Nasr's Introduction to Islamic Cosmological Doctrines.

Nasr's view of Islamic science takes this peculiar form as an
integral feature of his overall view of Islam among the world religions. In 1981 he was invited to give the Gifford Lectures at the
University of Edinburgh, which were later published in an

expanded and annotated form as *Knowledge and the Sacred*. The lectures turned out to be a prolonged eulogy for the books and ideas of René Guénon and Frithjof Schuon, respectively the founder and most prolific expounder of a set of ideas known as traditionalism, the perennial philosophy (*philosophia perennis*), *sophia perennis, religio perennis*, and *scientia sacra*. Some idea of Nasr's commitment to these writers and their ideas can be gathered from his description of Schuon: "Schuon seems like the cosmic intellect itself impregnated by the energy of divine grace surveying the whole of reality surrounding man and elucidating all the concerns of human existence in the light of sacred knowledge."[8]

Muhammad Salman Raschid has subjected *Knowledge and the Sacred* to a searching critique from the point of view of exoteric Islam and finds "looseness and ambiguity in his whole exposition." The main problem is Nasr's refusal, or inability, to define terms and make clear exactly what he is saying; this appears especially in his use of the term "knowledge," which makes the core of the book incoherent. In different parts of the text Nasr sometimes speaks of an intuitive, mystical knowledge of God and at other times of a discursive, secular knowledge of scriptures, doctrines, and the like, which Raschid labels knowledge I and II. Unfortunately, "These two logically and epistemologically distinct notions of knowledge are confused, or, more strictly conflated, by Nasr (presumably unwittingly) throughout his discussion and this seriously vitiates his whole case. . . ." After much further analysis of Nasr's incoherences, inaccuracies, and unwarranted assertions, noting his "generally excessively arrogant and dogmatic tone" and the "very many intemperate and injudicious remarks made about possibly rival views" Raschid concludes:

> As a Muslim I am bound to say that Professor Seyyed Hossein Nasr's book *cannot* be read as a *Muslim* statement since it does not represent the expression of Islamic (i.e., Quranic) ideas. It is rather based upon a confused mixture of what could be characterized as "Neoplatonized Semitic Theism with an admixture of

distorted Vedanta." If this sounds like an extraordinarily incoherent formulation I submit that it is a direct reflection of the
basic incoherence of Nasr's whole case.[9]

Raschid's characterization of Nasr's "case" is perfectly correct,
but it is not his case. Nasr is in fact little more than an apparently
respectable academic front man for traditionalism, a role he
shares with Huston Smith and, until recently, several other prominent academics in the field of Islamic studies and comparative
religion. There is an as-yet unrelated story here, which in this
place can be told only in part.

The basic idea of traditionalism or the perennial philosophy is
that behind all the exoteric forms of the major "orthodox" religious
traditions there is a single, esoteric, metaphysical Truth, which is
most explicitly expressed in the Advaita Vedanta doctrine of Hinduism. This Truth is known to be true by means of a superior mode
of knowing, a form of mystical/intellectual intuition termed Intellect. All men have Intellect by virtue of their being human, but in
the vast majority it is obscured by the passions of the empirical
ego. It follows that the Truth of traditionalism is known to be true
only by an Intellectual and moral elite, and anyone who denies its
truth is thereby demonstrating his Intellectual and moral deficiency, which accounts for the arrogant and dogmatic tone of
much traditionalist literature. This idea about the one Truth
behind the many religions is combined with an almost pathological
contempt for the modern world and all its works, which is regarded
as the Dark Age, or Kali Yuga, the last of the four ages of the world
before the final cataclysm that restores all things, an idea also
derived from Hinduism, although it has its Western analogues.
These ideas were first expressed in the works of the Frenchman
René Guénon (1886–1951), but were taken up and given their
fullest expression in the works of Frithjof Schuon (1907–1998).

Schuon was born in Basle, Switzerland, of a German Catholic
family, and the first indication of the future direction of his life
came when, at the age of seventeen, he discovered a copy of the
Bhagavad Gita in his father's bookcase. He read the words "The

Exalted One spoke," and as he says in his memoirs: "These few words from the *Bhagavad Gita* made upon me a powerful impression that was never to leave me; it was as if in these words I had recognized my deepest truest being."[10] As he told Muhammad Raschid: " '[S]trange to say' [the phrase is Schuon's: personal interview January 1978] it was patently clear to him that this scripture was also of divine origin; in consequence he could no longer continue to hold the simple Catholic dogma he was taught as a child."[11] These feelings were further enhanced by reading the works of René Guénon, from whom he learned the supreme truth of the Advaita Vedanta. Later, in the 1930s, he discovered Islam and traveled to Mustaghanem in Algeria, seeking an entry into Sufism at the hand of Sheikh Ahmad al Alawi. After receiving initiation, he requested that the sheikh make him a teacher (*muqaddam, naib*), or sheikh, but this was refused. Not long after, upon the death of Sheikh al Alawi, he claims to have received the grace to become a sheikh directly from God, so he is in fact a *Shaykh al Baraka*, a sheikh by special divine blessing, the highest thing possible.[12] These events are typical of Schuon's biography in that the main occasions are all of an intellectual, supernatural, or transcendent character, making his human relations merely secondary, carried on in the light of a seemingly ever more exalted inner life.

The result of these inner illuminations were eventually made known to the world in a series of publications, beginning with *The Transcendent Unity of Religions*, first published in French in 1948 and in English in 1953. This work lays the basis for the traditionalist thesis and was followed by some twenty-five further works, on all aspects of the world's religions. Several of these are devoted wholly to Islam, beginning with *Understanding Islam* (1963) and continuing with *Dimensions of Islam* (1969), *Islam and the Perennial Philosophy* (1976), and *Sufism, Veil and Quintessence* (1981), plus numerous essays on aspects of Islam in his other works, such as *Christianity/Islam: Essays on Esoteric Ecumenism* (1985). All these books have achieved considerable acclaim and made a reputation for Schuon as an unparalleled expositor of Islam at the highest intellectual level. Even orthodox, exoteric Muslims such as Raschid, who, as we have seen, is by no means uncritical of the traditionalist position, has said of *Understanding Islam* that it "represents, in my view, the most adequate exposition of the authentic mystical understanding and interpretation of the Muslim faith."[13] The book has been in print since its first publication and has recently appeared in an expanded edition (1994).

Most of those who know of Schuon know of him through his books, but the books are only the outward manifestation, so to speak, of Schuon's real presence. Being a *Shaykh al Baraka,* he could not be without his own *tariqa*, and this too came, as one might expect, from heaven itself. Journeying to Morocco by boat in 1965, suffering from asthma, feeling bitter and despondent, longing for paradise and trying to imagine it, he experienced what later became known as "The Great Vision"—"Then all at once the Divine Mercy overwhelmed me in a special manner; it approached me inwardly in a feminine form which I cannot describe, and which I knew to be the Holy Virgin; I could not think otherwise. And from this moment on I felt better and was in an ecstasy of love and happiness." Later, upon arrival in Fez: ". . . in the night the heavenly consolation streamed forth from the primordial femininity, came upon me once more and lasted for some three weeks, until we had returned home." It did not end there but continued in the background of his whole life, upsetting all his habits of soul: "as if I had been born into a new world."[14]

A parallel vision, sometimes called the Christmas vision, occurred twenty years later on Christmas Eve 1985. According to the account of Schuon's first wife, Catherine, "He heard on one side of him the *Ave Maria* being sung and on the other side *Ya Maryamu alaiki salam, ya Rahim* being sung. [This latter is now sung by his *fuqara*.] He was like a child, as he often is in these visions. He felt the breasts of the Virgin touching his back. Her legs were spread and she straddled him from behind. He put his hands on her thighs."[15] This vision is depicted in many of Schuon's paintings showing a naked Virgin and Child.[16]

It is from experiences such as this that the legitimation of Schuon's *tariqa Maryamiah* derives.

The description of the Christmas vision reveals the true nature of Schuon's visions of the Virgin. It is confirmed by Schuon's third "wife," Sa. Aminah, who has said that "he [Schuon] needed femininity because it was the perfect complement to his discrimination," and that when he came to a dead end, "God sent him a grace that had to do with the sexual parts of the Virgin. When he began to receive graces of this kind he was quite surprised. She appeared inside him and touched him on the inside. There was something erotic about it. She appeared inside of him. He didn't see her. It was more than seeing. He felt her inside." Sa. Aminah has also said that "it was as if the Virgin descended down upon him, naked, and she comforted his misery by consoling him with her sexual parts which she exposed to him inside him comforting his heart."[17] This makes sense when it is understood that for Schuon the sexual parts are the exteriorized heart.

In a suppressed chapter of the memoirs entitled *Sacred Nudity*, Schuon describes the effect that the Great Vision had on him:

> . . . I experienced a blessed contact with the Heavenly Virgin. And this had as its immediate result the almost irresistible urge to be naked like her little child; from this event onwards I went naked as often as possible, indeed most of the time, except when I was in the street, or receiving people, or saying the prayers; nevertheless I sometimes desired to wear a very simple white robe, as if I needed to rest from the wine of this grace. During that time there was for me only my nakedness together with the invocation and the nearness of the Virgin; it was as if the contact with the Virgin had sanctified my body. I recognized in nudity the garment of inwardness and the sign of kinship with all of God's creation. . . . [A] few years later—in the summer of 1973—this mystery came upon me again, and it did so in connection with the irresistible awareness that I am not a man like other men. The particular meaning of this is: just as in the Divine Name there is a simultaneous manifestation of Divine Truth and Divine Presence, so—or analogously—must one distinguish, in the sanctified man, between the teaching of the

Truth and a radiance that emanates from the body; and this applies to all degrees of participation in the one Logos.[18]

In short, Schuon regarded himself as both the lover and the adopted son of the Virgin, the paraclete, an incarnation of the Logos, and a unique avatara who embodied the quintessence of all the religions at the end of time. As a result of these extraordinary favors of heaven, his body was a living sacrament that radiated divine blessings, especially when naked. Among Schuon's female followers, this blessing was conveyed by physical contact in ceremonials known as primordial gatherings.

In 1980 Schuon moved from Lausanne, Switzerland, to Bloomington, Indiana. It was here that the *tariqa* blossomed and was combined with Native American ceremonial and other syncretic elements to form the primordial gatherings. None of these activities were known to anyone outside Schuon's immediate circle until 1991, when Mark Koslow, a disillusioned member of the *tariqa Maryamiah*, blew the whistle and brought a legal case against Schuon. On October 11, 1991, Schuon was indicted on the felony charge of child molestation. The indictment stated

> that Frithjof Schuon . . . did perform fondling or touching [on three girls] 13 years of age, 14 years of age and 13 years of age, respectively, with the intent to arouse or satisfy the sexual desires of Frithjof Schuon, in violation of I.C. 35-42 43. [And that] said persons were compelled to submit to touching by force or imminent threat of force, to wit: by undue cult influences and cult pressures, in violation of 35-42-4-81.

By the middle of November 1991, the case had been mysteriously dropped, despite a plenitude of evidence and the unanimous indictment of a grand jury. It is rumored that Schuon's supporters spent over a million dollars on lawyers and legal intimidation to silence critics and prevent prosecution. After 1991 much further evidence was gathered from several witnesses, but the authorities refuse to reopen the case. Although all this is well known in certain circles in the United States and elsewhere, very little has been published for fear of litigation.[19]

A minor revolt occurred among Schuon's followers in the period 1986–1988, when about ten people, including Cyril Glasse, Victor Danner, and Joseph Epes Brown, left the *tariqa*, objecting to Schuon's spiteful treatment and his claim to be an avatara. Many others, however, including Seyyed Hossein Nasr, Martin Lings, and Huston Smith, even after the events of 1991, refused to leave Schuon's group or denounce him in any way. Defending Schuon, Nasr told the *Bloomington Herald Times*, October 20, 1991: "[H]e belongs to a different world. He is very much a premodern man."[20] Asked by Mark Koslow to renounce Schuon as his master, Martin Lings replied that "Schuon is divine" and that there could be no question of doing such a thing.[21] Huston Smith has recently completed a series of programs for American television on world religions that expound Schuon's ideas throughout without once mentioning his name; Smith has been a member of Schuon's *tariqa* for over thirty years. Such is the honesty and judgment of some of the most prominent apologists for Islam in the West.

Since the scandal broke, many former admirers, while still adhering to Schuon's main ideas and expounding them in their books, refrain from mentioning his name or listing his books in their bibliographies. They may have come to their senses with regard to Schuon the man and managed to break away from his baleful influence, but they have by no means abandoned the kind of ideas he represents. Rama Coomaraswamy, son of the Anglo-Indian art historian and metaphysician Ananda Coomaraswamy, and the physicist Wolfgang Smith have both retreated to pre–Vatican II, traditionalist Roman Catholicism. William Chittick,[22] one of the foremost Ibn Arabi scholars, and Cyril Glasse, author of the very traditionalist *Concise Encyclopaedia of Islam*, have retreated to conventional Sufism; Glasse includes two books by Schuon in his bibliography but refers readers to the works of René Guénon for true guidance in traditionalism.

If these desertions are Schuon's loss, they are others' gain.

Those who have committed themselves to Islam and Sufism, and, of course, one cannot leave Islam without risk to life and limb, not to mention the social ignominy of having to admit to having been so foolish as to have taken it seriously in the first place, will be in need of further guidance, someone else to tell them how to lead their lives. For those in love with Sufism, which includes most Western intellectuals committed to Islam, that means a new *tariqa* and a new sheikh. For many this has meant the *Naqshbandiyya* and Sheikh Muhammad Nazim Adil al Haqqani.

Sheikh Nazim is in many ways an endearing figure, and there are no scandals of a Schuonian kind surrounding him; if he has faults, they are those inherent to Islam and Sufism. If Schuon, according to his own testimony, represents Sufism as gnosis (*jnana, ma'arifah*), Sheikh Nazim, also according to his own testimony, represents Sufism as love or devotion (*bhakti, mahabba*). No one is turned away for lack of intellectual, much less Intellectual, qualifications; all are welcome, from society's rejects to the highest in the land.

Sheikh Nazim was born in Larnaca, Cyprus, on April 23, 1922. His ancestors on his father's side claimed descent from Abdul Qadir Gilani, founder of the Qadiri *tariqa*, and on his mother's side from Jalaluddin Rumi, founder of the Mevlevi *tariqa*, popularly known as the whirling dervishes; thus, he inherited the Qadiri and Mevlevi Sufi orders and is also said to be Husani-Husayni, related to the family of the Prophet through the lineages of his grandfathers. A popular story about his youth, which presages his future life, concerns the grave of Umm Hiram, a companion of the Prophet. When the young Muhammad went missing, he was invariably found at the grave of Umm Hiram. When his mother came to bring him home, he would say: "Leave me here with Umm Hiram, she is one of our ancestors. Leave me, I am speaking with my grandmother who is in this grave."[23] This is essentially the Uwaysi phenomenon of communication with dead sheikhs, characteristic of the Naqshbandiyya and typical of the source of authority claimed by Sheikh Nazim throughout his life.

As a child he went to secular school by day and studied the religious sciences at night. After completing high school in Cyprus, in 1940 he moved to Istanbul, where his two brothers and one sister lived, and studied chemical engineering at the University of Istanbul. After completing his degree, his teachers wanted him to go into research, but he felt no attraction to modern science, preferring the religious sciences. During his first year in Istanbul he met his first spiritual master, Sheikh Sulayman Arzurumi of the Naqshbandi Order; he then studied chemical engineering by day and the Naqshbandi way by night. After some time he had a vision in which Sheikh Sulayman told him that permission had come from the Prophet for him to go and study with his real spiritual master in Damascus, Grandsheikh Abd Allah ad Daghestani. After a journey that took eighteen months, he eventually found Sheikh Abd Allah and spent one night with him, a night of tremendous spiritual experiences in which he was led through the highest spiritual stations. He was then ordered to return to Cyprus, a place he had not seen for five years, in order to spread the Naqshbandi Order and revivify Islam on the island. This was the beginning of a period of great traveling or wayfaring in the Muslim world, a way of life typical of Sufism that has survived to the present day.

Starting in 1974, Sheikh Nazim began to visit Europe, traveling each year from Cyprus to London by plane and returning to Cyprus overland by car. Beginning among the Turkish community in the Green Lanes area of north London, and later in Peckham, south London, the center of Sheikh Nazim's activities in Europe is now a large former priory in St. Ann's Road in the Tottenham area of north London. This impressive property was acquired and renovated due to the patronage of the richest man in the world, the Sultan of Brunei. Every year the sheikh spends the month of Ramadan and about six weeks thereafter at this center, after which he travels to France, Germany, and other centers throughout Europe. In 1991 he made his first trip to America and visited over fifteen states, which resulted in the establishment of more than thirteen centers of the Naqshbani Order and the conversion of over ten thousand people to Islam. Sheikh Nazim has also traveled extensively in the Far East, visiting Brunei, Malaysia, Singapore, India, Pakistan, and Sri Lanka, initiating thousands of people into the Naqshbandiyya *tariqa*, from common people to sultans and presidents.[24]

During the holy month of Ramadan, thousands of people from all over the world gather in London to spend the most sacred period of the Muslim year with the most illustrious sheikh; these gatherings are a manifestation of the Sufi virtue of companionship (*suhba*). This is the idea that it is spiritually beneficial to spend as much time as possible in the company of the friends of God (*awliya*) in order to observe their behavior, hear their teachings, and absorb their blessing (*baraka*); it is also an excellent device for enforcing group loyalty and solidarity. At these gatherings the sheikh gives talks intended to guide the faithful in the right understanding of Islam and the Sufi way; in Sheikh Nazim's case, these talks are recorded, video-taped, and turned into books, which form the main means of spreading his teachings, both among his followers and beyond. In one form or another, records of these talks go back to at least 1978 and amount to a substantial body of literature.

As might be expected, much of the material in these talks consists of stories drawn from the Koran, the Hadith, and the legendary lives of the prophets and saints, together with pious homilies on how to be a good Muslim, with emphasis on sincerity and good will to all people. In addition, because of Sheikh Nazim's special mission to the West, there are some surprising concessions with regard to what constitutes being counted a Muslim, even to the extent of one prostration a day being sufficient, as long as it is accompanied by sincere belief in God.[25] These attractive features of Sheikh Nazim's discourses are, however, interspersed with other material of a more dubious nature.

In the history of polemics between Islam and Christianity, the so-called Gospel of Barnabas holds a special place, especially in recent times. It is practically unknown in the West, apart from specialists in Christian apocryphal literature, but in the Muslim world it is regarded by many as an authentic eyewitness account of the life of Jesus written by a disciple, a disproof of the canonical Gospels and an unanswerable refutation of the Christian doctrine of Jesus' death and resurrection. At a Muslim-Christian conference held at Tripoli, Libya, in 1976, the host, Muammar al Qaddafi, asked one of the Catholic participants when the pope in Rome would at last produce the true gospel, Barnabas, which he had been trying to hide for centuries.[26] It could have been Sheikh Nazim speaking.

It is acknowledged by all competent scholars that the Gospel of Barnabas is a medieval forgery; this is recognized even by Guénonian traditionalists.[27] A complete Italian manuscript exists and was translated into English in 1907. It was thereafter translated into numerous oriental languages and published in pirated editions throughout the Muslim world. In the 1940s Sheikh Abu Zahra of al Azhar University, Cairo, the oldest and most prestigious center of learning in the Islamic world, used the Gospel of Barnabas in his religious classes to make polemical points against Christianity.[28] The main point at issue concerns the assertion of the Koran that Jesus was not crucified and did not really die; rather, "only a likeness of that was shown to them" (K.4:156). This is interpreted in Koran commentary (*tafsir*) by saying that God substituted another for Jesus but caused witnesses to perceive that other as Jesus. In the Gospel of Barnabas, as in many *tafsirs*, that other is Judas.

According to Sheikh Nazim, St. Barnabas was from Cyprus and is buried in Cyprus. When his grave was opened, the original Gospel of Barnabas was found on his chest; this is the copy that is now hidden in the Vatican, the Italian version being merely the first translation.[29] Apart from this unique twist to the story, the polemical use of Barnabas in the teachings of Sheikh Nazim is predictably Muslim: the Christian account of Jesus' passion, crucifixion, and resurrection is entirely false, indeed, knowingly and deliberately falsified, and only Muslims have the true story. In Sheikh Nazim's case, this conventional assertion is bolstered by a pretense of historical clairvoyance. When asked what really occurred with regard to Jesus' arrest and the substitution of another, an account from the *tafsir* of at Tabari is recounted, prefaced with the words "I am seeing it now."

The most persistent and pervasive feature of Sheikh Nazim's discourse is the invocation of the scenario surrounding the last days as this appears in Islamic tradition. If all Muslims are obliged to believe these teachings, since they appear so prominently in the Hadith, few would claim to have inside knowledge of the precise how, where, and when of such events. From his earliest days in the West, Sheikh Nazim has claimed such knowledge and has continuously been proved wrong. The last days are always presented as being within a few years of whenever they are mentioned or described. In 1978 he described how humankind was dividing itself into two camps, believers and unbelievers, just as the Prophet had foretold, and this was a sign that the end was near. The first camp are the followers of Mahdi and Jesus Christ, and the second camp are the followers of of Dajjal and the Antichrist. Soon Armageddon, the last great war, would occur, in which the members of the two camps would be sorted out by six out of every seven people being killed.[30] These events were presented as being imminent, bound to occur within the next two years.[31]

Such dire predictions set the pattern for all future references to the last times in Sheikh Nazim's talks. Some of the most remarkable exchanges on the subject occurred in Basle, Switzerland, in 1985, when he was invited to address the members of a Hindu community. He explained how it is impossible that the year 2000 will be completed, and how Dajjal, the Muslim equivalent of the Antichrist, is already physically present on earth, chained and imprisoned on an unknown island that no one can approach; he has already sent out thirty deputies to prepare for his coming. The opponent of Dajjal is the Mahdi, a descendant of the Prophet in the fortieth generation, and he too is already present on earth, living with ninety-nine helpers in the empty quarter of the Arabian peninsula between Saudi Arabia and Yemen, while his parents live at his birthplace near Jedda. Seen in a vision or dream, the Mahdi appears with a red turban and a deep red cloak and is identified by a spot of ashes on his right cheek that shines like a star.[32]

Sheikh Nazim claims to have taken an oath of allegiance (*bay'a*) with the Mahdi on the plain of Arafat, twelve miles southwest of Mecca, along with twelve thousand saints,[33] and rumors of people meeting the Mahdi at Mecca, Medina, and elsewhere are rife in certain circles. Fueled by the material on the Mahdi and the last times in the Hadith, speculation on the subject has become so febrile and obsessive in some quarters that many Muslims have become incapable of distinguishing fantasy from reality. Although this kind of speculation has always gone on in the Muslim world, especially in times of crisis, what appears to have precipitated it in recent times is the general crisis of Islam vis-à-vis the modern world. This is evident in the fact that Mahdi is now credited with the ability to neutralize technology,[34] so that in the end time, that which has been most instrumental in laying the Muslim world low will be found to be powerless. A desire for revenge against a technological and secularized world that refuses to take Islam seriously is sublimated into the inner animation of Mahdi and Dajjal and a scarcely concealed longing for an Armageddon that will wipe out all those with contrary views. Hatred of the modern world is what unites the conventional Sufism of Shaykh Nazim and the unconventional Sufism of Schuon and the traditionalists.

Despite a list of falsified predictions that would be too tedious to enumerate, in 1995, ten years after it was announced that the year 2000 would never be completed, Sheikh Nazim told those willing to listen that it is the twenty-first *century* that will not be completed. He is like a Muslim Jehovah's Witness, forever rescheduling the day of doom.[35] This perpetual prediction of the demise of the non-Muslim modern world is combined with an analysis of that world that betrays a woeful ignorance of both its nature and its history. This leads to remarks of an almost incredible crassness that make it difficult to understand how they are allowed to pass without question or demur; but this is what happens when someone surrounds himself with adoring followers willing to swallow, overlook, or make excuses for anything the master says. Like any bogus medium, Sheikh Nazim prefers that there be no negative or hostile listeners to his talks, since their presence is likely to impede the reception of his master's voice, that of Sheikh Abdullah Daghestani, who supposedly prompts whatever he says. This Uwaysi-style reliance on purported messages from dead sheikhs makes an apparently simple talk a cross between a séance and an exercise in controlled schizophrenia.

Many of Sheikh Nazim's crass remarks concern that stock-in-trade of lunatic conspiracy theorists: Jews and Freemasons. According to Nazim, the last Sultan of the Ottoman Empire was removed from power by Jews and Freemasons, who knew it would lead to the breakup of the Islamic world.[36] In America, everything is under the control of the Jews,[37] the Muslim world and the rest of the world is controlled by Jews,[38] the French Revolution was a Jewish trick,[39] and democracy is a Jewish *fitna* or cause of dispute.[40] On the principle that nothing occurs without a reason, six million Jews were killed in the Holocaust as a trial for them and for their spiritual improvement. If any people suffer, it is for a cleansing of their souls, their own fault or that of their ancestors, and they will be rewarded in paradise.[41] The present-day suffering of the Islamic world is because it is not Islamic enough but is running after technology and democracy and the wicked ways of the West. If only Muslims had sufficient faith, Allah would come to their aid and smite the unbelievers. Bosnian refugees were told that if Muslims in Bosnia prayed two cycles (*rakat*) of prayer every day enemy bullets would not touch them.[42] In short, the cause of all problems is lack of Islam, and the solution to all problems is more Islam.

That this kind of nonsense is taken seriously by intelligent, educated Westerners is hard to believe, but is true. Many have been willing listeners for twenty years or more and continue to cling to it with a pathetic loyalty born of a pusillanimous reluctance to question anything or think for themselves. Believers convince themselves that the Sheikh must be what he claims; otherwise, they must admit they are being deluded by a fraud. Therefore, there must be sublime reasons for whatever he says, reasons beyond the comprehension of lowly *murids*. This way of thinking is reinforced by the stipulation incumbent upon every member of the *tariqa*: "He must agree with the opinion of his sheikh completely, as the patient agrees with the physician."[43]

Most Britons who convert to Islam do so either through marriage or through Sufi groups. The Association of British Muslims (ABA) grew out of the group surrounding Sheikh Nazim, and the key to understanding its mentality can be gathered from a description of its membership: "The association represents the majority of converts, and a typical profile is middle class, professional, often public school educated, monarchist, conservative, and involved with genuine mystic paths and masters."[44] Sheikh Nazim's pronouncements are found congenial, or at least not particularly objectionable, since they coincide with the prejudices of such people. Indeed, one of the more amusing of Sheikh Nazim's eccentricities are his repeated pronouncements in favor of Prince Charles, who is lauded for praising Islam and being against tall buildings.[45] For the sheikh, monarchy is good and democracy is bad, and he advocates Charles's being made king with full powers and doing away with Parliament. This goes with Sheikh Nazim's constant calls for a king or caliph to rule over all Muslims in place of secular governments,[46] a plank from the platform of such extremist Islamic groups as Hizbat Tahrir.

This raises the question: What, after all, is the difference between Sufism and mainstream or fundamentalist Islam? In the end, very little. Sufism is fundamentalist Islam for those with a taste for mysticism. Sufism is fundamentalist because Islam is fundamentalist; an Islam that is not fundamentalist would not be Islam. A religion based on a text regarded as the direct word of God and on that account not to be critically examined in any way, as well as a religious law regarded as promulgated by God himself through the sayings and doings of his final Prophet, cannot *not* be fundamentalist. There is certainly a difference between an Islam that is fundamentalist by nature and an extremist Islam willing to use violent means to further such fundamentalist ideas, but the ideas are common to Islam in all its forms. Even Sufis of the stature of Ibn Arabi were fundamentalist with regard to the origin of the Koran and the Hadith, regardless of what extraordinary visions and interpretations they may have made out of them. The Naqshbandiyya *tariqa*, of which Sheikh Nazim is currently the most prominent representative, is notorious for combining strict adherence to the Sharia with the techniques of Sufism. The quarrels between Sufism and such relatively recent forms of exoteric Islam as Wahhabism are of an age-old type, whereby a Sufism that venerated saints and the tombs of saints had to justify such practices by retrojecting them to the time of the Prophet. Since the life of the Prophet has always been an empty vessel into which every party in Islam put whatever they found congenial, there is no more historical basis for one view over another.

The reasons non-Muslim Westerners convert to Islam are little different from the reasons they convert to any religious group; if the psychological need is there, it will be met in some form or other. The reasons people give for converting for the most part are rationalizations after the fact of belief itself, which comes upon them in ways they hardly know. Having the need for a belief of some kind and being ignorant of any cogent logical or historical reasons for not joining a particular group, many are members and committed before they know what has happened. Once inside a group, and this applies as much to major denominations as to any so-called cult, the psychological pressures to stay are irresistible for all but a few. Any critical attitude of mind, which may never have been present in the first place, becomes regarded as an act of treason, a sign of moral as well as intellectual obtuseness. It is for these sort of reasons that Muslims find it acceptable to advocate the death penalty for leaving the faith; what good word can be said for anyone who chooses of their own free will to turn their back on Truth? Human beings get enormous satisfaction from being members of any kind of group; if that group is considered to have privileged access to ultimate Truth and salvation, so much the better.

In the case of Islam, taking into consideration all the aspects of the subject considered in this book, when considered from a secular perspective, it is hardly an exaggeration to say that it does not have a sound intellectual leg on which to stand. The traditional account of its historical origin turns out to be a tissue of fabrications concocted in the second and third Islamic centuries to justify Arab rule of ancient civilizations. The purportedly revealed text on which it stands turns out to be an assemblage of fragments of diverse style and subject matter, collected over at least a century and put together in its canonical form by persons unknown, possibly with purposes in mind that have, as yet, hardly been recognized (see appendix); how much of it, if any, is to be attributed to the tribal warlord known as Muhammad is a matter of opinion. The Hadith literature should be classified as pious fiction. The so-called authentic collections are simply those traditions out of hundreds of thousands that happened to suit the purposes of those in power at the time. The Sharia consists of much of the ancient law of the Middle East given Muslim dress and attributed to the Prophet.

Islam maintains itself in existence in the modern world by refusing to look critically at its origins and by a systematic program of indoctrination of the young whereby their critical faculties are neutralized before they have a chance to develop. Forcing five-year-olds to learn the Koran by heart is an aspect of child abuse curiously overlooked by concerned liberals. As R. E. Burns has observed, "[T]he rote recitation of the Qur'an by young boys for hours at a time has a mentally unbalancing effect upon them."[47] The inner experiences that may result from such activities, which some would regard as their validation, are no more than might be expected from being a participant in a particular religious milieu; the argument for Islam from the evidence of religious experience fares no better in its case than in any other, even at the abstract level of *fana* and *baqa*.

For an intelligent, educated Westerner to convert to Islam is an act of mental suicide, a self-conscious infantilism born of the willful ignorance that refuses to look facts in the face, the adult equivalent of the rebellious teenager seeking a way to offend by choosing the antithesis of his or her parents' cultural values. The choice between Islam and the critical skepticism that has made the modern world is a choice between a return to the womb, the essence of the mystical experience, and going forward into the future without guide or refuge; if courage is the first of the virtues, the explorer has more than the stay-at-home. Traditionalism, the deliberate and knowing return to ways of thinking and living long abandoned, as urged by Guénon and his followers in the mystical-romantic school of Islamic studies, is a self-contradiction that even those immersed in a traditional world were self-aware enough to recognize. As al Ghazali noted long ago:

> There is certainly no point in trying to return to the level of naive and derivative belief (*taqlid*) once it has been left, since a condition of being at such a level is that one should not know one is there; when a man comes to know that, the glass of his naive belief is broken. This is a breakage which cannot be mended, a breakage not to be repaired by patching or by assembling fragments. The glass must be melted once again in the furnace for a new start, and out of it another fresh vessel formed.[48]

This was said within the womb of Islam; today, no one can live within the womb of Islam or any other religion, and the new start has to be made elsewhere.

Prominent advocates of Islam in the West, such as Frithjof Schuon and Sheikh Nazim, appear on close examination to be very human products of their environments and upbringing. In addition to being self-deluded, they are not above dissembling and cheap tricks to further the cause to which they have committed their lives. Being so committed, they are incapable of any objectivity and could no more critically examine the origin of Islam than they could admit the all-too-human and explicable reasons for their commitment. The same applies to those who, without really knowing how, find themselves within Islam's embrace. So finding themselves, an immense effort is needed to step back from their situation and come to their senses. Leaving something you have made the center of your life, even your very raison d'être, is immensely difficult and painful but by no means impossible. It has been the aim of this book to offer arguments for such a move and provide the intellectual basis on which it can be done.

Notes

1. See Z. Sardar, *Explorations in Islamic Science* (London: Mansell, 1989), p. 95.

2. D. Easterman, *New Jerusalems* (London: Grafton, 1992), p. 83.

3. F. Mernissi, *Islam and Democracy: Fear of the Modern World* (New York: Addison Wesley, 1992), p. 160.

4. See D. King, "Islamic Mathematics and Astronomy," *Journal for the History of Astronomy* 9 (1978): 212–19.

5. See Sardar, *Explorations in Islamic Science*, pp. 114–34.

6. Ibid., p. 116.

7. Ibid., p. 124.

8. Nasr, *Knowledge and the Sacred* (Edinburgh: Edinburgh University Press, 1981), p. 107.

9. M. Raschid, "Philosophia Perennis Universale Imperium," *Religion* 13 (1983): 155–71.

10. F. Schuon, *Memories and Meditations*, 1984, p. 10. This is an unpublished work circulated among members of Schuon's *tariqa*.

11. Raschid, "Philosophia Perennis," p. 156.

12. Schuon, *Memories and Meditations*, pp. 97, 127–28.

13. Raschid, "Philosophia Perennis," p. 157.

14. Schuon, *Memories and Meditations*, pp. 267–68.

15. M. Koslow, *An Account of the Schuon Cult*, p. 11; unpublished document circulated by the author.

16. See F. Schuon, *Images of Primordial and Mystic Beauty* (Bloomington: Abodes, 1992).

17. M. Koslow, *An Account of the Schuon Cult*.

18. Schuon, "Sacred Nudity," in *Memories and Meditations*, p. 1; unpublished, privately circulated document.

19. See Koslow, *An Account of the Schuon Cult, Telling Truth to Power* (1996), and *An Update on the Schuon Cult* (1996); circulated by the author.

20. Quoted in Z. Sardar, "A Man for All Seasons?" *Impact International* (December 1993): 33–36. See also ibid. (February 1994): 5–6.

21. Koslow, *Update*, p. 63.

22. Both Chittick and Coomaraswamy contributed essays to the *festschrift* for Schuon's eightieth birthday. See Nasr and Stoddart, eds.,

*Religion of the Heart: Essays presented to Frithjof Schuon on His Eight-
ieth Birthday* (Washington: Foundation for Traditional Studies, 1991).

23. M. H. Kabbani, *The Naqshbandi Way* (Chicago: Kazi Publications, 1995), pp. 378–81.

24. Ibid., p. 396.

25. See Nazim, *Mercy Oceans' Hidden Treasures* (London: Sebat,
1981), p. 195, and *Mercy Oceans of the Heart* (London: Sebat, 1985), pp.
37–42.

26. D. Sox, *The Gospel of Barnabas* (London: George, Allen and
Unwin, 1984), p. 11.

27. See the entry for *Barnabas, Gospel of*, in C. Glassé's *Concise
Encyclopaedia of Islam* (London: Stacey International, 1988), pp. 64-
65.

28. Sox, *Gospel of Barnabas*, p. 10.

29. See M. Nazim, *The Secrets Behind the Secrets Behind the
Secrets . . .* (Berlin: Dura, 1987), pp. 12–21.

30. These remarks are reminiscent of Schuon's: three-quarters of
the world's population deserves to be killed because they are profane and
do not believe in God. See Koslow, *An Account of the Schuon Cult*, p. 33;
unpublished document.

31. Nazim, *London Talks, Spring 1978*, pp. 12, 53; unpublished
typescript. See also Nazim, *Mercy Oceans*, part 2.

32. Nazim, *Secrets*, pp. 22–36.

33. Ibid., p. 140.

34. Ibid. p. 144.

35. M. Nazim, *Star from Heaven* (London: Zero Productions, 1996),
p. 33.

36. Ibid., p. 22.

37. M. Nazim, *Power Oceans of Love* (London: Zero Productions,
1995), p. 22.

38. Ibid., p. 24.

39. Ibid., p. 65.

40. Ibid., p. 68.

41. Nazim, *Secrets Behind the Secrets*, pp. 138–39.

42. M. Nazim, *Power Oceans of Light* (London: Zero Productions,
1995), pp. 105–6.

43. Kabbani, *The Naqshbandi Way*, p. 33.

44. *The Independent*, 26.8.91, quoted in P. Lewis, *Islamic Britain* (London: I. B. Tauris, 1994), p. 200.

45. M. Nazim, *Star from Heaven* (London: Zero Productions, 1996), pp. 11–12.

46. Nazim, *Power Oceans of Love*, pp. 24–25.

47. R. E. Burns, *The Wrath of Allah* (Houston: A. Ghosh, 1994), p. 163.

48. W. M. Watt, trans., *The Faith and Practice of Al Ghazali* (Oxford: Oneworld, 1994), p. 26.

Nineteen in the Koran: An Episode in Modern Islam

The story of nineteen in the Koran in modern times begins with the publication of *The Perpetual Miracle of Muhammad* (1976) by Rashad Khalifa. This work went through at least two further versions: *The Computer Speaks: God's Message to the World* (1981) and *Qur'an: Visual Presentation of the Miracle* (1982). The same material was also broadcast in numerous leaflets and articles and gained a further boost when taken up by the Islamic polemicist Ahmed Deedat in his booklet *Al-Qur'an the Ultimate Miracle* (1979). The latter work went through at least three editions, twenty thousand of which were printed for free distribution in England in 1985. However, because of the subsequent turn of events, all these items are now difficult to obtain.

Khalifa's basic thesis is that the structure of the Koran is based on the number nineteen and multiples of nineteen. This "fact" has been discovered by running the text through a computer and counting the number of letters, words, verses, and so forth. What this proves, at least to Khalifa, is that the Koran is truly God's word, a miracle, since no human being could possibly have contrived such an incredibly intricate feat. Thus modern,

201

infidel technology validates the age-old Muslim claim that the Koran is "God's message to the world" and that "it has been perfectly preserved."

Not surprisingly, this idea was at first enthusiastically welcomed in the Islamic world, and Khalifa became something of a celebrity. This enthusiasm was, however, short lived and rapidly subsided when he began making heretical statements. The chief of these was that all that Muslims needed was the Koran and that those who followed the *sunna* and *hadith* were idolaters. He also subsequently claimed to have worked out the date of the day of judgment, using numbers and multiples of nineteen in the Koran, and that, contrary to his first claims, the Koran had in fact been tampered with and was not perfectly preserved. These ideas forced most of his admirers in the Muslim world to denounce him and disassociate themselves from him, including his most fervent propagandist, Ahmed Deedat. It obviously could not be allowed that an outrageous heretic had found the secret of the Koran after all these centuries. Enthusiasm turned to ridicule and abuse, the final blow coming when one of the leading scholars of Saudi Arabia, Sheikh 'Abdullah ibn 'Abdul Aziz ibn Baz, issued a *fatwa* declaring Khalifa an apostate; he was later found dead in mysterious circumstances in his office in Tucson, Arizona, on January 31, 1990.

Emotional denunciations, culminating in death, however, were not sufficient to refute Khalifa's claims, based as they were upon the data produced by a computer. What was needed was a detailed analysis of the data, a denial that any such thing could possibly be true, and an explanation of how the nineteen idea is, and always has been, simply a platform for heresy. This was eventually produced by Abu Ameena Bilal Philips, a Jamaican convert of distinctly Wahhabi persuasion and author of numerous proselytizing books and pamphlets.

For a non-Muslim and an unbeliever, deciding upon the relative merits of the claims of Khalifa and Bilal Philips is rather like trying to decide which of two lunatics is the real Napoleon. That the task might be worth carrying out consists in the possibility that it could shed some light on the circumstances of the collection and arrangement of the Koran. If there really is a pattern or structure in the Koran based on nineteen and multiples of nineteen, it would imply that whoever decided upon the so-called order of revelation of the prophetic logia, and the arrangement of those logia in chapters and verses, were aware that they had to compete with similar patterns in the holy books of the Jews and Christians.

That there are numerical patterns in the holy books of Jews and Christians has come to light recently through the work of such scholars as A. G. Wright on Qoheleth (Ecclesiastes) and M. J. J. Mencken on the Gospel of John. Their findings of patterns and symmetries in these books are highly relevant in that they consist of a system of counting letters, words, and verses, very similar to that postulated by Khalifa for the Koran. For instance, Qoheleth is based on the number thirty-seven, the numeration of the word *hebel* (vanity), a word that occurs thirty-seven times in the book.[1] This is in addition to the long-known Qabalistic reading of biblical texts based on the numeration of words in a number-letter system. If the Koran as a canonical text made its appearance in an environment in which it was well known that authentic holy books contained hidden numerical patterns, it would have been well nigh obligatory that it contained something of the same kind. Hence, it is at least plausible that those who compiled the Koran in the odd form of 114 chapters of roughly decreasing length made sure that it did.

A large part of Khalifa's evidence concerns the *Muqatta'at*, or abbreviated letters, that stand at the head of twenty-nine chapters of the Koran. These mysterious letters have never been satisfactorily explained by either Muslim or non-Muslim scholars. A useful summary of previous theories concerning these letters can be found in Seale.[2]

We shall endeavor to examine the claims of Khalifa concerning the Koran by following the list of thirty-one "facts" set out in his 1981 book: *The Computer Speaks*. Bilal Philips's rebuttal, *The Qur'an's Numerical Miracle: Hoax and Heresy* (1987) refers mainly to Khalifa's 1982 work: *Qur'an: Visual Presentation of the Miracle*, which was unobtainable at the time of this writing. However, since the material cited by Philips appears to be identical for the most part to that in the 1981 work, this discrepancy should make little material difference to the main points at issue. The bulk of the evidence offered in Khalifa's book consists of nearly two hundred pages of computer printout, whereas Philips's critique attacks the principles upon which this evidence is based in a booklet of sixty-eight pages.

Nineteen in the Koran

FACT 1: The opening statement of the Koran, the *bismillah*, consists of nineteen letters.

Comment: Indisputable. Philips tries to dispute it (pp. 10–11) on the spurious ground that there are in fact three deleted *Alifs* in the statement, one unpronounced and the other two pronounced, so that the real number of letters is twenty-two. This is irrelevant since the whole argument is based on the written, not an ideal or pronounced, text. If anything, the fact that there are nineteen written letters and three deleted Alifs in the statement favors Khalifa's thesis, since it suggests that those who fixed the written text were aiming at a nineteen at the head of every chapter. Philips is here trying to defend the notion that the Koran is essentially an oral revelation, not a written text.

FACT 2: The first Koranic revelation (K.96:1–5) consisted of nineteen words.

Comment: Disputed by Philips on the ground that Khalifa follows a haphazard system of word identification "which contradicts both classical and modern rules of Arabic grammar and lexography" (p. 27). Again, there is a difference between pronunciation and the strict rules of word identification in Arabic grammar and the appearance of the written text. Strictly speaking, as

Philips points out (p. 28), Khalifa's word number eleven really consists of three words: *wa*, *rabb*, and *ka*. Nevertheless, it is written as one word, and it is the written word that counts in the present context. Philips's point is like insisting that "nevertheless" is three words not one.

FACT 3: The last Koranic revelation (K.110) consisted of nineteen words.

Comment: Disputed by Philips on the same grounds as fact two above.

FACT 4: The Koran consists of 114 chapters (19×6).
Comment: Indisputable. Not disputed by Philips.

FACT 5: The first chapter revealed (K.96) is found in position nineteen from the end of the Koran.

Comment: Indisputable. Not disputed by Philips.

FACT 6: The first chapter revealed (K.96) consists of nineteen verses.

Comment: Indisputable. Not disputed by Philips.

FACT 7: The first Koranic words ever revealed (K.96:1–5), the nineteen words of fact two, consist of seventy-six letters (19×4).

Comment: Indisputable. Not disputed by Philips.

FACT 8: The first chapter revealed (K.96) consists of 285 alphabet letters (19×15).

Comment: Disputed by Philips (pp. 10–11) on the grounds of pronounced but deleted Alifs. Curiously, he does not remark on the discrepancy between Khalifa's 1981 figures for the number of letters in K.96, quoted above, and his 1982 figures (304 = 19 × 16), quoted by Philips (p. 10).

FACT 9: The first word in the Koran's opening statement, the word "ism," is repeated in the whole Koran exactly nineteen times.

Comment: Disputed by Philips (pp. 31–32) on the ground that Khalifa illogically, and against his own stated principles, includes several different forms of the word in his count.

FACT 10: The second word in the Koran's opening statement, the word "Allah," occurs in the Koran 2,698 times (19 × 142).

Comment: Disputed by Philips (p. 32), since Khalifa later (1985) admits that this count is off by one and is actually 2,699, which is not an exact multiple of nineteen. Because of this Khalifa claims that the Koran has been tampered with and then goes into highly dubious explanations, which gives Philips a great opportunity to attack him at length (pp. 32–41) and discredit his whole position. However, it is interesting to note that Goitein[3] states that the number of "Allahs" in the Koran is 2,697, one less than Khalifa's original count. That the number of "Allahs" in the Koran is so close to an exact multiple of nineteen does suggest that such a thing may have been aimed at by the compilers. It could still be considered deliberate if it is in fact one over at 2,699, since by the conventions of gematria, to which the simple counting of letters and words is related by choice of the base number, being one off, *colel*, is considered to be good enough.[4] In this case the one "Allah" over would denote the one who created or manifested the 2,698.

FACT 11: The third word in the Koran's opening statement, *Al-Rahman*, is repeated in the whole Koran fifty-seven times (19 × 3).

Comment: Indisputable. Admitted to be so by Philips (p. 41).

FACT 12: The fourth word in the Koran's opening statement, *Al-Rahim*, is repeated in the whole Koran 114 times (19 × 6).

Comment: Disputed by Philips (pp. 41–42) on the grounds that Khalifa elsewhere[5] changes his mind and states that there are 115 occurences of *Al-Rahim*, and as before goes into highly dubious explanations. Khalifa also includes different forms of the word to get his total. However this may be, the fact that the total is so close to an exact multiple of nineteen suggests that such a thing may have been aimed at, especially since *Al-Rahim* completes the *bismillah* and 114 is a number signifying the whole Koran.

FACT 13: The number of *Bismillahs* in the Koran is 114, despite its being missing from the beginning of chapter 9. This deficiency is compensated at K.27:30, where an extra *Bismillah* is included in the text.

Comment: Indisputable. Not disputed by Philips; he simply ignores it.

FACT 14: Khalifa writes: "Not only is the missing 'Bismillah' of chapter 9 compensated in chapter 27, as we see in physical fact 13, but we find that the distance between the missing 'Bismillah' and the extra 'Bismillah' is exactly 19 chapters. In other words, when you count the chapters, starting at 9 [where the 'Bismillah' is missing], you will find that the chapter where the extra 'Bismillah' is found is number 19" (p. 96).

Comment: Indisputable. Not disputed by Philips; he simply ignores it.

FACT 15: The second Koranic revelation (K.68:1–9) consisted of thirty-eight words (19 × 21).

Comment: Disputed by Philips (pp. 26–27) on the same grounds as previous word counts. See facts two and three.

FACT 16: The third Koranic revelation (K.73:1–10) consisted of fifty-seven words (19 × 3). Thus we see that the first Koranic revelation, fact two, consisted of nineteen words (19 × 1), that the second Koranic revelation, fact fifteen, consisted of thirty-eight words (19 × 2), and that the third Koranic revelation consisted of fifty-seven words (19 × 3).

Comment: Disputed by Philips as above. That the number of words in the first three "revelations" approximates so closely a progressive ratio based on nineteen indicates that something of the kind may well have been aimed at by those who decided that order in the first place.

FACT 17: The fourth Koranic revelation brought the number nineteen itself. As this is crucial to Khalifa's case as a whole, we will quote him at length:

> The fourth revelation consisted of verses 1 through 30 of chapter 74, entitled, "The Hidden Secret." In retrospect, it turns out that this whole chapter is dealing with the Qur'an's 19 based numerical code, which remained a hidden secret during the last 14 centuries. The first few verses of this chapter exhort the "hidden secret" to shed its covers, and glorify its Lord.

> Then, verses 11 through 30 inform us that any person who does not recognize the Qur'an as the word of God, one who says that the Qur'an is "man-made" (v. 25), will be proven wrong "By the number 19" (v. 30).

> It should be noted here that the alteration of the written sequence of chapters, from the revelation sequence, is one of the effective means of "concealing" the hidden secret until the proper time for the unveiling. One good example is the fact that the first chapter revealed is located in slot 19 from the end of the Qur'an.

The importance of altering the written sequence from the revelation sequence becomes especially obvious when we look at physical fact No.18. (p. 100)

Comment: Disputed at length by Philips (pp. 6–8), mainly on the grounds that Khalifa mistranslates and misinterprets both the title and text of chapter 74. As verses 24–31 of chapter 74 are so crucial to the whole matter, it is best that we have them before us in the uncontentious translation of A. Yusuf Ali:

Sura LXXIV, Muddathir, or One Wrapped Up

24. Then said he: "This is nothing but magic, Derived from of old;

25. "This is nothing but The word of a mortal!"

26. Soon will I Cast him into Hell-fire.

27. And what will explain To thee what Hell-Fire is?

28. Naught doth it permit To endure, and naught Doth it leave alone!

29. Darkening and changing The color of man!

30. Over it are Nineteen.

31. And we have set none But angels as guardians Of the Fire; and We Have fixed their number Only as a trial For Unbelievers, — in order That the People of the Book May arrive at certainty, And the Believers may increase In Faith — and that no doubts May be left for the People Of the Book and the Believers, And that those in whose hearts Is a disease and the Unbelievers May say, "What symbol Doth God intend by this?" Thus doth God leave to stray Whom He pleaseth, and guide Whom He pleaseth: and none Can know the forces Of thy Lord, except He. And this is no other than A warning to mankind.[6]

Leaving aside whether Khalifa tendentiously mistranslates the title and text of chapter 74, it seems clear that there is something significant about the appearance of the number nineteen in a context of controversy about the divine credentials of the Koran. Even if we grant that the "it" in verse 30 refers to "Hell-Fire," as Philips insists, and not to the Koran, as claimed by Khalifa, we are still left wondering: Why that number? If the explanation is to be found in verse 31, as Philips believes, and nineteen refers to the number of angels set over hell-fire, we are still led to ask: Why that number? Especially in view of the following words: *"We have fixed their number only as a trial for unbelievers, — in order that the People of the Book may arrive at certainty, and the believers may increase in faith — and that no doubts may be left for the People of the Book and the believers, and that those in whose hearts is a disease and the unbelievers may say, 'What symbol doth God intend by this?'"* Why is the number nineteen a trial for unbelievers, and why does it give certainty to the people of the book? Indeed, "What Symbol doth God intend by this?" No answer has been forthcoming in the whole history of Islam until the advent of the heretic Khalifa. (It follows from K.74:31 that this text was invented and inserted in the Koran during the process of its arrangement in its canonical form.)

FACT 18: The fifth Koranic revelation placed the nineteen letters of *Bismillah* immediately following the number nineteen of verse 30, chapter 74. Khalifa writes:

As we saw from physical fact no. 17, the fourth revelation brought the number 19 itself. The fourth revelation stopped at verse 30 of chapter 74, which mentions the only number 19 in the Qur'an.

The fifth revelation brought the first complete chapter, namely, the chapter that is placed in position number 1 in the Qur'an, Al-Fatihah, "The Opener."

The first verse of chapter 1 is of course, *bism allah al-rahman al-rahim*, In the Name of God, Most Gracious, Most Merciful. The reader is by now aware that this verse represents the foundation upon which the Qur'an's numerical code is built. . . .

Placing the nineteen letters of "Bismillah" immediately following the number 19 of the fourth revelation is a direct indication that the 19 letters of the "Bismillah" are strongly connected with the role of no. 19 as described in chapter 74 and physical fact 17. (p. 102)

Comment: Facts seventeen and eighteen appear indisputable if Khalifa's version of the order of revelation is accepted. It is probably significant that Philips nowhere questions it. However, it is interesting to note that what Khalifa here describes as the fifth revelation, chapter 1, "The Opener," appears to be contradicted by what Ahmed Deedat describes as the fifth revelation: "the balance of Chapter 96 — the first revelation,"[7] that is to say, K.96:6–19. As Deedat is almost certainly dependent on Khalifa here, it implies that Khalifa has at some time changed his mind as to what constitutes the fifth revelation.

Further questions might be asked. If the fourth revelation ended at 74:30, and the fifth revelation consisted of chapter 1, to what number in the order of revelation does 74:31 belong? Presumably there is an answer to this somewhere in the traditional literature on the so-called occasions of revelation. If 74:31 explains the material in 74:24–30, as Philips thinks, why was it separated from it in the order of revelation and juxtaposed to it when the written order was decided? Can Philips, or anyone else, legitimately claim that 74:31 explains 74:24–30 if it belongs to a different revelation?

What this indicates is that those who decided the order of the oral revelations and those who decided the arrangement of their written versions were playing highly sophisticated games, the key to which has been missing for most of Islamic history.

FACT 19: Why is the Koran's secret numerical code based on the number nineteen? The Arabic word for "one" is *wahid*, consisting of the alphabet letters *Wa*, *Alif*, *Ha*, and *Dal*. The numerical values of these four letters are six, one, eight, and four, respectively. By adding the four values, we get the total nineteen. Therefore, nineteen = *wahid* = ONE.

Comment: Indisputable. Disputed by Philips (p. 47) on the grounds that this kind of numerology is a pseudoscience, non-Islamic, and heretical, which is simply a manifestation of his narrow minded Wahhabism. The traditionalist writer S. H. Nasr states that there are thirteen different systems of numerical symbolism, of which six are most frequently used. "The science of the numerical symbolism of letters, *'ilm al-jafr*, which is comparable to sciences of a similar nature that existed among the ancient Pythagoreans, the Hindus, and the medieval Kabbalists, is said by the masters of this science in Islam to have come down from 'Ali ibn Abi Talib."[8]

Interestingly, Philips also challenges fact nineteen on the grounds that Khalifa claims that the number nineteen at 74:30 is the only undefined number in the Koran and that this indicates its purely mathematical function. Philips points out that there is another unqualified number, namely, the number eight at 69:17, and that following methods similar to Khalifa's the number eight can be established as the basis of the Koran's numerical code (pp. 46, 50). Although Philips thinks this a great blow against Khalifa's thesis, it could well be true, since the number systems discovered by Wright and Mencken are not based on one number only but often have subsidiary systems within them based on other numbers.

The Quranic Initials: Khalifa writes:

The greatest portion of this numerical miracle was discovered in the "mysterious" alphabet letters which prefix 29 chapters of the Qur'an.

Fourteen alphabet letters, exactly half the Arabic alphabet, participate in the make-up of fourteen different sets of Quranic initials, and the 14 sets of initials are found in 29 chapters. Right away we see a connection between the Quranic initials and the number 19.

14 alphabet letters make up 14 sets of Quranic initials which prefix 29 chapters. This adds up to 57 which equals 19 × 3.

The 14 alphabet letters are: *Alif* (A), *Hā* (H), *Rā* (R), *Sīn* (S), *Sād* (S), *Tā* (T), *Ayin* (O), *Qāf* (Q), *Kāf* (K), *Lām* (L), *Mim* (M), *Nün* (N), *Hā* (H), and *Yā* (Y).

The 14 sets of Quranic initials are: N, S, Q, HM, YS, TS, TH, OSQ, TSM, ALM, ALR, ALMR, ALMS, KHYOS. (See illustration of initialed Chs.)

The Quranic initials are termed "miracles of the Qur'an" in 8 Quranic chapters. The expression used is, *tilka ayatul kitab*, and it is used exclusively in connection with the Quranic initials. The eight chapters and their verses are 10:1, 12:1, 13:1, 15:1, 26:2. 27:1, 28:2, 31:2.

It should be noted that the word *ayat* mentioned above is a multiple-meaning word. This multiplicity of meaning is important, and represents one of the Qur'an's miraculous features. The use of multiple-meaning words renders the Qur'an valid for many generations. Thus, before discovering the significance of the Quranic initials, as reported here, the previous generations understood the word *ayat* to mean "verses." But now that we have found out the great significance of these alphabet letters, it becomes obvious that the word *ayat* here means "miracles." (pp. 106–7)

Comment: Perhaps a better translation of *ayat* is "signs," rather than "miracles." This would in no way harm Khalifa's case.

FACT 20: The single Koranic initial *Qaf* is found in the *Qaf*-initialed chapters in frequencies of fifty-seven each (57 = 19 × 3). Khalifa writes:

> The Quranic initial *Qaf* is found in two chapters, namely, chapter 42 and 50. . . . When we count the letter *Qaf* in these two chapters we find that it occurs in each of the chapters exactly the same number of times, 57 and 57.

> It should be noted that chapter 42 is more than twice as long as chapter 50, which makes the equal occurrence of the letter in both chapters rather remarkable.

> It should be noted also that chapter 50 is entitled *Qaf* ("Q"), and that it contains the highest proportion of the letter "Q" among all the chapters of the Qur'an. . . .

> Another important point: when we add the frequency of occurrence of the letter "Q" in the two Q-initialed chapters, we find the total (57 + 57) = 114. The same as the total number of chapters in the Qur'an. It is reasonable to assume that the initial "Q" stands for "Qur'an." The fact that the letter "Q" occurs 114 times in the Q-initialed chapters, informs us that the 114 chapters constitute the Qur'an, the whole Qur'an, and nothing but the Qur'an . . . (pp. 109–11)

Comment: Indisputable. None of the above is disputed by Philips, even though he has a chapter entitled "Surah Qaf: False Claims." After dwelling at length on peripheral issues (pp. 43–45), he concludes that "the total of 57 *Qaf*s in *Surah Qaf* and *Surah Ash-Shura* is no more than a coincidence and can not in any way be considered proof for a 'miraculously intricate mathematical system' in the Qur'an" (p. 45). Those without a vested interest in denying such a system may beg to differ. It may not be miraculous, but it is unlikely to be coincidence either.

FACT 21: The Koranic initial *Nun* (N) occurs in the N-initialed chapter 133 times (133 = 19 × 7).

Comment: Disputed by Philips (pp. 21–23). The number is made up by spelling out the *Nun* at the head of chapter 68, N-U-N, and counting both *Nuns*. Khalifa gives highly dubious justifications for this procedure, which Philips easily demolishes. Once again, Khalifa is led into these spurious reasonings because he wants the pattern to be perfect or "miraculous," yet he finds it is one off, *colel*.

FACT 22: The Koranic initial *Sad* (Ṣ) occurs in the *Sad*-initialed chapters (7, 19, 38) a total of 152 times (152 = 19 × 8).

Comment: Disputed by Philips (pp. 23–24). Khalifa has certainly fiddled with the data in this case, and Philips makes the most of it. Once more, however, it is all occasioned by being one out, *colel*.

FACT 23: The two letters *Ya* (Y) and *Sin* (S) occur in the *Ya-Sin*-initialed chapter (36) a total of 285 times (285 = 19 × 15).

Comment: Indisputable. Not disputed by Philips in detail but denied in general terms (p. 18).

FACT 24: The two letters *Ha* (Ḥ) and *Mim* (M) occur in the seven *Ha-Mim*-initialed chapters (40–46) a total of 2147 times (2147 = 19 × 113).

Comment: Indisputable. Disputed by Philips (pp. 12–13) on the irrelevant ground that chapter 42 also has the letters *Ayin, Sin, Qaf* at its head. This is particularly churlish since he has to admit (p. 13) that the *Ayin Sin Qaf* total for chapter 42 is 209 (209 = 19 × 11). See below.

FACT 25: The three letters *Ayin* (O), *Sin* (S), and *Qaf* (Q) occur in the *Ayin-Sin-Oaf*-initialed chapter (42) a total of 209 times (209 = 19 × 11).

Comment: Indisputable. Khalifa writes:

The triple-lettered initial *Ayin Sin Qaf* (OSQ) is found in one chapter, namely, chapter 42. This particular chapter contains two sets of Quranic initials; verse no. 1 consists of the Quranic initials *Ha Mim* (see physical fact no. 24), while verse no. 2 consists of the initials *Ayin Sin Qaf*.

When we count the three letters in this chapter, we find that the letter *Ayin* (O) occurs 98 times, the letter *Sin* (S) occurs 54 times, and the letter *Qaf* (Q) occurs 57 times (see also physical fact number 20). Thus, the total occurrence of the three letters in this chapter is 209, a multiple of 19. (p. 136)

A. Yusuf Ali writes of the initial letters of chapter 42:

This Sura has a double set of Abbreviated Letters, one in the first verse, and one in this second verse. No authoritative explanation of this second set is available, and I refrain from speculation.[9]

It seems that the heretic Khalifa has found the explanation.

FACT 26: The three Koranic initials *Alif* (A), *Lam* (L), and *Mim* (M) occur in multiples of nineteen in the individual chapters prefixed with these letters (2, 3, 29, 30, 31, 32). Khalifa writes:

The letter *Alif* (A) was the most difficult to count, since it occurs in three different forms, namely, as an independent *Alif*, as an extension vowel, and as a *hamza* attached to some letter (*Waw* or *Ya*). Ironically, all three types of *Alif* exhibited some relationship to the number 19. However, the most powerful relationship is reported here, namely, where the numbers are multiples of 19 in the individual chapters. In this relationship, the independent

Alif and the *Alif* of extension are counted. The *hamza* which is part of another letter is not considered Alif. (p. 138)

Comment: Disputed at length by Philips (pp. 17–19). Philips writes: "Why do these 13 chapters [with initial *Alifs*] fit so nicely into the theory and the previous 12 do not? Actually none of these chapters fits the theory, but Dr. Khalifa has managed to make them fit by doctoring the count of *Alifs* in every case. He does this by counting the letter *Hamzah* as an *Alif* where it suits him and not where it does not" (p. 17). Using the data given in *Qur'an: Visual Presentation of the Miracle,* Philips then gives six examples (p. 18) that appear to contradict Khalifa's principle of counting explained above. It is difficult to know how far these are simply computer errors and how far they are deliberate falsifications. If Philips's six examples are all he can find in the thirteen *Alif*-initialed chapters, we might be inclined to give Khalifa the benefit of the doubt. If the miscountings are the difference between being an exact multiple of nineteen and being one out, as it usually is, it is still likely that an exact multiple of nineteen was being aimed at, especially in view of all the other exact multiples that are not in doubt.

FACT 27: The three Koranic initials *Alif* (A), *Lam* (L), and *Ŕa* (R) occur in multiples of nineteen in the individual chapters prefixed with these letters (10, 11, 12, 14, 15).

Comment: Disputed by Philips (p. 17) on the same grounds as fact twenty-six above.

FACT 28: The four Koranic initials *Alif* (A), *Lam* (L), *Mim* (M), and *Ra* (R) occur in the ALMR-initialed chapter (13) 1482 times (1482 = 19 × 78). Khalifa writes:

This set of initials occurs in one chapter, namely, Ch. 13. The frequency of occurrence of the four initials in this chapter were found to be 605, 480, 260, and 137, respectively. This makes the total occurrence of the four letters 1482 which is a multiple of 19. (p. 170)

Comment: Disputed by Philips on the same grounds as facts twenty-six and twenty-seven.

FACT 29: The four Koranic initials *Alif* (A), *Lam* (L), *Mim* (M), and *Sad* (S) occur in the ALMS-initialed chapter (7) 5320 times (3320 = 19 × 280). Khalifa writes:

> This set of initials occurs in one chapter, namely, Ch. 7. The frequency of occurrence of the four initials in this chapter were found to be 2529, 1530, 1164, and 97, respectively. This makes the total occurrence of the four letters 5320 which is a multiple of 19. (p. 172)

Comment: Not disputed in detail by Philips. However, these figures must be considered suspect in view of the discrepancies between the data published by Khalifa in 1976–1979 and 1981–1982, shown by Philips (p. 19).

FACT 30: The five Koranic initials *Kaf* (K), *Ha* (H), *Ya* (Y), *Ayin* (O), *Sad* (S) occur in the KHYOS-initialed chapter (19) 798 times (798 = 19 × 42). Khalifa writes:

> This set of initials occurs in one chapter, namely, Ch. 19. The frequency of occurrence of the five initials in this chapter were found to be 137, 175 343, 117, and 26, respectively. This makes the total occurrence of the five letters 798 which is a multiple of 19. (p. 178)

Comment: Indisputable. Not disputed by Philips. In view of the number of the chapter and there being five letters to total, this must be one of Khalifa's more impressive pieces of data.

FACT 31: Khalifa writes:

The initials *Ha* (H), *La* (T), *Sin* (S), and *Mim* (M) were found to interlock and interact with each other across five chapters, namely, 19 (*Ha*), 20 (*Ta Ha*), 26 (*Ta Sin Mim*), 27 (*Ta Sin*), and 28 (*Ta Sin Mim*). The total frequency of occurrence of these interlocking letters, in the 5 chapters, is 1767, which is of course a multiple of 19 (1767 = 19 × 93). (pp. 181–97)

Comment: Indisputable. Disputed by Philips on the ground that Khalifa chooses the letters arbitrarily in order to achieve his total (pp. 14–15). However, if we look at the list of chapters headed by letters (see illustration), chapters 19, 20, 26, 27, and 28 certainly appear to form an interrelated group, linked by the chapter numbers and visually by the letters that Khalifa counts.

Additional Facts: In two other publications Khalifa mentions two further "facts" relevant to his thesis.

(1) Since the Quranic evidence is based on the numerical code just presented, it was thought that the numbers mentioned in the Qur'an may also be involved. Indeed, a Muslim scholar from Homs Syria (Sidqi Al-Baik) reported that the Qur'an contains 285 numbers, and 285 = 19 × 15. When all 285 numbers mentioned in the Qur'an are added up, the total is 174,591, a multiple of 19. As if this is not enough, when we remove all repetitions, we find the total is 162,146, also a multiple of 19.[10]

(2) The total number of alphabet letters that make up the whole Book. This number was found to be 329,156 which equals 19 × 17,324.[11]

Comment: Neither of these "facts" are mentioned by Philips.

Conclusion

If, to begin with, we take only those facts labeled "indisputable" in the comment: 1, 4, 5, 6, 7, 11, 13, 14, 17, 18, 19, 20, 23, 24, 25, 30, 31, we find that the total is seventeen, or more than half. If, further, we give the benefit of the doubt to the word count and *Alif* "facts": 2, 3, 15, 16, 26, 27, 28, we find that the total rises to 24, or more than two-thirds. Finally, if we consider being one off, *colel*, good enough, then the total "facts" approaches something like a full house. If Khalifa's case has not been made in the way that he intended, it certainly has not been wholly demolished in the way that Philips intended.

Khalifa wanted the nineteen pattern in the Koran to be totally pervasive and completely perfect, since he wanted to present it as God's handiwork, unchanged since its first formation. In order to achieve the appearance of perfection, he resorted to specious arguments, and when errors were pointed out, he was not above doctoring the data to maintain his initial assertions. But, as we have seen, none of these dubious practices are necessary. If, in addition to the indisputable "facts" and the legitimacy of *colel*, human error is allowed for, a decent case can be made for a nineteen pattern in the Koran. The possibility of human error in the Koran is, however, what no Muslim can countenance for one moment, since it would undermine the whole edifice of Islamic certainty. If there is no infallible certainty in the text of the Koran, then there is no infallible certainty anywhere in Islam.

As Philips well realizes, and this provides his whole motivation, a nineteen pattern in the Koran, far from establishing that document's divine origin, as Khalifa naively thought, would prove precisely the opposite. It would prove that the text of the Koran had been written down and arranged in such a way as to demonstrate that it had a hidden, but recognizable, numerical pattern that rivaled or surpassed similar patterns to be found in the holy books of Jews and Christians. A very human act.

Moreover, since this pattern shows up not only in individual verses and chapters, but also in the distribution of those verses and chapters throughout the Koran as a whole, it implies that the text has been manipulated and interfered with, lengthened, shortened, and rearranged to an unimaginable extent. The Koran is far from being a perfect document, unchanged from the beginning, exactly representing the word of God as it issued from the mouth of Muhammad. It turns out to be one of the most doctored and corrupt texts in all religious literature. To anyone but a Muslim, this is exactly how it has always appeared: a collection of texts of varying provenance, character, and length stitched together in something of a hurry and given a spurious unity by the mechanical counting of letters, words, verses, and chapters.

Notes

1. A. G. Wright, "Additional Numerical Patterns in Qoheleth," *Catholic Biblical Inquiry* 45 (1983): 33.

2. M. S. Seale, *Qur'an and Bible* (London: Croom Helm, 1978), pp. 29–46; see also A. Y. Ali, *The Holy Qur'an* (London: Islamic Foundation, 1975), pp. 118–20, and individual initialed chapters; W. M. Watt, *Bell's Introduction to the Qur'an* (Edinburgh: Edinburgh University Press, 1970), pp. 61–65; H. Corbin, *Temple and Contemplation* (London: KPI, 1986), chap. 2, esp. pp. 81–103; D. Ovason, *The Zelator* (London: Century, 1998), pp. 186–87, 418; F. Rosenthal, "Nineteen," *Analecta Biblica* vo. 12 (1959), pp. 304–18.

3. S. Goitein, *Studies in Islamic History and Institutions* (Leiden: Brill, 1966), p. 30.

4. See D. Fideler, *Jesus Christ; Sun of God* (Wheaton: Quest Books, 1995), p. 206; J. Michell, *The Dimesions of Paradise* (London: Thames and Hudson, 1988), p. 60; and W. Stirling, *The Canon* (York Beach: Weiser, 1999), passim.

5. R. Khalifa, *Qur'an: The Final Scripture* (Tucson: Renaissance Productions, 1981), p. 472.

6. Ali, *Holy Qur'an*, pp. 1643–44.

7. A. Deedat, *Al Qur'an* (London: n.p., 1985), p. 30.

8. See Nasr, *An Introduction to Islamic Cosmological Doctrines* (Cambridge: Harvard University Press, 1964), pp. 49–52, 162, 209–12. See also D. Hulse, *The Key of It All* (St. Paul: Llewellyn, 1993–1994), vol. 1, pp. 179–221.

9. Ali, *Holy Qur'an*, p. 1305, n. 4527.

10. Khalifa, *Qur'an*, app. 1. See also E. G. McClain, *Meditations Through the Koran* (York Beach: Weiser, 1981), pp. 79–83 and passim.

11. R. Khalifa, *The Evolution of Creationism* (Tucson: Renaissance Productions, 1982), p. 15.

The Chapters of the Koran with Initial Letters

Chapter Numbers	Initial Letters	
2	A L M	
3	A L M	
		3
7	A L M Ṣ	
		2
10	A L R	
11	A L R	
12	A L R	
13	A L M R	
14	A L R	
15	A L R	
19	K H Y O S	
20	T H	
		5
26	T S M	
27	T S	
28	T S M	
29	A L M	
30	A L M	

Chapter Numbers	Initial Letters
31	A L M
32	A L M
	3
36	Y S
38	Ṣ
40	H M
41	H M
42	H M O S Q
43	H M
44	H M
45	H M
46	H M
50	Q
	17
68	N

$$38 = 19 \times 2$$

14 letters
in 14 different combinations
in 29 chapters

$$\overline{57} = 19 \times 3$$

Glossary

Abbasids	second dynasty of Islam (750–1258)
'abd	slave, servant
adab	polite behavior, good manners
adhān	the call to prayer
ahadiyya	oneness, unity
ahwāl (pl. of *hāl*)	mystical states
akhira	the next world, opposite of *dunya*
'ālam al ghayb	world of hidden things, spirits, angels
'ālam al khayāl	world of imagination
'ālam al mithal	world of images
'ālam al shahāda	world of the visible, manifestation
Allah	Arabic for God
anbiyā (pl. of *nabī*)	prophets
'aql	mind, reason, intellect
Arafat	a plain twelve miles southwest of Mecca
'arīf	knower, gnostic.
arkān	pillars, the five pillars of Islam: *shahāda*, *salāt*, *zakāt*, *sawm*, *hājj*.
asbab an nuzul	occasions of revelation

225

asmā dhātiyah	names of the divine essence
asmā sifātiyah	names of the divine qualities, attributes
awliyā (pl. of *wali*)	friends of God, saints
ayāt	signs of God, verses of the Koran
'ayn thābita (pl. *a'yān thābita*)	immutable essence
'ayn al qalb	eye of the heart, organ of intellectual intuition .
baqa'	survival, subsistence, duration of the soul of the mystic in the qualities or attributes of God. Usually combined with *fana*
baraka	blessing
barzakh	isthmus, interface, intermediary state or world
basīra	inner certainty
batīn	inner, hidden, esoteric., opposite of *zahir*
bay'a	oath of allegiance
bid'a	innovation
bismillah	the formula *bismi Llah ar Rahman ar Rahim*, In the Name of God, the Merciful, the Compassionate
dahri (from *ad dahr*, time)	atheist, one who thinks that only time destroys, hence *ad dahriyyah*, atheism
Dajjal	Muslim equivalent to Antichrist; opponent of Mahdi
dhāt	essence
dhikr	remembrance, invocation
dīn	religion
dunya	this world, in the sense of profane distraction
fana'	passing away, extinction of the human aspects of the soul of the mystic in the qualities or attributes of God. Usually combined with *baqa*.
faqr	poverty, hence *faqir*, poor man, Sufi

fath	spiritual opening, illiunination, hence *al fatiha*, the opening chapter of the Koran
fatwā	legal pronc ncement, religious decree
fiqh	jurisprudence, law
fitra	primordial nature
ghafla	heedlessness
al ghayb	the invisible, hidden
ghusl	major ritual ablution necessary after sexual emissions and menstruation
hadarat	divine presences
hadīth	any report, oral or written, about the sayings and doings of the Prophet
Hadith	the science or literature of Islamic tradition
hadīth qudsi	extra-Koranic saying of God
hāfiz	someone who has memorized the Koran
hajj	pilgrimage
hāl (pl. *ahwāl*)	mystical state, usually of a temporary nature, contrasted with *maqam*
halal	lawful, permitted, contrasted with *haram*
harif	pre-Islamic monotheist
al haqq	the Truth, Reality
haram	unlawful, forbidden
hijāb	veil
Hijaz	region of Saudi Arabia bordering the Red Sea and containing the cities of Mecca and Medina
hijra	emigration
hulūl	incarnation
al hurūf al muqatt 'āt	the isolated letters that stand at the head of twenty-nine *surahs* of the Koran
'ibada	worship
iblīs	Satan
ihsān	sanctifying virtue, spiritual beauty

ikhlās	sincerity, purity, of intention
ilhām	inspiration
'ilm	knowledge
imām	leader, especially of congregational prayer
imān	faith, belief
al insan al kamil	the Perfect Man
irtidad (or *riddah*)	apostasy, hence *murtadd*, apostate
Islam	submission
isnād	chain of transmission, especially of *hadith*
ittihad	mystical state interpreted as unitive fusion with God
jahiliyya	age of ignorance, time before Islam
jibrīl	Gabriel
jihād	striving, strenuous effort, holy war
jinn	spirits, good and evil, said to be created from fire
juma'	Friday congregational prayer
Kaaba	lit. cube, the sanctuary at Mecca
kalām	theology
karāmāt	miracles
kashf	unveiling, revelation
khalifa	caliph, deputy
khalq	creation
khalwa	seclusion, spiritual retreat
khatm al-awilya	seal of the saints
khirqa	mantle, patched frock of the Sufis
Koran	lit. reading, recitation, the holy book of Islam
kufr	unbelief, ingratitude, hence *kafir*, unbeliever
laylat al qadr	night of power; night during Ramadan when the first verses of the Koran are believed to have been revealed to Muhammad

madhhab	school of Islamic jurisprudence, i.e., the Hanafi, Shafi'i, Maliki, and Hanbali
mahabba	love
Mahdi	divinely guided one; ideal messianic figure expected to appear at the end of time
maqam (pl. *maqamat*)	spiritual station of a permanent nature
ma'rifa	knowledge, gnosis
mi'rāj	ascension (to heaven), especially that of the Prophet
mukashala	unveiling
munafiq	hypocrite
murīd	disciple or follower of a sheikh
murshid	teacher, spiritual guide
nabi (pl. *anbiya*)	prophet
nafs	soul, person, especially the lower soul or empirical ego
naskh	abrogation
niyyā	intention
nūr	light, especially the divine light experienced by the mystic
nūr al yaqin	light of certainty
qadar	God's decree, fate, destiny
qalb	heart
qibla	direction faced when praying
qiyāma	day of judgment
Quraysh	tribe of the Prophet
qutb	Pole, the most exalted spiritual person at any particular time
rabb	lord
rahma	mercy
Ramadan	ninth month of the Muslim year, the month of fasting

rasūl	envoy, messenger (from God), propagator of a new sacred law.
riba	usury, forbidden at K.2:275–80
ruh	spirit, the higher soul
sabr	patience
sadaqa	charity
sahāba	companions, early associates of the Prophet
sahih	sound, highest grade of *hadith*
sajda	prostration
salāt	prayer
sawm	fasting
shahada	bearing witness, confession of faith, the formula *la ilaha illa Llah,* there is no god but God; *Muhammadun rasul Allah*, Muhammad is the Prophet of God
Sharia	lit. road, the revealed law of Islam
sharif	descendant of the Prophet
sheikh	lit. old man, head of family, tribe, or religious order
Shia	lit. party, usually *shi'at Ali*, the party or followers of Ali, the second largest group in Islam after Sunnis
shirk	ascribing divinity to anything other than God
sidq	honesty, truthfulness
silsila	chain, line of descent, especially of a Sufi order
sira	biography of the prophet
Sufi	a follower of Sufism, the esoteric mysticism of Islam (see *tasawwuf*)
suhba	association, companionship, especially with a Sufi sheikh
sunna	custom, usage, especially the practices of the Prophet
Sunnis	the largest group of Muslims who recognize the first four caliphs, hence *ahl as sunnah*

	wa-l-ima', the people of the sunna and the consensus.
sura	lit. a row, a chapter of the Koran
tafsir	commentary on the Koran
tajalliyat (pl. of *tajalli*)	theophanies, divine revelations
tariqa	lit. way, road, path, one of the Sufi orders
tasawwuf	Sufism, wearing wool (from *suf*, wool), following the beliefs and practices of Sufism, trying to become a Sufi
tawakkul	trust in God
tawba	repentance
tawhid	affirmation or experience of God's Oneness
ta'wil	allegorical interpretation of scripture
ulama	the learned class, especially in religious matters
Umayyads	the first dynasty of Islam (661–730)
umma	the community of believers
umra	the lesser pilgrimage, performed at any time.
Uwaysi	like Uways, who communicatd with the Prophet telepathically or posthumously
wahdat al wujud	oneness of being
Wahhabi	followers of Ibn Abd al Wahhab (d. 1787). A strict version of the Hanbali *madhhab*, mostly confined to Saudi Arabia and the Gulf
wahy	divine revelation
wajd	ecstasy
wali (pl. *awilya*)	friend of God, saint
wudu	ritual ablution obligatory before prayer
zahid	renouncer, ascetic
zahir	outer, apparent, exoteric, opposite of *batin*
zakat	almsgiving

| Zamzam | the sacred well at Mecca |
| *zawiya* | lit. a corner, a spiritual retreat, place for Sufi activities |

Bibliography

Addas, C. *Quest for the Red Sulphur*. Cambridge: Islamic Texts Society, 1993.

Affifi, A. E. *The Mystical Philosophy of Muhyid'Din Ibnul-'Arabi*. Cambridge: Cambridge University Press, 1936.

Ali, A. Y., *The Holy Qur'an*. London: Islamic Foundation, 1975.

Ali, M. M. *A Manual of Hadith*. London: Curzon, 1978.

Arberry, A. J. *The Doctrine of the Sufis*. Translation of Kalabadhi's *Kitab at ta'arruf*. Cambridge: Cambridge University Press, 1935.

————. *Sufism: An Account of the Mystics of Islam*. London: George Allen and Unwin, 1950.

————. *The 'Ruba'iyat' of Jalaluddin Rumi*. London: John Murray, 1959.

————. *Discourses of Rumi*. London: John Murray, 1961.

————. *The Koran Interpretted*. Oxford: Oxford University Press, 1966.

————. *Muslim Saints and Mystics*. Excerpts from 'Attar's *Tadhkirat al awliya*. London: Routledge and Kegan Paul, 1966.

————. *A Sufi Martyr*. Translation of 'Ayun'l Qudat's *Apology*. London: George,, Allen and Unwin, 1969.

At Tabari. *The History of at Tabari, Vol. 6, Muhammad at Mecca*, edited and translated by Watt and McDonald. New York: SUNY Press, 1990.

Austin, R. W. J. *The Bezels of Wisdom*. Translation of Ibn Arabi's *Fusus al hikam*. London: SPCK, 1980.

233

————. *Sufis of Andalusia*. Translation of Ibn Arabi's *Ruh al quds and Al durrat al fakhirah*. Sherborne: Beshara Publications, 1988.

Ayoub, M. M. *The Qur'an and Its Interpreters*. Vol. 1. New York: SUNY Press, 1984.

Azami, M. M. *Studies in Early Hadith Literature*. Indianapolis: American Trust Publications, 1978.

————. *On Schacht's Origins of Muhammadan Jurisprudence*. Oxford: Islamic Texts Society, 1996.

Baldick, J. *Mystical Islam*. London: I. B. Tauris, 1989.

————. "The Legend of Rabi'a of Basra: Christian Antecedents, Muslim Counterparts." *Religion* 20 (1990): 233–47.

————. *Imaginary Muslims: The Uwaysi Sufis of Central Asia*. London: I. B. Tauris, 1993.

Bashear, S. *Arabs and Others in Early Islam*. Princeton: Darwin Press, 1997.

Bell, R. *The Origin of Islam in Its Christian Environment*. London, 1926.

————. *The Qur'an, Translated, with a Critical Rearrangement of the Surahs*. Edinburgh: Edinburgh University Press, 1937–1939.

Bennett, J. G. *Sufi Spiritual Techniques*. High Burton: Coombe Springs Press, 1984.

Brock, S. P. "Syriac Views of Early Islam." In *Studies on the First Century of Islamic Society*, edited by G. Juynboll. Carbondale: Southern Illinois University Press, 1982.

Bulliet, I. H. *The Camel and the Wheel*. Cambridge, Mass.: N.p., 1975.

Burckhardt, T. *The Wisdom of the Prophets*. Translation of excerpts from Ibn Arabi's *Fusus al hikam*. Aldsworth: Beshara Publications, 1975.

————. *Art of Islam: Language and Meaning*. London: World of Islam, 1976.

————. *Mystical Astrology According to Ibn Arabi*. Aldsworth: Beshara Publications, 1977.

————. *Universal Man*. Translation of excerpts from Abd al Karim al Jili's *Insan al kamil*. Sherborne: Beshara Publications, 1983.

————. *Mirror of the Intellect: Essays on Traditional Science and Sacred Art*. Cambridge: Quinta Essentia, 1987.

————. *An Introduction to Sufism*. London: Thomsons, 1995.

Burns, R. E. *The Wrath of Allah*. Houston: A. Ghosh, 1994.

Burton, J. "Those are the high-flying cranes," *Journal of Semitic Studies* 15, no. 2 (1970): 246–65.

———. *The Collection of the Qur'an*. Cambridge: Cambridge University Press, 1977.

———. *The Sources of Islamic Law*. Edinburgh: Edinburgh University Press, 1990.

———. Review of *The History of At Ribari, Vol. 6, Muhammad at Mecca. Bulletin of the Society of Oriental & African Studies* 53 (1990): 328–31.

———. *An Introduction to the Hadith*. Edinburgh: Edinburgh University Press, 1994.

Calder, N. "From Midrash to Scripture: The Sacrifice of Abraham in Early Islamic Tradition." *Le Museon* 101 (1988): 375–402.

Chittick, W. C. "The Five Divine Presences: From al Qunawi to al Qaysari." *Muslim World* 80 (1982): 107–28.

———. *The Sufi Path of Love: The Spiritual Teachings of Rumi*. New York: SUNY Press, 1983.

———. "Eschatology." In *Islamic Spiritualiy: Vol. 1, Foundations*, edited by S. Nasr. London: SPCK, 1987.

———. *The Sufi Path of Knowledge: Ibn al Arabi's Metaphysics of Imagination*. New York: SUNY Press, 1989.

———. "Ibn Arabi and His School." In *Islamic Spirituality: Vol. 2, Manifestations*, edited by S. Nasr. London: SPCK, 1991.

———. *Faith and Practice of Islam: Three Thirteenth-Century Sufi Texts*. New York: SUNY Press, 1993.

———. *Imaginal Worlds: Ibn al Arabi and the Problem of Religious Diversity*. New York: SUNY Press, 1994.

———. *The Self-Disclosure of God*. New York: SUNY Press, 1998.

———. *Sufism: A Short Introduction*. London: Oneworld, 2000.

Chittick, W. C., & S. Murata. *The Vision of Islam*. New York: Paragon House, 1994.

Chodkiewicz, M. *Les Illuminations de la Mecque (The Meccan Illuminations: Selected Texts)*. Paris: Sindbad, 1988.

———. *An Ocean Without Shore: Ibn Arabi, the Book, and the Law*. New York: SUNY Press, 1993.

———. *Seal of the Saints: Prophethood and Sainthood in the Doctrine of Ibn Arabi*. Cambridge: Islamic Texts Society, 1993.

———. *The Spiritual Writings of Amir Abd al Kader*. New York: SUNY Press, 1995.

Cook, M. *Early Muslim Dogma: A Source Critical Study*. Cambridge: Cambridge University Press, 1981.

———. *Muhammad*. Oxford: Oxford University Press, 1983.

Coomaraswamy, A. *The Destruction of the Christian Tradition*. London: Perennial Books, 1981.

———. *The Problems with the New Mass*. Rockford, Tan, 1990.

Conrad, L. "Abraham and Muhammad: Some Observations a propos of Chronology and Literary Topoi in the Early Arabic Historical Tradition." *Bulletin of the Society of Oriental and African Studies* 50 (1987): 225–40.

Corbin, H. *Creative Imagination in the Sufism of Ibn Arabi*. Princeton: Bollingen, 1969.

———. *The Man of Light in Iranian Sufism*. Boulder: Shambhala, 1971.

———. *Spiritual Body and Celestial Earth*. Princeton: Bollingen, 1977.

———. *Avicenna and the Visionary Recital*. Dallas: Spring Publications, 1980.

———. *Cyclical Time and Ismaili Gnosis*. London: KPI, 1983.

———. *Temple and Contemplation*. London: KPI, 1986.

Coulson, N. J. *A History of Islamic Law*. Edinburgh: Edinburgh University Press, 1964.

Cragg, K. "Hadith, Traditions of the Prophet." In *Encyclopaedia Brittanica*. Vol. 22, 1974, pp. 10–12.

———. *The Mind of the Qur'an*. London: George, Allen and Unwin, 1973.

———. *Readings in the Qur'an*. London: Collins, 1988.

Crone, P. *Slaves on Horses: The Evolution of the Islamic Polity*. Cambridge: Cambridge University Press, 1980.

Crone, P., & M. Cook. *Hagarism: The Making of the Muslim World*. Cambridge: Cambridge University Press, 1977.

———. *Meccan Trade and the Rise of Islam*. Oxford: Blackwell, 1987.

———. *Roman, Provincial and Islamic Law*. Cambridge: Cambridge University Press, 1987.

Crone, P., and M. Hinds *God's Caliph: Religious Authority in the First Centuries of Islam*. Cambridge: Cambridge University Press, 1986.

Crowley, A. *Magick*. Book 4, parts 1–4. York Beach, Weiser, 1994.

Danner, V. "The Necessity for the Rise of the Term Sufi." *Studies in Comparative Religion* 6, no. 2 (1972.): 71–77.

————. *The Islamic Tradition: An Introduction*. New York: Amity House, 1988.

Deedat, A. *Al Qur'an: The Ultimate Miracle*. London: N.p., 1983.

Easterman, D. *New Jerusalems: Reflections on Islam, Fundamentalism and the Rushdie Affair*. London: Grafton, 1992.

Eaton, G. *The Concept of God in Islam*. London: The Islamic Cultural Centre, n.d.

————. *King of the Castle: Choice and Responsibility in the Modern World*. London: Bodley Head, 1977.

————. Islam and the Destiny of Man. London: George, Allen and Unwin, 1985.

Eliade, M. *Shamanism: Archaic Techniques of Ecstasy*. Princeton: Bollinger, 1972.

Elmore, G. "Ibn al-'Arabi's Testament on the Mantle of Initiation (*al-Khirqah*)." *Journal of the Muhyiddin Ibn 'Arabi Society* 26 (1999): 1–33.

Fahkry, M. *A History of Islamic Philosophy*. London: Columbia University Press, 1985.

Fales, E. "Mystical Experience as Evidence." *International Journal for the Philosophy of Religion* 40 (1996): 19–46.

————. "Scientific Explanations of Mystical Experiences." *Religious Studies*, 32, no. 2 (1996): 143–63; no. 3 (1996): 297–313.

Fideler, D. *Jesus Christ, Sun of God: Ancient Cosmology and Early Christian Symbolism*. Wheaton: Quest Books, 1995.

Firestone, R. *Journeys into Holy Lands: The Evolution of the Abraham–Ishmael Legends in Islamic Exegesis*. New York: SUNY Press, 1993.

Flew, A., and A. MacIntyre. *New Essays in Philosophical Theology*. London: SCM, 1963.

Fuller, B. A. G. *The Problem of Evil in Plotinus*. Cambridge: Cambridge University Press, 1912.

Glassé, C. *The Concise Encyclopaedia of Islam*. London: Stacey International, 1988.

Goldziher, I. *Muslim Studies*. 2 vols. London: George, Allen and Unwin, 1966–1971.

————. *Introduction to Islamic Theology and Law*. Princeton: Princeton University Press, 1981.

Goitein, S. D. *Studies in Islamic History and Institutions*. Leiden: Brill, 1966.

Graham, W. A. *Divine Word and Prophetic Word in Early Islam*. The Hague: Mouton, 1977.

Guénon, R. *East and West*. London: Luzac, 1941.

———. *Introduction to the Study of Hindu Doctrines*. London: Luzac, 1945.

———. *Man and His Becoming According to the Vedanta*. London: Luzac, 1945.

———. *The Reign of Quantity and the Signs of the Times*. London: Luzac, 1953.

———. *Symbolism of the Cross*. London: Luzac, 1958.

———. *The Crisis of the Modern World*. London: Luzac, 1962.

———. *The Lord of the World*. Moorcote: Coombe Springs Press, 1983.

———. *The Multiple States of Being*. New York: Larson, 1984.

———. *Studies in Hinduism*. New Delhi: Navrang, 1985.

———. *The Great Triad*. Cambridge: Islamic Texts Society, 1991.

———. *Fundamental Symbols: The Universal Language of Sacred Science*. Cambridge: Quinta Essentia, 1995.

Guillaume, A. *The Life of Muhammad*. Translation of Ibn Ishaq's *Sirat Rasul Allah*. Oxford: Oxford University Press, 1955.

———. *Islam*. Harmondsworth: Penguin Books, 1956.

Halifax, J. *Shaman: The Wounded Healer*. London: Thames and Hudson, 1982.

Harwood, N. *Mythology's Last Gods*. Amherst, N.Y.: Prometheus Books, 1992.

Hawting, G. R. "The Origins of the Muslim Sanctuary at Mecca." In *Studies in the First Century of Islamic Society*, edited by G. Juynboll. Carbondale: Southern Illinois University Press, 1982.

———. *The First Dynasty of Islam: The Umayyad Caliphate A.D. 661–750*. London: Croom Helm, 1986.

———. *The Idea of Idolatry and the Emergence of Islam: From Polemic to History*. Cambridge: Cambridge University Press, 1999.

Hick, J. *An Interpretation of Religion*. Basingstoke: Macmillan, 1989.

Hirtenstein, S. *The Unlimited Mercifier: The Spiritual Life and Thought of Ibn 'Arabi*. Oxford: Anqa Publishing, 1999.

Hulse, D. A. *The Key of It All: An Encyclopaedic Guide to the Sacred Languages of the World*. 2 vols. St. Paul: Llewellyn, 1993–94.

Hussaini, A. S. "Uways al Qarani and the Uwaysi Sufis." *Muslim World* 57 (1969): 103–13.

Izutsu, T. *The Structure of Ethical Terms in the Koran: A Study in Semantics.* Tokyo: Keio University, 1959.

———. *God and Man in the Koran: Semantics of the Koranic Weltanschauung.* Tokyo: The Keio Institute of Cultural and Linguistic Studies, 1964.

———. *The Concept of Belief in Islamic Theology: A Semantic Analysis of Iman and Islam.* Tokyo: Yurindo Publishing, 1965.

———. *The Concept and Reality of Existence.* Tokyo: The Keio Institute of Cultural and Linguistic Studies, 1971.

———. *Sufism and Taoism: A Comparative Study of Key Philosophical Concepts.* Los Angeles: University of California Press, 1984.

———. *Creation and the Timeless Order of Things: Essays in Islamic Mystical Philosophy.* Ashland: White Cloud Press, 1994.

James, W. *The Varieties of Religious Experience.* London: Collins, 1960.

Jeffrey, A. *Materials for the History of the Text of the Qur'an.* Leiden: Brill, 1937.

———. *Foreign Vocabulary in the Qur'an.* Baroda: Oriental Institute Baroda, 1938.

Jones, R. H. *Mysticism Examined: Philosophical Inquiries into Mysticism.* New York: SUNY Press, 1993.

Juynboll, G. H. A., ed. *Studies in the First Century of Islamic Society.* Carbondale: Southern Illinois University Press, 1982.

———. *Muslim Tradition.* Cambridge: Cambridge University Press, 1983.

———. *Studies on the Origins and Uses of Islamic Hadith.* Cambridge: Cambridge University Press, 1996.

Kabbani, M. H. *The Naqshbandi Sufi Way: History and Guidebook of the Saints of the Golden Chain.* Chicago: Kazi Publications, 1995.

Katsh, A. *Judaism in Islam.* New York: New York University Press, 1954.

Katz, S., ed. *Mysticism and Philosophical Analysis.* London: Sheldon Press, 1978.

———, ed. *Mysticism and Religious Tradition.* Oxford: Oxford University Press, 1983.

Khalifa, R. *The Perpetual Miracle of Muhammad.* Tucson: Renaissance Productions, 1976.

————. *Mu'jizah Al Qur'an Al Karim*. Tucson: Renaissance Productions, 1980.

————. *The Computer Speaks: God's Message to the World*. Tucson: Renaissance Productions, 1981.

————. *Qur'an: The Final Scripture*. Tucson: Renaissance Productions, 1981.

————. *The Evolution of Creationism*. Tucson: Renaissance Productions, 1982.

————. *The Law of Creation*. Tucson: Renaissance Productions, 1982.

————. *Qur'an, Hadith and Islam*. Tucson: Renaissance Productions, 1982.

————. *Qur'an: Visual Presentation of the Miracle*. Tucson: Renaissance Productions, 1982.

King, D. "Islamic Mathematics and Astronomy." *Journal for the History of Astronomy* 9 (1978): 212–19.

King, F., ed. *Astral Projection, Ritual Magic, and Alchemy: Golden Dawn Material by S. L. MacGregor Mathers and Others*. Wellingborough: Aquarian Press, 1987.

Kister, M. J. *Concepts and Ideas in Early Islam*. Abingden: Variorum, 1997.

Koslow, M. *An Account of the Schuon Cult*. Unpublished, 1991.

————. *Telling Truth to Power*. Unpublished, 1996.

————. *An Update on the Schuon Cult*. Unpublished, 1996.

Kurtz, P. *The Transcendental Temptation: A Critique of Religion and the Paranormal*. Amherst, N.Y.: Prometheus Books, 1986.

Lings, M. (Abu Bakr Siraj Ed-Din) *The Book of Certainty: The SufiDoctrines of Faith, Vision, and Gnosis*. New York: Weiser, 1970.

————. *A Sufi Saint of the Twentieth Century: Shaykh Ahmad al Alawi*. London: George, Allen and Unwin, 1971.

————. *The Quranic Art of Calligraphy and Illumination*. London: World of Islam, 1977.

————. *Ancient Beliefs and Modern Superstitions*. London: Perennial Books, 1980.

————. *What Is Sufism?* London: George, Allen and Unwin, 1981.

————. *Muhammad: His Life Based on the Earliest Sources*. London: Islamic Texts Society, 1983.

————. *The Eleventh Hour: The Spiritual Crisis of the Modern World in the Light of Tradition and Prophecy*. Cambridge: Quinta Essentia, 1981.

———. *Symbol and Archetype: A Study of the Meaning of Existence*. Cambridge: Quinta Essentia, 1991.

Lewis, P. *Islamic Britain*. London: I. B. Tauris, 1994.

———. *The Secret of Shakespeare*. Cambridge: Quinta Essentia, 1996.

Mahmud, A. H. *The Creed of Islam*. London: World of Islam, 1978.

Margoliouth, D. S. "Mecca," "Muhammad," "Qur'an." In *Encyclopaedia of Religion and Ethics*, edited by J. Hastings. Vols. 8, 10. Edinburgh: T. & T. Clark, 1967.

Martin, R. C., ed. *Approaches to Islam in Religious Studies*. Tucson: The University of Arizona Press, 1985.

Massignon, L. *The Passion of al Hallaj*. 4 vols. Translated by H. Mason. Princeton: Bollingen, 1982.

McCarthy, R. J. *Freedom and Fulfilment: An Annotated Translation of Al Ghazali's "al Munqidh min al Dalal" and Other Relevant Works of al Ghazali*. Boston: Twayne, 1980.

McClain, E. G. *Meditations Through the Quran: Tonal Images in an Oral Culture*. York Beach: Nicolas Hays, 1981.

Meier, F. "The Mystery of the Kaaba." In *The Mysteries*. Princeton: Bollingen, 1971.

Menken, M. J. J. *Numerical Literary Techniques in John: The Fourth Evangelist's Use of Numbers of Words and Syllables*. Leiden: Brill, 1985.

Merkur, D. *Gnosis: An Esoteric Tradition of Mystical Visions and Unions*. New York: SUNY Press, 1993.

Mernissi, F. *Islam and Democracy: Fear of the Modern World*. New York: Addison Wesley, 1992.

Michell, J. *The Dimensions of Paradise: The Proportions and Symbolic Numbers of Ancient Cosmology*. London: Thames and Hudson, 1988.

Morris, J. "The Spiritual Ascension: Ibn Arabi and the Mi'raj." *Journal of the American Oriental Society* 107 (1987): 629–52; 108 (1988): 63–77.

———. "Ibn Arabi's Spiritual Ascension." In *Les Illuminations de la Mecque*, edited by M. Chodkiewicz. Paris: Sinbad, 1988.

Morwedge, P. *Neoplatonism and Islamic Thought*. New York: SUNY Press, 1992.

Murata, S. "The Angels." In *Islamic Spirituality: Vol. 1, Foundations*, edited by S. Nasr. London: SPCK, 1989.

————. *The Tao of Islam: A Sourcebook of Gender Relationships in Islamic Thought*. New York: SUNY Press, 1992.

Nasr, S. H. *Three Muslim Sages: Avicenna–Suhrawardi–Ibn Arabi*. Cambridge: Harvard University Press, 1964.

————. *An Introduction to Islamic Cosmological Doctrines*. Harvard: Belknap, 1964.

————. *Ideals and Realities of Islam*. London: George, Allen and Unwin, 1966.

————. *Science and Civilization in Islam*. Cambridge: Harvard University Press, 1968.

————. *Sufi Essays*. London: George, Allen and Unwin, 1972.

————. *Islam and the Plight of Modern Man*. London: Longman, 1975.

————. *Islamic Science: An Illustrated Study*. London: World of Islam, 1976.

————. *Sadr al Din Shirazi and His Transcendent Theosophy*. Tehran: Imperial Iranian Academy of Philsophy, 1978.

————. *Knowledge and the Sacred*. Edinburgh: Edinburgh University Press, 1981.

————., ed. *The Essential Writings of Frithjof Schuon*. New York: Amity House, 1986.

————., ed. *Islamic Spirituality*. 2 vols. London: SPCK, 1989–91.

————. *Traditional Islam in the Modern World*. London: KPI, 1989.

————. *The Need for a Sacred Science*. London: Curzon Press, 1993.

————. *A Young Muslim's Guide to the Modern World*: Cambridge: Islamic Texts Society, 1993.

Nasr, S. H., and Stoddart, eds. *Religion of the Heart: Essays Presented to Frithjof Schuon on His Eightieth Birthday*. Washington: Foundation for Traditional Studies, 1991.

Nazim, M. *Mercy Oceans*. Book 2. London: Sebat, 1980.

————. *Mercy Oceans' Hidden Treasures*. London: Sebat, 1981.

————. *Mercy Oceans' Endless Horizons*. London: Sebat, 1982.

————. *Mercy Oceans' Pink Pearls*. London: Sebat, 1983.

————. *Mercy Oceans' Divine Sources*. London: Sebat, 1984.

————. *Toward the Divine Presence*. Book 1. London: N.p., 1984.

————. *Mercy Oceans of the Heart*. London: Sebat, 1985.

————. *Toward the Divine Presence*. Book 2. London: N.p., 1985.

————. *Mercy Oceans' Rising Sun*. London: Sebat, 1986.

————. *Toward the Divine Presence*. Book 3. London: n.p., 1986.

————. *Mercy Oceans*. Serendib edition, part 1. Colombo: Arafat Publishing, 1987.

————. *Ocean of Unity*. Konya: Sebat, 1987.

————. *The Secrets Behind the Secrets Behind the Secrets. . .* Berlin: Dura, 1987.

————. *Power Oceans of Love*. London: Zero Publications, 1993.

————. *Power Oceans of Light*. London: Zero Publications, 1995.

————. *Star from Heaven*. London: Zero Publications, 1996.

Needleman, J., ed. *The Sword of Gnosis*. Baltimore: Penguin Books, 1974.

Netton, I. R. *Muslim Neoplatonists: An Introduction to the Thought of the Brethren of Purity*. London: George, Allen and Unwin, 1982.

Newby, G. D. *A History of the Jews of Arabia: From Ancient Times to Their Eclipse Under Islam*. Columbia: University of South Carolina Press, 1988.

————. *The Making of the Last Prophet: A Reconstruction of the Earliest Biography of Muhammad*. Columbia: University of South Carolina Press, 1989.

Nicholson, R. A. *A Literary History of the Arabs*. Cambridge: Cambridge University Press, 1956.

————. *The Mystics of Islam*. London: Routledge and Kegan Paul, 1963.

————. *Rumi: Poet and Mystic*. London: Unwin, 1978.

————. *Studies in Islamic Mysticism*. Cambridge: Cambridge University Press, 1978.

————. *The Tarjuman al Ashwaq*. Translation of Ibn Arabi's *Interpreter of Desires*. London: Theosophical Publishing House, 1978.

————., trans. *The Mathnawi of Jalalu'ddin Rumi*. 3 vols. Cambridge: Gibb Memorial Trust, 1982.

Noll, R. *The Jung Cult: Origins of a Charismatic Movement*. Princeton: Princeton University Press, 1996.

————. *The Aryan Christ: The Secret Life of Carl Gustav Jung*. London: Macmillan, 1997.

Ovason, D. *The Zelator: A Modern Initiate Explores the Ancient Mysteries*. London: Century, 1998.

Palacios, M. A. *Islam and the Divine Comedy*. London: Cass, 1968.

Peters, F. E. *Children of Abraham: Judaism/Christianity/Islam*. Princeton: Princeton University Press, 1982.

———. *Muhammad and the Origins of Islam*. New York: SUNY Press, 1994.

Perry, W. N. *A Treasury of Traditional Wisdom*. London: George, Allen and Unwin, 1971.

———. *Gurdjieff in the Light of Tradition*. London: Perennial Books, 1978.

———. *The Widening Breach: Evolutionism in the Mirror of Cosmology*. Cambridge: Quinta Essentia, 1995.

———. *Challenges to a Secular Society*. Oakton: Foundation for Traditional Studies, 1996

Philips, A. A. B. *The Qur'an's Numerical Miracle: Hoax and Heresy*. Jeddah: Abdul Qasim Bookstore, 1987.

———. *The Fundamentalism of Tahweed*. Riyadh: Tawheed Publications, 1990.

Plotinus, *Enneads*. Translated by A. H. Armstrong. 7 vols. London: Harvard University Press, 1989.

Rahman, F. *Avicenna's Psychology*. Oxford: Oxford University Press, 1952.

———. "Dream, Imagination and *'Alam al Mithal.*' " *Islamic Studies* 3, no. 2 (1964): 167–79.

———. *Islam*. Chicago: University of Chicago Press, 1979.

———. *Prophecy in Islam: Philosophy and Orthodoxy*. Chicago: University of Chicago Press, 1979.

Raschid, M. S. *Iqbal's Concept of God*. London: KPI, 1981.

———. "Philosophia Perennis Universale Imperium." *Religion* 13 (1983): 155–71.

Regardie, I. *The Complete Golden Dawn System of Magic*. Phoenix: Falcon Press, 1985.

Rippin, A. "The Exegetical Genre *Asbab Al Nuzul*: A Bibliographical and Terminological Survey." *Bulletin of the Society of Oriental and African Studies* 48 (1985): 1–15.

———. "Literary Analysis of *Qur'an*, *Tafsir*, and *Sira*: The Methodologies of John Wansbrough." In *Approaches to Islam in Religious Studies* 48 (1985): 151–65.

———. "The Function of Asbab Al Nuzul in Quranic Exegesis," *Bulletin of the Society of Oriental and African Studies* 51 (1988): 1–19.

————. *Muslims, Their Religious Beliefs and Practices*. Vol. 1: *The Formative Period*. London: Routledge, 1990.

————. *Muslims, Their Religious Beliefs and Practices*. Vol. 2: *The Contemporary Period*. London: Routledge, 1993.

————., ed. *The Qur'an: Formative Interpretation*. Abindon: Variorum, 1999.

————., ed. *The Qur'an: Style and Contents*. Abindon: Variorum, 2000.

Robinson, F., ed. *Cambridge Illustrated History of the Islamic World*. Cambridge: Cambridge University Press, 1996.

Rosenthal, F. "Nineteen." *Analecta Biblica*, Vol. 12 (1959).

Rosser-Owen, D. G. *Social Change in Islam—The Progressive Dimension*. London: Open Press, 1975.

Rubin, U. *The Eye of the Beholder: The Life of Muhammad As Viewed by the Early Muslims*. Princeton: Darwin Press, 1995.

Sardar, Z. *Explorations in Islamic Science*. London: Mansell, 1989.

————. "A Man For All Seasons." *Impact International* (December 1993): 33–36.

Sardar, Z., and Z. A. Malik. *Muhammad for Beginners*. London: Writers and Readers, 1994.

Schacht, J. *The Origins of Muhammadan Jurisprudence*. Oxford: Oxford University Press, 1979.

————. *An Introductio · to Islamic Law*. Oxford: Oxford University Press, 1991.

Schaya, L. *The Universal Meaning of the Kabbalah*. London: George, Allen and Unwin, 1971.

Schimmel, A. *Mystical Dimensions of Islam*. Chapel Hill: University of North Carolina Press, 1975.

————. *As Through a Veil: Mystical Poetry in Islam*. New York: Columbia University Press, 1982.

————. *And Muhammad is His Messenger: The Veneration of the Prophet in Islamic Piety*. Chapel Hill: University of North Carolina Press, 1985.

————. *The Mystery of Numbers*. New York: Oxford University Press, 1993.

————. *Deciphering the Signs of God: A Phenomenological Approach to Islam*. Edinburgh: Edinburgh University Press, 1994.

Scholem, G. G. *On the Kabbalah and Its Symbolism*. London: Routledge and Kegan Paul, 1965.

Schuon, F. *The Transcendent Unity of Religions.* London: Faber and
Faber, 1953. Rev. ed., Harper and Row, 1974.
———. *Spiritual Perspectives and Human Facts.* London: Faber and
Faber, 1954.
———. *Gnosis: Divine Wisdom.* London: John Murray, 1959.
———. *Stations of Wisdom.* London: John Murray, 1961.
———. *Understanding Islam.* London: George, Allen and Unwin, 1963.
———. *Light On the Ancient Worlds.* London: Perennial Books, 1965.
———. *In the Tracks of Buddhism.* London: George, Allen and Unwin,
1968.
———. *Dimensions of Islam.* London: George, Allen and Unwin, 1969.
———. *Logic and Transcendence.* New York: Harper Torchbooks, 1975.
———. *Islam and the Perennial Philosophy.* London: World of Islam,
1976.
———. *Esoterism as Principle and as Way.* Bedfont: Perennial Books,
1981.
———. *Sufism: Veil and Quintessence.* Bloomington, Ind.: World
Wisdom Books, 1981.
———. *Castes and Races.* London: Perennial Books, 1982.
———. *From the Divine to the Human.* Bloomington, Ind.: World
Wisdom Books, 1982.
———. *Memories and Meditations.* Unpublished, 1984.
———. *Christianity/Islam: Essays on Esoteric Ecumenism.* Bloom-
ington, Ind.: World Wisdom Books, 1985.
———. *Survey of Metaphysics and Esoterism.* Bloomington, Ind.:
World Wisdom Books, 1986.
———. *In The Face of the Absolute.* Bloomington, Ind.: World Wisdom
Books, 1989.
———. *The Feathered Sun: Plains Indians in Art and Philosophy.*
Bloomington, Ind.: World Wisdom Books, 1990.
———. *To Have a Center.* Bloomington, Ind.: World Wisdom Books, 1990.
———. *Roots of the Human Condition.* Bloomington, Ind.: World
Wisdom Books, 1991.
———. *Images of Primordial and Mystic Beauty: Paintings by Frithjof
Schuon.* Bloomington, Ind.: Abodes, 1992.
———. *The Play of Masks.* Bloomington, Ind.: Abodes, 1992.
———. *The Transfiguration of Man.* Bloomington, Ind.: Abodes, 1995.

——. *The Eye of the Heart*. Bloomington, Ind.: Abodes, 1997.

Seale, M. S. *Qur'an and Bible: Studies in Interpretation and Dialogue*. London: Croom Helm, 1978.

Sextus Empiricus. *Outlines of Pyrrhonism*. Translated by R. G. Bury. London: Harvard University Press, 1990.

Shamash, L., and S. Hirtenstein. "From the Preface to the Futuhat Al-Makkiya by Ibn Arabi." *Journal of the Muhyiddin Ibn Arabi Society* 4 (1985): 4–6.

Siddiq, A. Translated by Darwish. *Al Mahdi, Jesus, and the Anti-Christ*. London: As-Siddiquyah, 1985.

Siddiqi, M. Z. *Hadith Literature: Its Origin, Development, Special Features and Criticism*. Calcutta: Calcutta University Press, 1961.

Smith, H. *Forgotten Truth: The Primordial Tradition*. New York: Harper Colaphon Books, 1976.

——. *Beyond the Post-Modern Mind*. Wheaton, Ill.: Theosophical Publishing House, 1989.

——. *The World's Religions*. San Francisco: Harper, 1991.

Smith, M. *The Way of the Mystics: The Early Christian Mystics and the Rise of the Sufis*. London: Sheldon Press, 1976.

——. *An Early Mystic of Baghdad: A Study of the Life and Teaching of Harith B. Asad al Muhasibi, A.D. 781–857*. London: Sheldon Press, 1977.

——. *Rabia the Mystic and Her Fellow Saints in Islam*. Cambridge: Cambridge University Press, 1984.

Smith, W. *Cosmos and Transcendence*. Peru, Ill.: Sherwood Sugoler and Company, 1984.

——. *The Quantum Enigma: Finding The Hidden Key*. Peru, Ill.: Sherwood Sugoler and Company, 1995.

Sox, D. *The Gospel of Barnabas*. London: George Allen & Unwin, 1984.

Staal, J. F. *Exploring Mysticism*. Harmondsworth: Penguin Books, 1980.

Stace, W. T. *Mysticism and Philosophy*. London: Macmillan, 1960.

Stade, R. C. *Ninety-Nine Names of God in Islam*. Translation of the major portion of al Ghazali's *Al Maqsad Al Asma.* Ibadan: Daystar Press, 1970.

Stirling, W. *The Canon: An Exposition of the Pagan Mystery Perpetuated in the Cabala as the Rule of All the Arts*. York Beach: Weiser, 1999.

Stoddart, W. *Sufism: The Mystical Doctrines and Methods of Islam*. Wellingborough: The Aquarian Press, 1984.

Tabatabai. *Shi'ite Islam*. Translated by Nasr. Houston: Free Islamic Literature, n.d.

Takeshita, M. *Ibn Arabi's Theory of the Perfect Man and its Place in Islamic Thought*. Tokyo: Institute for the Study of Languages and Cultures of Asia and Africa, 1987.

Tart, C. T., ed. *Altered States of Consciousness*. San Francisco: Harper-Collins, 1990.

Torrey, C. *The Jewish Foundations of Islam*. New York: Ktav Publishing House, 1967.

Trimingham, J. S. *The Sufi Orders in Islam*. Oxford: Oxford University Press, 1971.

———. *Christianity Among the Arabs in Pre-Islamic Times*. London: Longman, 1979.

Valiuddin, M. *The Quranic Sufism*. Delhi: Motilal Banarsidass, 1959.

———. *Love of God: A Sufic Approach*. Farnham: Sufi Publishing Company, 1972.

———. *Contemplative Disciplines in Sufism*. London: East West Publications, 1980.

Waite, A. E. *The Hermetic and Alchemical Writings of Faracelsus the Great*. 1894. Reprinted, New York: University Books, 1967.

Wansbrough, J. *Quranic Studies: Sources and Methods of Scriptural Interpretation*. Oxford: Oxford University Press, 1977.

———. "Review of Burton's *The Collection of the Qur'an*." *Bulletin of the Society of Oriental and African Studies* 41 (1978): 370–71.

———. "Review of of P. Crone and M. Cook's *Hagarism: the Making of the Muslim World*." *Bulletin of the Society of Oriental and African Studies* 41 (1978): 155–56.

———. *The Sectarian Milieu: Content and Composition of Islamic Salvation History*. Oxford: Oxford University Press, 1978.

Warraq, I. *Why I Am Not a Muslim*. Amherst, N.Y.: Prometheus Books, 1995.

Waterfield, R. *René Guénon and the Future of the West: The Life and Writings of a Twentieth-Century Metaphysician*. London: Crucible, 1987.

Watt, W. M. *Muhammad at Mecca*. Oxford: Oxford University Press, 1953.

———. *Muhammad at Medina*. Oxford: Oxford University Press, 1956.

———. *Bell's Introduction to the Qur'an*. Revised by W. Montgomery Watt. Edinburgh: Edinburgh University Press, 1977.

————, trans. *The Faith and Practice of Al Ghazali*. Oxford: Oneworld, 1994.

Wilson, P. L., and N. Pourjavady. *The Drunken Universe: An Anthology of Persian Sufi Poetry*. Grand Rapids, Mich.: Phanes Press, 1987.

————. *Scandal: Essays in Islamic Heresy*. New York: Autonomedia, 1988.

————. *Sacred Drift: Essays on the Margins of Islam*. San Francisco: City Lights, 1993.

Wolfson, H. *The Philosophy of the Kalam*. Harvard: Harvard University Press, 1976.

Wright, A. G. "Numerical Patterns in the Book of Wisdom." *Catholic Biblical Quarterly* 29 (1967): 524–38.

————. "The Riddle of the Sphinx: The Structure of the Book of Qoheleth." *Catholic Biblical Quarterly* 30 (1968): 314–34.

————. "The Riddle of the Sphinx Revisited: Numerical Patterns in the Book of Qoheleth." *Catholic Biblical Quarterly* 42 (1980): 38–51.

————. "Additional Numerical Patterns in Qoheleth." *Catholic Bibilical Quarterly* 45 (1983): 32–43.

Zaehner, R. C. *Mysticism, Sacred and Profane*. Oxford: Oxford University Press, 1957.

————. *Hindu and Muslim Mysticism*. New York: Schocken Books, 1969.

Zayd, A. *Al Ghazali on the Divine Predicates*. Translation of chapters from al Ghazali's *Al Iqtisad fil I'tiqad*. Lahore: S. H. Muhammad Ashraf, 1970.

Index

251